Revolution in Psychology

REVOLUTION
IN PSYCHOLOGY

Alienation to Emancipation

IAN PARKER

Pluto Press

LONDON • ANN ARBOR, MI

First published 2007 by Pluto Press
345 Archway Road, London N6 5AA
and 839 Greene Street, Ann Arbor, MI 48106

www.plutobooks.com

British Library Cataloguing in Publication Data
A catalogue record for this book is available from the British Library

Hardback
ISBN-13 978 0 7453 2536 1
ISBN-10 0 7453 2536 X

Paperback
ISBN-13 978 0 7453 2535 4
ISBN-10 0 7453 2535 1

Library of Congress Cataloging in Publication Data applied for

10 9 8 7 6 5 4 3 2 1

Designed and produced for Pluto Press by
Chase Publishing Services Ltd, Sidmouth EX10 9QG, England
Typeset by Newgen Imaging Systems (P) Ltd, Chennai, India
Printed and bound in the European Union by
CPI Antony Rowe Ltd, Chippenham and Eastbourne, England

Contents

Acknowledgements

This book would not have been possible unless there had been objections to psychology right from the early days of the discipline. The voices against psychology have been diverse – anti-capitalist, anti-racist, ecological and feminist – and some of the recent critics have been willing to discuss the ideas in this book and help me sharpen the arguments. The arguments in the chapters were rehearsed as a series of lectures in 2005 in Guadalajara, Mexico (in the Departamento de Psicología Aplicada, Universidad de Guadalajara), and I would particularly like to thank Erica Burman, Bernardo Jiménez-Domínguez, Rosa Margarita López Aguilar, Juan Alberto Hernández, Raul Medina and Alfredo Salmerón. A seminar series in 2005–06 in Manchester, UK (in the Discourse Unit, Manchester Metropolitan University) was then devoted to the chapters, and thanks again to those who listened and contributed; Alex Bridger, Jill Bradbury, Geoff Bunn, Khatidja Chantler, Paul Duckett, Thekla Giekeimi, Jeannine Goh, Romy Graichen, John Griffiths, Rebecca Lawthom, Ken McLaughlin, Sue Makevit Coupland, Vera Marten, Ilana Mountian, Teija Nissinen, Christine Paalsrud, Julia Robinson, Asiya Siddique, Judith Sixsmith and Emma Wilmer.

Introduction

This book is about psychology, the way the discipline of psychology betrayed its promise to understand and help people, and what we need to do to make psychologists work for social change rather than against it. The discipline of psychology as a field of academic study and professional practice aims to discover how we behave and think and feel, but the knowledge and technology that psychologists produce is designed to adapt people to society. Because present-day society is organised around exploitation and subordination, even the most well-meaning psychologist contributes to alienation, to the separation of our selves from others and from our own creative abilities.

The book is for those who want to change the world, for those trying to make sense of their own psychology and to make connections between psychology and radical politics. Activists involved in anti-capitalist, anti-racist and feminist politics often try to connect big political change with change at the more intimate level of everyday relationships. They are quite right to make this connection, and one of the lessons of failed revolutions and authoritarian 'socialist' societies is that this apparently 'psychological' level is woven into political change. Activists need to know about psychology, and what needs to be done to prevent it from operating only as an instrument of social control.

We Encounter Psychology Indirectly in Political Debate

Psychology is important not because it is true but because it is so useful to those in power. Psychological descriptions of individual action are often enthusiastically taken up by those who have most to lose from those descriptions; and those who benefit from persuading people that a problem can be reduced to the way someone thinks or feels also, quite understandably, really believe in psychology themselves. Psychology is an increasingly powerful component of ideology, ruling ideas that endorse exploitation and sabotage struggles

1

against oppression. This psychology circulates way beyond colleges and clinics, and different versions of psychology as ideology are now to be found nearly everywhere in capitalist society.

Personality profiles of political leaders are increasingly used to explain away political issues, for example, and here psychological ideology seeps into the way we understand the world, making it seem as if there is nothing we can do to change it. The historical conditions in which certain figures give orders and other people follow them then, as far as the psychologist is concerned, simply serve as the backdrop to how individual motivations and decisions are played out. The focus on the childhood of political enemies then psychologises politics, and the activity of those engaged in political resistance is sidelined, marginalised as something irrelevant and useless. This reduction of political struggle to what is going on inside the minds of individual characters then reduces the rest of us to being mere spectators.

Advice about personal improvement takes the place of social transformation, and the psychologisation of social life already encourages people to think that the only possible change they could ever make would be in the way they dress and present themselves to others. Confession, reconciliation and 'makeover' thus operate as sites of psychologisation on television; sometimes the expert counsellor is quite explicit about how a person or relationship needs to change, but often the participants have already absorbed enough psychological ideology to be able, without much guidance, to burst into tears, own up to their faults and ask forgiveness. There is always a message about what healthy psychological functioning is like here, and how it is the root of everything else.

Ideas about sex and race divide people from each other, and psychological theories have played an important role in making us believe that differences between people are essential, necessary qualities of human beings that can never be changed. Psychology provides ever more sophisticated and so more effective arguments for sexism and racism than the old biological theories, and this new psychology as ideology serves to justify violence and reinforce stereotypes. Notions from so-called 'evolutionary psychology', for example, supplement the worst old religious arguments about differences between men and women. The shift of attention from racial classifications to cultural differences, from biology to psychology, follows the same logic, and treats underlying mental processes as responsible for economically structured white privilege.

Popular arguments about 'human nature' make it seem as if social change is out of the question, and psychological theories undermine those who believe that another world is possible. Psychological explanations for war, invasion and mass-murder not only mislead us, and draw attention away from economic, political and historical conditions, but they also sap the confidence of those committed to change. Every theory of human nature that tells us what cannot be changed at a deep psychological level has insidious economic functions and dangerous political consequences. Taking a distance from psychology will enable us to refuse to accept the mistaken view that brutality is wired in to our brains and behaviour.

We Encounter Psychology Directly in Political Activity

Psychological ideas not only float around in day-time television, providing false explanations for problems in the world and misleading us as to how we could make this world a better place. Psychology as ideology is not just the stupid stuff that can be avoided while we are doing real politics, not merely the froth on the surface of our lives that can be quickly skimmed off. Psychology has also come to be structured into the way we have learnt to think about ourselves as individuals, and so it also enters into the way people think of themselves as political agents. It impacts on how we interpret and how we try to change the world.

We are subject to categories of ability and intelligence in school, for example, that leave deep scars on what we been made to think of as our own individual 'psychology'. The sorting and grading of people into different kinds of school mark the class position and identity of every child. An individual path through school is experienced as something 'psychological'; each child comes to live their failure as something from which they are alienated, as if it were something deep within themselves which they could never really comprehend or escape. Then, as our own children suffer from an ever-increasing system of assessments and decisions about what they cannot do, we feel even more helpless.

Most of us are encouraged to change the way we behave and the way we speak in order to adapt ourselves to this world. Capitalist society is dependent on those who work for a living, the working class that is still the mass of the population, but society presents itself to itself as middle class, as if workers were an unfortunate and dwindling minority. This contradiction between image and reality, a lie about who we are, means that as we fit ourselves in we also start to live out certain assumptions about what is wrong with us and what is right about the strategies we adopted to survive. Individual choices that cover over structural inequalities feed more psychologisation, and the ability to chatter about feelings and personal journeys becomes more evidence to others and our selves that we will not cause trouble. We are taught to give up on social change, and accept that the aim of changing the world was itself the product of psychological motivations like envy and resentment at the success of others.

Those who refuse, those who remained steadfast in socialist and feminist politics and those who are now building the new social movements, are often able to keep psychologisation at bay, keep psychology in its place, but even then it remains a potent force. We are sometimes stressed, burnt out or traumatised by our struggles, and when we collapse in exhaustion and despair it is vital to know what demands to make on professionals who make it their business to patch individuals up when they fall apart. Because psychology is part of the problem – individualising and essentialising social processes – we need to know how to treat the problems we experience as social processes instead of handing ourselves over to those who will turn them into psychology again.

Unbearable misery is treated by psychology as if it were a disorder, failure or illness. One of the most destructive aspects of alienation is the separation of people from feelings of misery and anger, either at their own plight or the plight of others. Our own oppression is then turned by psychologists into 'negative thinking' that we feel bad about finding within ourselves, and the oppression of others is turned into fateful misfortune at the hands of maladjusted people. In capitalist society driven by profit and the imperative to consume, there is a premium placed on 'positive psychology' so that happiness has come to be viewed as the normal state. Self-activity and solidarity are replaced by anti-depressants and charity.

The Domain of Psychology is a Political Issue

Psychology as a discipline has come to play a very precise function under capitalism, and the academic theories and professional practices that comprise psychology in schools, companies, hospitals and prisons fit hand-in-glove with power. This in itself should be enough to put psychology on the agenda for those involved in radical politics. There is also another more pressing reason for tackling psychology, however, which is that the domain of individual experience that we call 'psychology' was itself formed under capitalism, and close analysis of this psychology will help us understand something deeper about the functioning of capitalism itself. A close analysis of the development of psychology can actually enable us to understand something about the nature of alienation in capitalist society and the role of different forms of oppression within it.

The 'psychologisation' of everyday life under capitalism is not an optional extra, nor is it a simple political device used by those in power to divide and rule us; psychologisation is essential and necessary to capitalism. And this is why the phenomena of racism and sexism, for example, are interlaced with capitalism. Some aspects of oppression appear to be more 'psychological' precisely because they complement and underpin what is, to some, more immediately visible exploitation.

This capitalist society is exploitative and alienating, and for sure it intensifies individual experience, but it also constitutes that individual experience as something 'psychological', as something that operates as if it were inside each person. Whether it is viewed as a mental or emotional process it operates as something simultaneously as the particular property of the individual and as something that cannot be completely comprehended by them. Alienation is not merely the separation of our selves from others but a kind of separation from our selves in which we experience our selves as inhabited and driven by forces that are mysterious to us. These mysterious forces include economic forces that structure our lives as beings who must sell our labour power to others; however, psychologisation of the different dimensions of oppression that have made capitalism possible also condenses 'race' and 'sex' into highly charged, sometimes exciting and sometimes frightening, forces out of our control.

There is an intimate connection between private experience, personal relationships and the state that calls upon this 'psychological' realm and mobilises it so that threats to private property can be defended against. Psychologisation has become such a deeply embedded part of life under capitalism that it is now not only the psychologists who blame individuals and treat them as those who are being 'defensive' when racism and sexism are mobilised. Attacks on immigrants, for example, accompany rational political debate so that middle-class folk can show themselves to be psychologically minded, thoughtful and emotionally literate at the same time as another 'psychology' that is supposed to belong to the working-class mob is incited. So, at the very same moment that psychologisation functions to express through racist violence the role of the state as the economic-political mechanism to defend the 'nation' against outsiders, psychology as ideology is able to smugly confirm once again that there is something wrong with human nature.

This is why radical politics has nothing to do with simply releasing things that have been 'repressed', pent-up frustrations and energies that the 'system' has not allowed to be expressed; revolution does not simply 'resist' oppression, inciting people to rise up against power. That image of forces pushed down deep within us and bubbling away ready to erupt when the lid comes off is exactly what the process of psychologisation encourages, part of the most dangerous and reactionary side of psychology as ideology. Against the barbarism of capitalist society, evident to those who live on pittance wages as the hidden workforce that makes consumer society possible, and against the barbarism that capitalism unleashes against those who resist it at home or abroad, revolutionary movements have always been concerned with maintaining what has been gained by the oppressed so far. Revolutionary changes require social and personal change that prefigures a better world, and this means that detailed analysis, reflection and theory have always been necessary; this analysis, reflection and theory should not be mistaken for psychology, however.

The link between the personal and the political in revolutionary politics has been put on the agenda again by feminism. The socialist movement had, in the early years, treated the personal and political as interlinked, and many revolutions would not have been possible if sexual and cultural liberation had not figured explicitly alongside economic demands. Unlike psychology, however, these movements link the personal and political in such a way as to bring to the fore the collective nature of human activity. They challenge the reduction of social phenomena to the level of the individual, and historical change transforms what seemed to be essential fixed qualities of human behaviour. The universalising of the struggle for change then also challenges and transcends the exploitative globalisation brought about by capitalism.

Psychologisation is an Obstacle to Emancipation

Those who think they know little about psychological theory are often in the best position to resist it; their starting assumption, that most of psychology is rubbish, is a fairly good place to begin investigating how it operates as ideology. However, this assumption also needs to be treated with care, and that is one reason why this book is necessary. As with any ideological system, those who start to learn about psychology tend to experience much of it as chiming uncannily with commonsense, and this can make it seem appealing. It is this very intuitive appeal of psychology that is part of the problem, and because psychology as ideology now suffuses so much commonsensical reasoning about behaviour it can also even reappear in the lives of those who think they have nothing to do with it. Psychology needs to be tackled at two levels: when it is explicitly wheeled out by the so-called experts on other people's lives, and when it is implicitly drawn upon to frame political arguments and shut down prospects for radical change.

As one aspect of our task, we need to understand how the domain of psychology (individual experience separated from others) and the discipline of psychology (a particular body of knowledge and techniques) appeared in the world. The other aspect of the task is to find ways to intervene and transform it into something different. From outside psychology, those already involved in radical political change have to take the realm of experience carved out by the discipline seriously. Anti-globalisation and peace movements have appeared around the world as a response and alternative to miserable conditions, and solidarity with those struggling against misery is one way of bearing the unbearable. This also means tackling the psychologisation that reinforces the personal private misery of those who have been taught to believe that they are responsible for what has happened to them.

Psychology is indeed a fake science that abuses the public, but it calls upon forces that have come to operate deep within us as human beings who have come to be who we are so we can work and survive in capitalist society. Those coming into psychology, and those already suffocating inside it, will need now to do something quite different. Those who choose to train as psychologists often do so because they want to help others, and so this book includes resources to help students on courses that include psychological theories to get through their studies and hold true to what they hoped of psychology. While the main text presents an argument about the development and function of psychology in contemporary society, the footnotes provide detailed references so that those who are working inside psychology can track through the arguments and

develop them further. Many psychologists know that there is something deeply wrong with the discipline, and we will now show how
we can shift the terrain of debate in and against the discipline so
that we can move beyond psychology as social control toward
individual and social emancipation.

1
What Is Psychology?
Meet the Family

There is no one definition of what our human psychology is or how it should be understood, and the discipline of psychology is just as difficult to define. Psychology comprises many incompatible theories and research traditions, some counter-intuitive and some common-sensical, mostly useless and sometimes dangerous. This chapter shows how psychology as a separate discipline came into existence at a specific point in history in a certain part of the world. We will see how the psychologists defined themselves against other approaches to understanding and treating individuals, and how they carved out a particular role for their discipline based on a mistaken view of what people are and what they can be.

Psychologists do not agree with each other about
what psychology really is

Sometimes psychology textbooks seem very certain as to what psychology should be about, but this is precisely because there is such sharp disagreement among psychologists. The disagreements are often smoothed over so that a particular position can be argued for all the more forcefully. Because they do not even agree on what the most important disputes are, most introductions to psychology cover this over by pretending to weigh up and judge different vantage points. This feeds the illusion that it all fits together somehow.

Some psychologists argue that the discipline should be 'concerned primarily with establishing cause and effect relationships',[1] or that it should be seen as 'a branch of biological science which studies the phenomenon of conscious life and behaviour'.[2] Others, strict

---

[1] Neel (1977), p. 7. This solid US American text outlines main theoretical systems in the English-language tradition in a very traditional manner.

[2] Drever (1964), p. 232. This little dictionary of psychology from Edinburgh which was first published in 1952 gives a very detailed outline of terms used in laboratory-experimental psychology, untouched by anything outside that 'scientific' tradition. There is not much plot, but it explains every word as you go along.

behaviourists, focus on learning at the expense of any attempt to look inside the head,[3] while rival approaches build models of cognitive mechanisms to explain how we remember and why we forget.[4] Each view of what psychological science should be like is partial, but you should not believe any psychologist who claims they can tell you with confidence what they all agree on.

Different areas of study in psychology are competing, not complementary

One way of holding together the ragbag of different models of psychology in the same discipline has been to divide it into separate areas of study, but this only serves to highlight the disagreements between psychologists still further. The different kinds of psychologists do not usually think of their particular domain of work as putting new pieces of knowledge into a bigger picture. Instead, the pictures of the human being that emerge from the different areas of psychology overlap, and their proponents aim to blot out the explanations given by other psychologists.

Cognitive psychologists – who specialise in mental processing of information and memory recall – try to explain why people engage in 'social behaviour', for example, but they reduce the interaction between people to cogs and glitches inside individual heads.[5] Meanwhile social psychologists – who are supposed to account for patterns of behaviour in collections of people – aim to show the reasons for differences in 'individual development', but the only social factors they really take seriously are small-scale ones that can be

---

[3] Ivan Pavlov is the father of 'classical' conditioning in the Russian tradition, best known for conditioning dogs to salivate, linking sound to food so that the dog responds to the sound, for which a good (but conservative) introduction is Gray (1979). B. F. Skinner is the best known figure from the US American so-called 'radical' behaviourist tradition, and famously reduced human language to 'verbal behaviour' (Skinner, 1957). Chomsky's (1959) refutation of Skinner's argument did itself rest on some explicitly Cartesian, and so psychological, assumptions (see Chomsky, 1979). Skinner's ideas about the political consequences of his approach are neatly summed up in *Beyond Freedom and Dignity* (Skinner, 1973) and in a science-fiction novel about a community run on behaviourist lines, *Walden Two* (Skinner, 1962).

[4] George Miller's (1966) book reviewing different psychological theories and lives of psychologists provides one of the most compelling arguments for the development of a 'cognitive' approach as the highest point of development of the discipline. This book, which was dedicated to another arch-propagandist in the history of the discipline, E. G. Boring (1929), is still worth reading as a historical document, but care should be taken about adopting the view of human beings contained in it. Ulric Neisser (1967) was one of the first to use the phrase 'cognitive psychology'.

[5] For an example of the reduction of social psychology to cognition (even though it pretends to give a 'social' account) see Eiser (1986).

manipulated and measured.[6] Developmental psychologists – focusing on when and how an infant learns to think like an adult – aim to show how cognition and social action are linked together, and hope to pull the rug from beneath their colleagues so that research on children is given priority. And so it goes, with every bid to be open and inclusive concealing an agenda to define what psychology really is. This is rocky terrain for those who are already inside psychology, and it is bewildering for those coming in on the disputes from the outside with no map to guide them. But how did we get into this mess in the first place?

There Are Certain Interlinked Conditions for 'Psychology' to Become Possible

We should not take for granted the existence of psychology as a separate domain of research. Instead, we will learn far more about the discipline if we examine the historical conditions for this particular way of understanding people to have appeared in the world. There were rich traditions of thought about thought in different cultures before the term 'psychology' was introduced into the English language by the poet Coleridge in the early nineteenth century and then exported into other languages. Psychologists often like to trace back their own history to the ancient Greeks, but this is a little bit of story-telling that serves to make their work seem wiser and older than it actually is.[7]

The quite recent birth of psychology was toward the end of the nineteenth century, and some spectacular changes were occurring in European society that made the study of individual 'psychology' possible, and necessary. Changes in property relations, the family and the state called upon the services of a new discipline that would study and maintain social order at the level of the individual. It was so successful that many people now take for granted that this discipline is the one that unlocks the secrets of the self. We need to look closely at how these elusive secrets came to be seen in there.

Private property entailed the idea that mental processes are 'owned' by each individual

The growth of capitalism in Europe entailed a fundamental change in the way that each person would understand their place in

---

[6] Examples which uncannily, but not surprisingly, interlock with the Eiser (1986) text are to be found in the US 'international edition' texts (e.g., Aronson et al., 2004) and in the 'European' text by Hewstone and Stroebe (2001).

[7] One example is the chronological guide produced by Lawry (1981).

the world. The owners of the new industries had to accumulate sufficient capital to build factories and employ workers, and their competition with each other in the marketplace encouraged them to understand their own activity as being powered by self-enclosed unique creative abilities. This is not at all to say that there was no conception of personal creativity before this point in history, but now, at the very moment when the individual was glorified, it was assumed that it could only flourish inside the new cage of the 'self'. People were, at each moment of their activity, separated and set against their competitors and they became all the more convinced that their plans for growth were their own private property.[8]

Workers, meanwhile, had to compete against each other to sell their labour power in order to make money for themselves and their families to survive. Labour and creativity became something that they came to experience as something possessed by them, until it was sold to someone else. Even if the life of the worker was judged as less than that of the employer, something significant changed that called upon new explanations of individual differences and how they might have developed. The old Christian image of the rich man in his castle and the poor man at his gate – one that seemed to account for why people's fates were so different – continued to function in a new society that was also intensely hierarchical. But now there was a search for something in human nature that would explain why people struggled against each other and why some people would not accept their lowly place in the order of things. When people could acquire more and more, and buy the labour of others in the process, the stage was set for a form of 'possessive individualism' that posed a puzzle for the new generation of gentleman scientists and university scholars.[9]

The nuclear family required intense dependence, and anxiety about separation

Women were very present in the workforce in early capitalism, but they were still responsible for life at home and for the care of

---

[8] A very nice little book on this topic is Morris' (1972) study of the 'discovery of the individual', and Williams (1976) includes a brief review of how the word 'individual' has come to have its present-day meaning.

[9] Macpherson (1964) provides an account of the way that 'possessive individualism' became one of the dominant conceptions of self under capitalism, and in psychological culture the individual comes more and more to believe that they 'possess' themselves. For a good discussion of Macpherson's work, see Townshend (1998).

children. There is a complicated process at play here through which the life of the child was transformed as it was prepared for the world of work and through which the women became more confined to the increasingly separate sphere of the nuclear family. In addition, as social commentators looked back on life before capitalism in the early years of industrialisation, and as they wrote histories of conditions in the factories later on, there was another turn in the fate of women and how their lives should be understood.[10]

These new social conditions transformed one kind of patriarchal system into another, carrying the traces of that old system to the present so that the burdens placed on women became all the more complex.[11] The change in relations of production, with large privately owned enterprises replacing locally organised work on the land, separates work as time in the factory from the home; and it separated work from leisure, giving rise to the newly distinct realm of childhood, the cradle of what later came to be 'developmental' psychology.[12]

Compared with the competition and exploitation of industrial capitalism, the family became the 'heart of a heartless world'; this phrase, which was coined by Karl Marx to describe how religion offered some space of comfort in a society built on ruthless exploitation,[13] also highlights how escape into the bosom of the family home was a mixed blessing. From the factory furnaces into the frying pans of

---

[10] Marcus (1974) gives a marvellous account of Engels in Manchester and the early history of capitalism that addresses these issues. It is tempting to look back on pre-industrial Europe and imagine that women were not subordinated to men before capitalism, and then to imagine that women did not work as capitalism became dominant; for an argument against this view, see Beechey (1979).

[11] Millett (1977) – in one of the defining texts of 'second wave' feminism of the 1960s and 1970s (in which the suffragette struggle for women's votes at the beginning of the twentieth century is part of the 'first wave' and the queer movement independent of any political party at the start of the twenty-first century is part of a 'third wave') – argues that patriarchy is a system of social control in which men dominate women and older men dominate younger men. Even before the so-called 'men's movement', then, there is a concern in feminist politics with the negative impact of patriarchy on men as well as women. For a good overview of socialist, radical and revolutionary strands of second wave feminism, see Beechey (1979).

[12] Ariès (1962) is the key reference for a strand of historical work on the historical construction of 'childhood', and this work has been taken forward in a number of volumes, in particular the collection of papers edited by Kessel and Siegel (1981), which includes as appendix a reprint of the significant contribution by Kessen (1979).

[13] It is Marx's (1844) argument that 'Religious suffering is, at one and the same time, the expression of real suffering and a protest against real suffering. Religion is the sigh of the oppressed creature, the heart of a heartless world, and the soul of soulless conditions. It is the opium of the people.'

sizzling resentment at home, the place of the family and its internal shape served all the more to separate the world of women from the world of men. It also made all those who grew up in families more dependent on this little world, and fearful about what lay outside. The dialectical relation between family life and work life is one that has from the beginning entranced psychologists who study first the one side of the relation and then the other, giving advice to those on either side, but not realising that psychology came onto the scene to make the impossible choices for each individual caught in their vice-like grip just a bit more bearable.[14]

The nation state became a key player in discipline and identity, at work and at home

While each individual worker was set against the others to find employment and each nuclear family was becoming a separate place to raise children, competition was becoming more intense between different enterprises and between different parts of Europe. The logic of competition in this burgeoning capitalism, however, was something that increasingly called upon the state to protect and support it. One paradox of 'free enterprise' is that while individual capitalists often complain about state interference in their economic affairs, they need the state to maintain law and order.[15]

Each particular capitalist nation state must have an apparatus charged with guaranteeing the property of its inhabitants and each nation state is then caught up in competition against outsiders. The military was often already in the vanguard of the push to develop health care for its own personnel and for prostitutes who serviced the troops, and the discussions over discipline in the army balanced against therapeutic support for those suffering mentally increased in intensity.[16]

The integrity of the state was faced with threats from outside – from those who resisted occupation or those who defied the companies

[14] Zaretsky (1976) provides a wonderful little account of how 'personal life' is separated off from the public sphere under capitalism so that the family then functions as a refuge from a world in which we are unable to show intimacy to others.
[15] See Engels (1972) for the classic argument – originally made in 1884 – that the family, private property and the state were necessarily intertwined from the birth of capitalism.
[16] The study of 'shell-shock' in the twentieth century was another manifestation of the need for military efficiency rather than being an expression of benevolent care for the soldiery. Shephard (2001) traces the development of the notion from when it was first identified to its current manifestation as 'post-traumatic stress disorder'.

searching for profits overseas – and concern then grew over the task of dealing with enemies from within. Suspicion of outsiders now mutated into new more virulent forms of racism, and it was only a matter of time before psychological explanations of essential differences between peoples was stirred in. The question could not be settled by simply declaring that non-European races were less than human; instead, more sophisticated racist descriptions of the characteristics of different segregated 'communities' were mobilised to explain why the foreigners were liable to be disloyal to their host country. Immigrant workers who are productive and well behaved will be tolerated, but only insofar as they can be assimilated to a workforce that identifies with its own employers in a common struggle against those of other nations.[17]

The competition for markets and new sources of cheap labour as industry expanded then took this nationalist element of capitalism to a further more world-shaping point with the emergence of imperialism. The idea that capitalism was the only road to civilised development was interlinked with the exploitation of colonised countries, and these parts of the world were systematically 'underdeveloped', reduced to providing raw materials and labour power.[18]

Those who refused to adapt needed to be observed, treated and brought back into line

Employers do not like to be told to ensure safety at work, to keep within maximum hours of labour in a day or, still less, to agree to minimum levels of pay. However, the welfare of the workforce is also, to an extent, in their interests, and the state started to play an increasingly influential role alongside the family in looking after the health of existing workers and the upbringing of potential employees. Individuals and their families were still expected to do most of the actual day-to-day care work, while the state undertook the regulation of standards for health and, bit by bit, what came to be seen as 'mental' health. The government welfare programmes operating alongside independent charitable bodies did not always intervene

[17] Cohen (2006) outlines the history of immigration controls and how they function to strengthen the nation state.
[18] Rodney (1973) provides the classic argument that Europe 'underdeveloped' Africa, and it is in this sense that we can see 'underdevelopment' as a general process that is intensified by neoliberal globalisation (see Cammack, 2003), a process which 'overdevelops' certain countries (such as the United States) as part of the ecological crises faced by capitalism (see Bookchin, 2004).

directly in the family to tell parents exactly how they should bring up their children. However, the combination of particular laws and moral advice in the 'public' sphere outside the family served to carve out a certain space in which the family was supposed to operate, a certain kind of shape with certain responsibilities for those in the 'private' sphere of the home.[19]

Capitalists who make rash decisions about investment or behave in bizarre ways that endanger a particular enterprise are not really much of an immediate problem for the economy, and even now rich eccentrics can get away with a lot without drawing the attention of the state authorities. The problem that concerns the state is that workers of any kind – those in the factory, the shop or the home – may be unwilling or unable to work; while an individual worker who only refuses to sell his or her labour power may merely starve on their own, such irrational behaviour may infect others, men and women.

The images of disorder that were most disturbing to the authorities during the popular uprising which formed the Paris Commune in 1871 were those that showed the active participation of women; collective activity against capitalism is bad enough, but when that activity breaks down the distinction between work and home things are really serious.[20] The police may be able to deal with deliberate political agitation that threatens production, but for cases of individual irrationality that may spill over into collective discontent a new body of professionals was needed; enter stage right, the psychologists.

Psychology as a Discipline Sought Knowledge, but This Was Tied to Power

The development of capitalism was of new relations of production, new social relations, and the economic transformations in the nineteenth century were intertwined with changes in the family and in the place of women. This new political-economic system required increasingly intense control and segregation of time; of the length of the work day, of leisure and of holidays. The space in which people lived and worked was also organised to ensure that the family was an efficient mechanism for producing and caring for the

[19] See Donzelot (1979) for a study of the way the French state intervened in the family and determined its internal shape.
[20] Edith Thomas (1967) describes the activity of women during the Paris Commune, and the horror of the authorities.

workforce – architecture reflected and reproduced new spaces of public housing and private space and the connections between them.[21] Capitalism consisted of new relations of power that included exploitation of labour, exploitation of natural resources and exploitation of those colonised by imperialism. Those relations of power sustained a particular kind of search for knowledge and what researchers imagined they might do with knowledge once they found it.

The Western Enlightenment tradition that began toward the end of the eighteenth century provided inspiration for a form of knowledge that was intimately bound up with the development of capitalism, necessary to it. The best of that tradition from the early phase of the Enlightenment is still alive in modern science and in the value placed on the pursuit of truth as such; but the worst of it, from the time it started to degrade at the end of the nineteenth century, lingers on in the discipline of psychology as one of its offspring.[22]

Early studies of psychology separated the experimenter from the individual subject

We can see how things started to go wrong from the first days, or at least from what psychologists still like to treat as the first days of their discipline. The founding moment of psychology is often presented as being when Wilhelm Wundt carried out his experimental studies in an attic in Leipzig in 1879, but what is quickly covered over is that Wundt's first experiments involved the experimenter and his 'subject' changing places and investigating each other.[23] This is not to say that just anyone could be a subject in this kind of research; in fact, Wundt's experimenter and subject were both required to be highly trained experts in the practice of observing and reporting their experience. Experimental psychology was right from the very start sealed off from the real world, and was concerned with investigating and describing itself. When the 'subjects'

---

[21] See Joyce (2003) for an account of the historical production of private living spaces and the architecture that separates and enables observation and control of families and individuals.

[22] Kramnick (1995) provides an excellent selection of key texts from the Enlightenment period which starts with Immanuel Kant's (1784) essay 'What is Enlightenment?'. On occasion the European Enlightenment writers saw other, 'native' cultures as less advanced; there is a good discussion of Kant's racism and consequences for psychology by Teo (1999).

[23] Danziger (1990) provides an excellent account of the historical context for Wilhelm Wundt's research and an earlier paper by Danziger is a classic study of the way the later positivist psychologists screened out the aspects of Wundt's methodology that did not fit a strict reductionist laboratory-experimental methodology (Danziger, 1979).

of psychological research came to include the general public, however, things got even worse.

Too quickly for most psychologists now to notice, the figure of the experimenter became separated from his object of study. This object, which is still called the 'subject' in most mainstream research, is now someone else who is not a psychologist. So, here we have two steps toward reification, toward the turning of people and relationships into things:[24] the first step is the separation of the investigator from what they describe – the experimenter studies the 'subject' – while the second step is to turn that 'subject' into someone who must now by definition be someone who is not a psychologist, must be an object to be manipulated and measured because they are not accorded the expertise to describe what they do themselves accurately enough. This reification cannot simply be solved by telling psychologists not to call their objects of study 'subjects'; quite the opposite, for this leaves experimental procedures in place.[25]

The laboratory-experimental method defined its own history and development

One of the key defining texts for the new discipline, *The History of Experimental Psychology* by the suitably named E. G. Boring in 1929 was a programmatic document.[26] It was a manifesto for the

[24] Reification – in which social relationships are turned into things – is the mainstay of the 'social constructionist' tradition in sociology (Berger and Luckmann, 1971). Marxism sees human relationships under capitalism as 'reified', for everything in this society is turned into a commodity to be bought and sold, including human creative labour (see Bottomore, 1991). This aspect of reification is not really taken seriously by 'social constructionist' academics because they are usually not interested in understanding and challenging capitalism; not surprisingly, 'reification' is then screened out from social constructionism when it finds its way into psychology, not even making it into the index of some of the otherwise quite good introductory books on the topic (Burr, 2003). For an account of reification in psychology, see Ingleby (1972).

[25] The term 'subject' to refer to active human agents is something that is taken into psychology and distorted, and then because laboratory-experimental psychologists refer to 'subjects' of their studies when they are treating them like objects, it is understandable that people try to avoid this term. Some psychologists prefer not to talk about 'subjects' but they then, quite hypocritically, carry on as usual. The issue, of course, is not what term we use to refer to people – and 'subject' is still the most appropriate way of conceptualising a human agent in philosophy and political theory – but whether their activities are valued or demeaned in the practice of investigation, and whether it makes it more difficult for non-experimental researchers to accord value to 'subjects' as active agents.

[26] Boring (1929); for a good account of how Boring's book was designed and used as a political intervention to swing US American psychology toward a laboratory-experimental approach, see O'Donnell (1979).

discipline that would be based on laboratory-experiments conducted by a scientific investigator observing and measuring the behaviour of individual 'subjects'. Boring stitched together a variety of different studies to show an unbroken lineage from Wundt to modern psychology, and this meant that many of Wundt's speculations about social processes had to be filtered out. Psychology would look very different today perhaps – not necessarily better, but maybe not so obsessed with laboratory-experimental studies – if Wundt's writings on 'folk psychology' had also been translated into English. These latter writings showed that Wundt saw the study of individual psychology as only part of the story, and his folk psychology was concerned with collective cultural processes that were crucial to the way human beings perceived the world, thought about it and remembered things of significance to them.

Boring's approach was deliberately and explicitly positivist, a vision of science as based on the steady accumulation of findings that could be treated as 'facts' within a complete system of knowledge.[27] The new science of psychology was supposed to be based on findings about individuals. This is ironic, for Boring had already selected certain 'facts' about the discipline of psychology to tell a story of the development of a laboratory-experimental discipline. We can already see from this official history that a strict positivist programme is actually impossible, for there are no neutral facts that stick out ready to be slotted in the right place into a story about human beings.[28] Every story about society and human nature has to select certain pieces of information that then take on a certain kind of sense in the overall narrative. When experimental psychology was taken up and developed in the United States, for example, it was hitched to the work of Francis Galton, and so to a version of evolutionary theory that told a story that fitted well with ideology in capitalist society; the fittest and best individuals are those that are

[27] The version of positivism that laboratory-experimental psychology championed was very different from the 'positivism' of the French founder of sociology, Auguste Comte (for a good outline of how sociology developed, and how it functioned as an academic alternative to Marxism, see Therborn, 1976). Comte's scientific Enlightenment spirit is still very much alive in the slogan on the Brazilian flag 'order and progress'. Here we have another example of how the discipline of psychology screened out things from other academic areas of study that it did not like (Samelson, 1974). Psychology ended up with a version of 'science' that would be unrecognisable to other natural scientists as well as social scientists (Harré and Secord, 1972).

[28] Krige (1979) provides a good challenge to positivist notions in an article that is very relevant to the way psychology treats its 'discoveries'.

successful and wealthy, and the poor are the losers in the struggle for survival.[29]

Categories of the gifted and the stupid became a key concern

There was a two-fold pressure on psychologists at the beginning of the twentieth century; first, that they show that their knowledge could claim to be grounded in evidence rather than idle speculation – psychology had to break away from philosophy to find this new more secure ground – and second, closely linked to the kind of 'evidence' that the authorities had in mind, that they come up with a kind of knowledge that will successfully predict behaviour. Prediction of cause and effect relationships – relationships between things rather than between people – also had to be linked with control; when psychologists say that they want to develop a science based on 'prediction and control' they really mean it.[30] Ideally this prediction and control of behaviour should operate from cradle to grave, and some of the earliest investigations – aiming for 'facts' to distance psychology from philosophical ruminations about the nature of the 'noble savage' and suchlike – were focused on the earliest years of life.[31]

The fate of studies into 'gifted' children who might benefit from education shows that the requirements of mass education to produce a workforce able to deal with increasingly sophisticated working conditions forced its own agenda on psychology and added further pressures. The early researchers were certainly carrying out a form of 'psychological research', and this study of children who are

---

[29] For an excellent collection of papers on the way Galton's work functioned in the context of the development of psychological testing in the US, see Block and Dworkin (1977). For good accounts of the way these ideas fuelled racism in the US, see Blum (1978) and Lawlor (1978). One of the proponents of genetic theories of intelligence tried to smear his critics by labelling them as Marxists (Eysenck, 1982); of course Marxism provides a quite different account of how 'individual differences' are produced, and is quite right to do so. Galton adapted and perverted Darwinian theories of evolution, as do many psychologists who now call themselves 'evolutionary psychologists'; for arguments against evolutionary psychology, see Rose and Rose (2001).

[30] Although it is sometimes thought that behaviourist psychologists are the only ones obsessed with the 'prediction and control' of behaviour (e.g., Mills, 1998), the phrase actually appeared first in an article by William James (1892), who is now seen as a guiding light of the humanist and spiritually inclined 'transpersonal' psychotherapists (Rowan, 2005). Morawski (1982) shows that the idea that the discipline should be concerned with 'prediction and control' informed behaviourist and non-behaviourist psychology in the US.

[31] A good review of historical connections between psychological research on the development of children and broader notions of the development of civilisation is provided by Malson and Itard (1972).

supposed to be very intelligent does continue today.[32] However, the discipline of psychology was organised around a much more practical task, practical from the standpoint of those wanting to ensure that individual members of the population would work efficiently to produce profit for those who employed them. It might be interesting to identify gifted children, but it became clear that it was more useful, more economically expedient to identify the stupid ones who would not benefit from education.[33] There was thus a rapid shift of focus, from those who were different and needed more attention to those who were abnormal, not the merely work-shy but those constitutionally unsuited to the work capitalism required of them, those that needed to be regulated.

Psychological problems were explained by inheritance and familial relationships

One of the most powerful warrants for the free market was provided by the idea that economic processes were in line with evolutionary principles of natural selection and the survival of the fittest. The early years of intelligence-testing in the United States and restrictions on immigration from cultures deemed to be more prone to 'feeble-mindedness' were connected with this Galtonian version of evolutionary theory.[34] The theory provided one explanation for why some people were very successfully wealthy and others fell by the wayside, but another set of explanations also started to gain currency; these explanations focused on why it was that most people succeeded in adapting to the world of economic competition while other particular individuals failed.

Racist studies of intelligence were now complemented by equally racist ideas about the nature of different cultures, and how people brought up outside the structure of the normal nuclear family might be less able to adapt to the new industrial society. Larger 'extended families' are sometimes admired and sometimes disdained, but they

---

[32] Burks et al. (1930) argue that this 'giftedness' is genetic and that special attention should be given to those children. For an analysis of the work of the psychologist Lewis Terman on the 'gifted' child and the relationship to gender, see Hegarty (in press).

[33] The logic of this focus on those whom parents and educators think are 'gifted' means that the labelling of children with psychiatric disorders is often not opposed, simply that special pleading is made that the 'gifted' children have been 'misdiagnosed' (James et al., 2005).

[34] Kamin (1974) provides a classic history, of the way intelligence-testing was part of eugenic programmes in the US that included sterilising those categorised as 'feeble-minded' and enacting immigration legislation to keep out less intelligent 'races'.

came in for special attention either way as psychology in the 'West' tried to make sense of those it saw as 'other' than itself.[35]

The family was now assumed to be the crucible of the self, and so it became plausible to argue that inherited abilities and deficits might be influenced by, or be even less important than, family processes.[36] Psychology has often puzzled over the role of 'environmental influences' in the development of intelligence, and it tries to weigh up those influences against the 'genetic component'.[37] By 'environment' it usually means the family and it often then turns to the difference between families in different cultures. Psychological theory is always a child of its time, and the theories do adapt and survive in the intellectual marketplace as the survival of the fittest ideas for capitalism.

Psychology Had to Mark Itself Out Against Rival Approaches to the Individual

The domain of individual psychology became a concern for people invested in the success of capitalist society, a concern both for the state authorities and for individuals who more and more experienced themselves as separate and distinct from others. However, the discipline of psychology as a contender for being the discipline that would provide the most convincing explanations for why things sometimes went wrong, and come up with the goods to put people back on track, was still not fully formed. Fortunately the question as to who should have priority in studying and helping individuals is still not settled today, and psychologists have to spend a good deal of energy explaining to other people what differentiates them from psychiatrists, psychoanalysts and psychotherapists. This extended family of what we can term the 'psy professions' is an annoyance and embarrassment to many psychologists, and most non-psychologists want to know what makes psychology as such so special.

[35] Said (1978) shows how 'orientalist' images were used to assure those in the 'West' that they were civilised, and although Said is not concerned directly with psychology, his cultural and literary study is very relevant to an understanding of how psychology viewed those from other cultures. This work is taken further to address questions of gender by Lewis (1996).

[36] John Bowlby's (1944) psychoanalytic study of 'forty-four juvenile thieves' was a key intervention here, shifting the ground so that psychologists would research family history and, crucially, the role of the mother (see Riley, 1983).

[37] In addition to the Kamin (1974) history and the Block and Dworkin (1977) collection, another critical review of theories of 'race' and intelligence in the context of British psychology is that of Richardson and Spears (1972).

Psychology claims expertise in education and
social welfare alongside medicine

Psychology presents itself as having distinctive knowledge about development, personality and behaviour in training for nurses, occupational therapists, social workers and others involved in health and social care. One way that people in other professions first come across psychology is when they are taught the 'facts' about child behaviour or mental disorders. The knowledge that psychologists pretend to have about these things is slotted into the curriculum of other disciplines, even when practitioners have long known that they do not work well in practice. The discipline of social work, for example, has often, quite rightly, been very scathing about psychology, which is not to say that everything is rosy in social work as a self-declared progressive alternative.[38]

In state and voluntary training courses psychologists try to pull rank over what they see as lesser disciplines, and one way psychology tries to award itself higher status is to ally itself with medicine. It has in the past even laid claim to an area of 'medical psychology',[39] and if psychologists now were able to get as much respect as medical doctors it seems they would be very happy. There is an uneasy truce with rival professions in most parts of the world, sometimes interrupted by skirmishes conducted from the safer ground of private practice and sometimes smoothed over through participation in multidisciplinary teams in clinics or schools.[40] Advice based on 'evidence' that is built on the mistaken assumption that interventions in education can be sampled and measured is one recent ploy by psychologists to show that they can be useful.[41]

---

[38] For a good account of this question, focusing on therapeutic assumptions among British social workers, see K. McLaughlin (2003a).

[39] Even so, the section for 'medical psychology' in the British Psychological Society was actually more psychoanalytic, and the clinical discussions were framed in psychoanalytic terms. This was the setting for the influence of John Bowlby's psychoanalytic work on 'attachment' in the discipline of psychology in the UK.

[40] Squabbles with other competing approaches that deal with mental health make peaceful coexistence with rival professions difficult, however, and for a time in Britain, for example, clinical psychologists feared that they could be completely sidelined and even disappear as a separate profession. They fought back and are now busy persuading themselves and others that they have a particular expertise that will complement psychiatry and psychotherapy (see Pilgrim and Treacher, 1990).

[41] The American Psychological Association is up to its neck in this game, as the title 'Wanted: politics-free, science-based education' of one of the articles in the APA *Monitor on Psychology* makes clear (Murray, 2002).

Psychology claims expertise in cognitive
therapy against psychiatry

Medical approaches to mental distress are historically crystallised in psychiatry, and psychologists have to deal with the inconvenient fact that although psychiatrists are sometime seen as having lesser status than their fellow medics they are certainly accorded more status than the psychologist. One tactic that psychology has used to differentiate itself from psychiatry, and to make it seem as if it has something distinctive to offer, is to claim that 'cognitive therapy' is a useful alternative. Cognitive-behavioural approaches to distress are thus pitted against the medical psychiatric diagnoses that tend to treat them as underlying 'organic' illnesses.[42]

The strategy here is to try and complement the medical specialists, those psychiatrists whom they cannot hope to defeat. If psychiatrists can be persuaded to focus on disorders that are supposedly 'organic' – a product of chemical imbalances to be treated with drugs – then psychologists hope that this will leave the field free for specialising in the mind – the 'cognitions' that are supposed to guide our behaviour. Psychologists would love to have prescribing rights for drug treatments as well, of course, and they rarely tackle the medical model in psychiatry head on.[43] The psychiatrists are friends they would rather not have, and this means that psychology is always jostling for position, and offering alternatives that are not much better than the medical model. Claims that 'schizophrenia' is caused by child abuse rather than faulty genes, for example, still reinforce the quite erroneous idea that there is such a thing as a 'schizophrenic', and it still locks someone who is suffering into a category that is fixed and permanent.[44]

---

[42] See, for example, Haddock and Slade (1995).

[43] There are exceptions, such as the book on 'schizophrenia' edited by Bentall (1990), which is very useful as a resource to challenge psychiatric models, but which is still making a bid for psychologists to address the 'symptoms' of schizophrenia with cognitive-behavioural treatments.

[44] For a detailed study of the evidence for the existence of a discrete illness 'schizophrenia' which concludes that this thing does not exist, see Boyle (2002). This has not stopped psychologists trying to claim 'schizophrenia' as something psychological rather than medical, a move that does not do anyone any favours, least of all those who are made to live with the label (see James, 2003). For a slightly better account, but one that still tends to put psychology in the place of psychiatry, see Bentall (2004); ironically, the most radical accounts come from within psychiatry (e.g., Double, 2006), and these are then invaluable resources for those struggling against diagnoses in and against psychology.

Psychology claims scientific knowledge about
change against psychoanalysis

Psychiatrists have historically had a much closer association than psychologists with psychoanalysis, even though psychoanalysis is an approach that does not rely on a medical model of 'mental illness'. Instead, it should be a theory and treatment of the unconscious and of the effects of the unconscious that keep childhood memories at play throughout adult life. Psychoanalysts have in many countries been required to do medical training and this has then made their work in practice into something that can be just as problematic as psychiatry or psychology,[45] but psychoanalysis still has a quite distinct approach to distress based on speaking and interpretation rather than the administration of a 'treatment'. The close links that psychoanalysis enjoyed with psychiatry have been disturbing and sometimes incomprehensible for psychologists, and made all the worse by the assumption that psychoanalysis is not based on what they think of as scientific study.[46]

Psychologists use the quasi-scientific watchwords 'prediction' and 'control' to do battle with psychoanalysis and to claim that only 'scientific' psychology can tell you how people change and exactly what you have to do to them to make them change in the right way. Some humanistic psychologists in the English-speaking world do not like psychoanalysis because it is mechanistic, but this rejection of psychoanalysis is a mirror image of the same mistake that the 'scientific' psychologists make; in some contexts psychoanalysis is an alternative to psychology, and in other contexts it is just as bad.[47] Outside the English-speaking world, particularly in Latin America, psychologists are sometimes a beleaguered minority who

[45] Jacoby (1975) shows how psychoanalysis comes to operate as part of mainstream psychology and psychiatry when it attempts to adapt people to society, and he follows this argument up in a fascinating study of the way émigré psychoanalysts arriving in the US from Europe after fleeing fascism had to adapt themselves to medical knowledge, and so adapted psychoanalysis itself to forms of medicine and medical psychology (Jacoby, 1983).
[46] Hans Eysenck, when he was not touting theories of racial differences in intelligence (see Billig, 1979), produced a much-quoted paper on the failure of psychotherapy, which at the time the paper was written was predominantly psychoanalytic (Eysenck, 1952), and then followed this up with increasingly vociferous attacks on the 'unscientific' nature of psychoanalysis (Eysenck and Wilson, 1973) which ended in some massive wish-fulfilment fantasies about 'the decline of the Freudian empire' (Eysenck, 1985).
[47] The psychoanalyst Bruno Bettelheim (1986) argued that psychoanalysis in the original German used everyday terminology, but was distorted in order to make it fit natural-scientific models when it was translated into English.

cling to their US American textbooks to try and do battle with the psychoanalysts, who are much more powerful.[48]

Psychology claims expert knowledge in and against psychotherapy and counselling

The pretend-scientific approach adopted by psychology also gives it an edge, so it thinks, against other approaches in therapy that are not supported by the kind of investigation psychology approves of. This has led it to build its own supposedly more scientific variety of 'counselling psychology'. In practice, a 'counselling psychologist' may do much the same as another counsellor working with a similar theoretical framework, but the scientific aura given to the treatment is often a source of comfort to the practitioner when they think of themselves as being a 'psychologist'. A false sense of security is given to this kind of counsellor who claims knowledge about the self against rival professions.[49]

Here the status game is quite naked, and institutional struggles for prestige are fought out over the precise labels that different practitioners should be allowed to claim for themselves. Psychologists are making a big push to be recognised as distinctive key players in the hierarchies between counsellors, who are usually at the bottom of the pecking order, and psychotherapists. The magical word 'evidence' is used to support attempts to develop courses in 'counselling psychology' and separate registers for psychologists who practise as psychotherapists, but in the end the discipline knows that it is recognition by the state that will weigh most.[50] Victory, as far as the psychologists are concerned, will be signalled by government regulation of all the psy professions which prohibits anyone without a certificate being allowed to use the label 'psychologist'. The word 'psychology' has been snatched from popular use, and now it is jealously guarded by the discipline; and, like Gollum's ring, it has given a baleful and terrible power to those who have seized it.[51]

[48] Psychology is not always dominant as an academic or clinical approach, though with increasing globalisation it is becoming more powerful, and psychoanalysis in France and Spanish-speaking countries is now under siege from cognitive behavioural approaches (which were developed by Aaron Beck, who trained first as a psychoanalyst and then defected to psychology).
[49] At the same time, some counselling psychology practitioners in the UK have tried to hold open a space for radical critiques of mainstream counselling and psychotherapy (e.g., Woolfe et al., 2003).
[50] For accounts of the attempt to regulate counselling and psychotherapy in Britain, see Mowbray (1995) and House and Totton (1997); see also the Independent Practitioner Network perspectives at http://ipnosis.postle.net.
[51] The reference here is, of course, to Gollum in *The Lord of the Rings* (Tolkien, 1969), not to any particular obscure experimental psychologist of that name.

**Psychological Training Produces Specific Approaches
to the 'Normal' and 'Abnormal'**

A psychologist undertakes a specific kind of training that so often gives rise to a strange mindset for understanding other people, a rather unpleasant attitude to what the causes of problems are and what should be done about them. Students who begin psychology degrees often do so because they genuinely want to understand something about themselves and help others. There are many pathways that students take into psychology training, and some of these routes enable them to maintain their integrity and vision. However, these are the minority, and most students are taught very early on in their course that there are certain questions they must not ask about their own experience and motivations; they learn that their objects of research are other people who, they assume, must be unlike themselves.

*Other people are the subjects to be studied closely,
and deceived if necessary*

Most psychological investigation works on the premise that if you tell people what you are studying they will change the way they behave, and, rather curiously, in the research context this capacity of people to reflect on what they do and change is seen as a bad thing. It is assumed to be more scientific to deceive objects of study, to draw their attention away from what is being measured. The stuff of psychology that is reported in the journals and relayed to students in the textbooks, then, is based on what people do when they have no agency. The behaviour that is recorded and reported is that which takes place when someone else, usually the psychologist, is in control.

Even this control is not much of a source of comfort to the psychologist as researcher. It seems as if the psychologist is the active subject and the person called the 'subject' in the study is reduced to the status of an object; but even their own status as 'subject' is betrayed. The poor psychologist does not even have the right to assume the position of conscious active agent in their account of what happened in a psychological experiment, for they are required to write in the third person, as if they were not really present themselves. They certainly cannot say what actually happened in their interaction with participants in a study – those whom they must not smile at because it would be a 'confounding variable', for example. The experiments are thus 'depopulated' of actual living, thinking people, and the psychologists themselves have to efface themselves.[52] There is a sad assumption on the part of most psychologists that they would be too 'subjective' and therefore too 'biased' if they were actually to research something they were genuinely interested in, and this assumption lies at the root of the often rather pointless dull studies reported in the mainstream journals.[53]

Laboratory-experimentation is at the core of psychology, with some dissident approaches

Psychology is not only divided into different specialist areas of study – cognitive, developmental, social, and so on – but also into warring methodological camps. The main approach is still firmly quantitative, and it rests on the idea that laws of cause and effect can be discovered by manipulating behaviour and measuring it. The measurement may be of things ranging from 'reaction times' to 'attitudes', but the underlying assumption is always that the psychologist knows in advance what that thing is that they are going to target and record. Against this dominant methodology, there have over the years been arguments by 'humanistic' psychologists concerned with the meaning people give to their actions, and there have been valiant attempts to show that a quantitative approach is a mistaken 'paradigm'; a new more scientific paradigm, they have argued, would be qualitative in nature and would 'for scientific purposes treat people as if they were human beings'.[54] These attempts failed, and not merely because the advocates of the 'new paradigm' were not clever enough; the 'new paradigm' that they hoped for would not, if successful, have ended up being psychology as we know it at all.

The closely controlled environment in which 'variables' are manipulated to discover whether predictions about behaviour are confirmed, and whether the models that specify laws of cause and effect can be supported, is still necessary to the dominant research paradigm for psychology. Even in studies that are carried out in the 'field' outside the laboratory, assumptions about the importance of

---

[52] For an account of this problem and some amusing ways to redress it, see Billig (1994); see also Stam et al. (1998).

[53] Psychologists busy themselves with squashing any manifestation of subjectivity in those they do research on, and they are equally worried about any manifestation of subjectivity on their own part, and so they become obsessed with 'bias', as if it is necessarily a bad thing to be interested in what they research (Rosenthal, 1966).

[54] Harré and Secord (1972), p. 84.

controlling 'independent variables' and measuring 'dependent variables' still provide the conceptual frame to justify what the psychologist does to other people. Objections to these assumptions have been beaten back, mainly because psychologists have taken fright at what the consequences would be if they had to face their sponsors in government and private enterprise and admit that they cannot really measure, predict and control how people behave and think.

Psychological research requires certain assumptions about what counts

Prediction and control of behaviour can only be guaranteed by stripping away the meaning people give to why they do things, and by producing measurements that replace and obscure that meaning. It is not that there is then no meaning as such in psychology; there is plenty of meaning, bucket-loads of ideological assumptions about the nature of human beings and what they are able to do. That ideological meaning is what is put into the measurements by way of the interpretation of the results by the psychologist.

The most obvious ideological meanings appear by way of assumptions about categories of behaviour or identity that can be specified and measured, and here we are faced with questions of content. Some cases are now obvious to psychologists, and they would not now, for example, assume that there was a category of disorder called 'drapetomania' that would supposedly explain why slaves ran away from plantations.[55] Many, perhaps most, psychologists would not now assume that homosexuality is a disorder that can be cured with aversion therapy.[56] The most insidious ideological meanings appear in the formal structure of psychological knowledge rather than in the content, and we see this formal structure at work in appeals to the notion of a 'normal distribution' in statistics.[57] A psychologist who assumes that anything about a person's experience or activity fits a 'normal distribution' is already working inside ideology, and it is then a slippery slope to specific limiting assumptions about human beings.

[55] Littlewood and Lipsedge (1993) provide a good account of the way that cultural differences often lead psychiatrists to treat behaviour that they cannot understand as pathology.

[56] An indicative example (in a book edited by Hans Eysenck) is the discussion by Freund (1960). For a further critical discussion of this practice, see Tatchell (1997).

[57] There is nothing necessarily wrong with statistics as such, but there is a serious problem when psychologists try to use statistics to abstract and reify observations about people and then arrange human populations on so-called 'normal distributions'. For good reviews of the way statistics is misused by the social sciences generally, see the collections by Irvine et al. (1979) and Dorling and Simpson (1999).

Studies of decision-making and identity-formation are still the mainstay of cognitive psychology and developmental psychology, and these studies fit very well with the agenda of understanding people so that those in power can be sure that they know what their subjects will do next. Those who do not fit the normative models of how a human being should develop and think are given special attention and, if they are very unlucky, 'treatment'. Those who are unpredictable are still the ones who might at any point disrupt the smooth running of the economy.

Psychology has remained all too faithful to its earliest history, the worst of that history. It rests on ideas about 'normal' distributions and the other 'skewed' distributions that are measured against what they assume the world should be like. It emphasises individual behaviour as separate from other people; it makes the difference between men and women one of its main concerns, puzzling over how it is that some men do not seem to be as competitive as the rest of their mates.[58] It aims to enable people to lead productive lives within the limits of present-day political-economic systems that are based on competition and profit.

Psychologists Are Not What They Think They Are

Most psychologists are not consciously dedicated to the survival of capitalism, but their failure to reflect on what they actually do is as great as the cognitive failures that they expect to find in those who are not psychologists. They do not play the grand role they sometimes imagine they should.[59] Even the history of psychology is not what psychologists think it is the history of.[60] That is why I have had to give an account in this chapter that grounds the history of the discipline in the development of capitalism; a kind of history that most psychologists would think is quite bizarre. They imagine that a scientific approach to understanding individuals appeared around a century ago, that we are all very lucky that it helps discover more about people, and that is that.

[58] See Eagly (1995) on the assumption that research in psychology should compare men and women, and some attendant problems with this assumption. The attention to ostensibly complementary 'sex differences' also serves to normalise heterosexuality as the bedrock of the nuclear family and pathologise gay parents and their children (Anderssen, 2001).

[59] As has been pointed out, 'Psychologists claim to be social engineers, but turn out to be really maintenance men' (Ingleby, 1972, p. 57).

[60] For a good exploration of this problem, see Smith (1988), and for an outstanding history of psychology that fleshes out a lot of the detail in my cursory account, see Richards (1996).

Psychology is not scientific, and it is not clear that it could
be a separate distinct science

When you come into psychology you have to meet the whole extended family of the psy professions as well as the individuals that psychologists like to study. The discipline has from the very beginning tried to distance itself from philosophy as a sustained reflection on what it is to be a human being, and it has tried to make itself useful by making alliances with adjacent disciplines like management and criminology.[61]

The most interesting 'findings' from laboratory-experiments actually have the status of powerful anecdotes, but these anecdotes become poisonous ideology when they treat people as objects driven by process which only an expert can understand.[62]

Psychology is a constellation of practices that divide people
from each other and produce experts on others' lives

We should not be surprised that a lot of academic psychology appears to outsiders as being like shredded and recycled commonsense. If that first dismissive judgement were maintained, then psychology as a discipline would not have much prestige and power. Capitalist society grinds people down and leads them to experience their powerlessness and misery as lying inside individuals, to be treated at the level of the individual. Some individuals thrive, and psychology has certainly done well out of it, even if some psychologists are fairly dismal characters and a good number have been quite dangerous.

Psychology is not only about individuals but it is also a way of theorising and managing social relationships. It does this by focusing

---

[61] It is striking that psychology as a discipline increased massively in popularity in Britain during the rule of Margaret Thatcher, who made the famous claim that 'There is no such thing as society. There are only individual men and women and their families.' Thatcher was a scientist, trained as a chemist; how disappointed she would be with the fake science that is psychology.

[62] An example here is the famous Milgram (1963) study of 'obedience'. Stanley Milgram provided a powerful anecdote about how people might behave when they are told by 'experts' to do bad things to other people (in his experiment it was to deliver electric shocks to other 'subjects'). However, his study also treated the actual subjects that gave the shocks as objects; other, later studies have shown that it is possible to get the same kinds of results if the 'subjects' know exactly what is going on and are deliberately performing their obedience (Mixon, 1974). So, it is possible to have the powerful anecdote without the demeaning dehumanising practice of the deceptive laboratory experiment that psychology organises its world around; you do not need psychology to give you moral lessons about human nature.

on the individual and breaking up the individual into measurable components. The main problem is not that it does not work. The main problem is that it works so well because it confirms some of the most dehumanising practices that many people take for granted, practices that are a necessary part of the fabric of capitalist society.

2
Psychology as Ideology: Individualism Explained

One very useful aspect of psychology as a collection of theories about human beings and social relationships is that it captures and reflects back to us the dominant ideas of capitalist society. It is, in this sense, ideology crystallised, and if we examine it closely we can understand more about the mistaken assumptions we make about who we are in everyday life. Psychology is the *Star Trek* of the human sciences, and it is so interesting and enjoyable precisely because it portrays and puzzles over the things that we usually take for granted. Good science fiction poses complicated thought-experiments about human nature, but there are always intriguing blind spots where some features are taken as given, unquestioned. It remains trapped within its own horizons, and that is why we need to interpret it. This chapter explores the limited horizons of psychology and the way it makes us in its own image as it carries out its research.

Psychology searches for universal processes
that will explain human behaviour

Most psychologists think that it is possible to discover underlying laws which link the causes of human behaviour with the effects they scrutinise. Different kinds of psychology picture these underlying laws as operating in various specific ways in different places. In many cases what the psychologists dabble in is not psychology at all; research into the so-called 'biological basis of behaviour', for example, might tell us something interesting about biology, but what exactly it tells us about psychology as such is highly dubious. The distinctive qualities of our human nature are thus betrayed by the psychologists, for while we do indeed require certain material biological processes to be able to function and survive and relate to each other, our psychology is something that varies according to how we reflect on our human nature and the political choices we make about what to do with it.[1]

For a biological human being to become a human subject there needs to be a network of other subjects to provide the conditions for recognition of self and others, and our reflexive capacities to interpret and change the world are a function of our experience as social beings. To define these activities as 'psychology' is to make a serious conceptual error, an ideological mistake about what human nature actually is. There is no 'psychology' as such that will explain what we do; the abstract behaviour and individual mental processing that are studied by psychologists is fiction, science fiction, but then becomes lived out by those alienated from others and from themselves. The reduction and distortion of human social activity occurs today through psychologisation, and that psychologisation is carried out by academics and professionals who take research from biology, for example, and represent it to us as if it told us something about our psychology hidden deep inside ourselves.[2]

It also tries to explain what differentiates
human beings from each other

At the same time as psychologists search for underlying mechanisms to explain how we perceive and think and feel, most research

---

[1] Studies of brain function written by psychologists are actually sometimes quite good, but it is the claim that the descriptions about physiology are therefore also necessarily about psychology that is problematic; see, e.g., Stirling (1999). The most interesting parts of a psychology degree are usually not psychology at all, and the psychology departments would collapse if the research was moved to the actual disciplines their work draws on. The best writers on evolutionary theory are very cautious about extrapolating their findings to psychology (e.g., Gould, 1996; Lewontin, 2001), and biologists working on the brain do not then claim to be able to tell us how we think (e.g., Rose, 2006). In fact, these evolutionary and biological researchers have been active in challenging attempts to define what 'human nature' really is like and speculation about psychological differences between groups of people (e.g., Rose et al., 1990).

[2] Geras (1983) makes a compelling case that Marxists, who are often caricatured as wanting to reject any biologically grounded human needs, must have some notion of human nature if they are to argue against injustice and unequal distribution of resources under capitalism. The evolutionary process that gave rise to the human species with a particular biological make-up also, of course, enabled human beings to develop language and culture through which they reflect and transform their 'first nature' into something much more complex, what we are able to conceptualise as the thoroughly non-psychological human 'second nature' which is elaborated in further detail in later chapters of this book. Feminist and anti-racist writers have argued along exactly these lines, showing that 'gender' and 'culture' are reproduced and transformed over the course of history; see, for outstanding examples, Haraway (1989), Mamdani (2005), and, on the nature of 'barbarism' specific to different forms of civilisation, Achcar (2006).

programmes are organised around differences between human beings. When psychologists are stuck for a topic to research they usually fall back on the most banal option and ask if there are any 'sex differences'; they know this will easily chime with common-sensical ideas about men and women, and the term 'gender' is then often employed to connect with biological explanations rather than to question how we construct different versions of 'gender' around what we think is our biological sex.[3] Research on gender and sexuality operates as a powerful politically charged dividing practice which runs alongside the segregationist logic of the study of 'race' differences that were so popular in psychology in the first half of the twentieth century. These supposed 'racial' differences are still the template for much contemporary research, and nothing makes a psychologist happier than when they are able to map differences in 'intelligence' or 'personality' onto the difference between cultures.[4]

It is the pretence to be addressing 'psychological' issues when biological research is carried out that can make the discipline very dangerous. The process of psychologisation transforms biological, anthropological or social research into essential differences between 'sexes' or 'races', and portrays certain kinds of sexuality as normal and other kinds as abnormal. In this way psychologists pretend to have a symbiotic relationship in their interdisciplinary research projects with colleagues from other academic departments, but they are actually parasites. They feed on other forms of knowledge and turn that knowledge into a form of social control, and in this way individualism in the discipline quickly folds into a form of totalitarianism.[5]

[3] Detailed historical research on the way human beings interpret sex differences shows that there is no natural correspondence between biological sex and our sense of who we are by way of separate genders or different sexualities. The supposed biological difference between male and female was for many years, for example, seen as something that contradicted an identical genital structure rather than confirmed it (Lacquer, 1990), and even the Christian Church in medieval Europe was willing to bless same-sex marriages (Boswell, 1994). This research is well before the arrival of 'queer theory' and the argument that our experience of 'sex' is determined by the way we are assigned to and experience 'gender' (e.g., Butler, 1990, 1993), a useful corrective to essentialist stories told by psychologists who cannot conceptualise what they see and so take what they see for granted as a starting point in research (e.g., Lynn and Irwing, 2004).

[4] Race research often pretends that it is not concerned with those who are less intelligent, and likes to point to 'research' showing that Japanese score higher in order to avoid the accusation that the researcher is just peddling White supremacism (see, e.g., Lynn, 1982).

[5] For a good analysis of the connection between individualism and totalitarianism in psychology, see Ratner (1971). Critical approaches to 'development' and the development of the individual in psychology have taken a similar theoretical tack (see, e.g., Broughton, 1987). On the 'biologising' of childhood, see Morss (1990).

All Models of the Mind in Psychology Are Culturally Specific

What we think we know about ourselves is bound up with culture, and it is always from a position in culture that we reflect on what makes us different from others. However, cultural differences in views about human psychology do not simply float around together, jostling up against each other to provide a richer multicultural dish. Psychology is not the melting pot or the tossed salad of academic research but the sorting machine that selects and grades people according to categories that most times are worse than useless, and often a little tasteless. The principles upon which psychology as a kind of sorting machine works are bound up with cultural power, with ideas and practices that are 'hegemonic', those that are dominant. The battle of ideas in a culture is a battle for hegemony, but this battle always takes place within limits set by forms of economic exploitation and oppression. We can see the structure of this hegemonic view of the world and the people in it when we look at where psychological research is carried out, and who carries it out on whom.[6]

The dominant defining centres of the discipline have shifted from Europe to US America

If psychology began as a discipline where capitalism began, in Europe, it really took off where capitalism and imperialism have come to remake the whole world in its own image, in the United States. This shift of gravity in the centre of psychological research has had far-reaching consequences for the kind of knowledge that psychology aims at, and there is a close fit between two dominant ways of conducting research in the English-speaking world. On the

[6] The most influential theorist of 'hegemony' in political theory was the Marxist Antonio Gramsci, and his work is sometimes interpreted as meaning that a battle of ideas has now replaced political-economic struggle between social classes (Gramsci, 1971). However, Gramsci's discussion of ideological struggle was concerned primarily with the battle within different classes rather than between them; the working class, then, was seen as a field of struggle in which revolutionaries of different kinds battled with reformists, and the 'hegemony' of certain analyses and theories of change within the working-class organisations would lead to certain kinds of strategy to confront the bourgeoisie and the state. For a discussion of this aspect of Gramsci's writing, see Anderson (1976–77). The idea that ideological struggle runs across classes and that it could replace the overthrow of the state is an interpretation of Gramsci's work that leads it toward a reformist politics (e.g., Laclau and Mouffe, 2001). The hegemony of different forms of psychology within the academic world and professional practice is, by the same token, of interest to those concerned with social change, but it is not in our interests to participate in this discussion about the best way to ensure social control; instead, the debates we should have are to do with how we can develop strategies to connect the personal and political without drawing on psychology at all.

one side is the US American tradition of pragmatism, a focus on behaviour and how it can be guided. For a pragmatist what is 'true' is what works. On the other side is the English empiricist tradition, a more cautious focus on what can be directly observed; an empiricist wants hard evidence for something that claims to be 'true'.[7]

In US American psychology there is an optimistic view that each individual can become a self-managing unit, while the English research tradition tends to construct more pessimistic theories of mechanisms that constrain behaviour. Choices we are invited to make in both research traditions, however, are those that concern individual behaviour. The tension between freedom and limits gives rise to a kind of compromise formation in the discipline of psychology. The debate between 'agency' and 'structure' in fruitless attempts to develop a proper 'social psychology' is one example of such a compromise formation in which the researcher goes around in a circle, trapped inside the terms of the debate and so helplessly experiencing the limits themselves.[8] It is possible to see this ideology of individual choice against the background of individual constraints described in the massive course texts that are so influential in defining what the study of psychology should be like around the world.

The tension within Anglo-American psychology, between US and English modes of research, is a good example of hegemonic struggle; here it is a battle for influence between those who have power. Notice that in this struggle, one that is pretty well won by the US, there is little space for other traditions of research. The special relationship between the two dominant traditions shuts out, and is now wiping out, other forms of psychology and alternatives to psychology in other parts of the world. Notice also that the voices of

[7] On empiricism as an approach that came to be associated with the 'English' philosophical tradition, see Norton (1981), and on empiricism as a wider structuring force in English culture, see Fox (2004). For a discussion of the difference between pragmatism as a form of ideology and Marxism as a theory and practice of change, see Novack (1975); for discussion of these issues directly related to the problem of psychology, see Newman (1999), and for the elaboration of philosophical problems and a 'performative' alternative, see Newman and Holzman (1996).

[8] Apart from run-of-the-mill laboratory-experimental paradigm 'social psychology' journals that are content to report studies of small-scale interaction, and do not bother themselves much with questions of social structure, there are academic journals devoted to the endless task of teasing out the relationship between 'structure' and 'agency' – such as *Journal for the Theory of Social Behaviour* – and much discussion of 'third way' theories of 'structuration', which have been a dead-end in sociology and politics and are now just as useless in social psychology (see, e.g., Giddens, 1979, 1998).

those who are subjected to psychological research are entirely absent from these struggles.

Most psychological research is conducted by men,
with corresponding methods

The new psychology that was studied in Europe and brought to the US was handed from men to men, and the 'sex differences' that pre-occupied so many researchers have effectively also been differences between the male researcher and his 'female subjects'. Even today most psychology students in most classes are women, while leading researchers still tend to be men. The prospect of more women taking up senior positions in psychology has led to some concerns voiced, by the men, that the 'feminisation' of the discipline would lead to a loss of status in relation to other disciplines.[9]

There is also another different undercurrent of anxiety in this concern, which is that women might carry out the research in a less scientific way. Here, of course, there are powerful assumptions about what 'science' should be like. If you simply want to make things work smoothly – as the pragmatists do – or observe the way objects behave, which is the empiricist way, then it might actually be better to have men at the helm. These two perspectives find a meeting point in the idea that knowledge develops through a gradual accumulation of 'facts' along the road advocated by positivists, for whom the watchwords are 'order' and 'progress'. Positivist psychology, then, is able to balance pragmatist and empiricist views of science because it is in line with what works for those with power now. Psychology is organised like the world of work, with stereotypically masculine values of prediction and control structuring how the studies are set up.[10]

---

[9] A new wave of feminist writing in psychology has been devoted to the demeaning images of women purveyed by the discipline. Key texts anticipating 'second wave' feminism outside psychology explored how knowledge in patriarchy is infused with masculine assumptions of prediction and control (e.g., De Beauvoir, 1968). Inside the discipline, Ussher (1989) showed how women's bodies are pathologised in psychology, and Walkerdine (1988) explored links between notions of rationality and masculinity that are assumed in psychological models of child development. For an analysis of masculinity tied to cognitive 'development' as a disciplinary process (focusing on Piaget's work), see Broughton (1988). Burman (1990) tackled the images of women in the discipline and the control exercised by men in academic and professional psychology.

[10] For a good review of this issue, see Morawski (1997). The argument of feminist 'standpoint' theorists has been directed to this problem (e.g., Hartsock, 1987), and standpoint arguments were taken up within psychology by feminists concerned with the importance of subjectivity in research (e.g., Hollway, 1989).

Research agendas in the US are structurally 'white',
even when non-whites do research

As one would expect, the cultural composition of psychology is also weighted in favour of those with power in society. The key issue is not how many psychologists of colour there are, though this is important, but how the 'whiteness' of psychology seeps into the way researchers see the world. White research agendas are so powerful because the whiteness of most of those who pursue them is invisible to the researchers. Those who are 'other' to the psychologist are those with the colour, and the standard against which they are measured is assumed to be neutral and colourless. In this way the supposedly 'objective' observations of the researcher are formalised in an 'observation language' that screens out differences that matter in the real world.[11]

There is an intimate connection between the way psychology functions as a peculiarly US American way of describing people – with a European perspective singing in harmony with it – and the balance of power between the imperialist centres and countries that have been colonised, those still treated as peripheral to the real stuff. Colonisation – where those who are outside have to speak in the language of those with power – is then a structuring force in psychology as it becomes a global phenomenon. Then 'internal colonisation' ensures that when different cultural groups are included it is on the basis of their adherence to the values of white, male psychology.[12]

Most research studies are based on undergraduate students

The power relations inside psychology are very apparent if we look at the kinds of 'subjects' that usually participate in the experiments. In many psychology departments in the US, and increasingly in

[11] On the exclusion of black people from US American psychology, see, e.g., Guthrie (1976), and for a thorough analysis of the way psychology has advanced racist agendas, see Richards (1997). Howitt and Owusu-Bempah (1994) provide an impassioned argument against representations of black people in psychology but then appeal to what they assume to be a real 'black psychology' derived mainly from US American studies. Mama (1995) discusses how this idealisation of the black family as an alternative to white families can be oppressive to women, and Fine (2004) includes different perspectives on the importance of 'colouring in whiteness' in psychology.

[12] The 'internal colonisation' argument needs to be treated with care, of course; this argument can lapse so easily into psychological diagnosis of those subjected to colonialism and thus to forms of victim-blaming; discussions of the work of the radical black psychiatrist Frantz Fanon (1967, 1970) have grappled with this task of tackling the deep subjective effects of racism without leading the 'victims' into therapy as if that were a solution to the problem (Bulhan, 1985).

other countries, undergraduate students are required to take part in studies as part of research carried out by their professors. This gives the researcher an easy-to-access pool of people, but it also then means that the 'subjects' are all the more likely to be already selected for particular cognitive skills and studied carrying out academic tasks in isolation. The problem then goes well beyond the domain of studies in social psychology, where there have already been complaints that this practice of recruiting students 'presents the human race as composed of lone, bland, compliant wimps who specialize in paper and pencil tests'.[13]

This limited research base is only part of the problem, because the attempt to broaden out the picture in comparative studies on those in other 'experimental conditions', in other cultures or in other countries still buys into the categories that psychologists base the comparisons on.[14] The use of students as subjects is only one side of the equation – the other necessary condition for this kind of research is that the research questions are set by academics with a particular limited view of what the world is like. The pecking order in the academic world then sets its own limits on what those academics study and where they are able to publish. The status hierarchies between research institutions are structured by the class positions of those who are permitted to enter and succeed in that limited privileged world and then act as gatekeepers for the kind of questions that can be asked.[15]

---

[13] Sears (1986), p. 527.

[14] While 'cross-cultural' psychology which compares those in the West with those viewed as less civilised is bad form now, there is still a strong orientalising gaze directed across at Japan, which often provides a kind of 'limit case' for examining cultural factors in psychological development; for a discussion of this issue, see Burman (in press).

[15] Peters and Ceci (1982) showed how articles submitted to psychology journals were more likely to be published if they came from prestigious institutions, even if the same article had been rejected by that journal before when submitted from another place. Lubek's (1976, 1980) early study of the rights to speak in the power structure of psychology was followed up some years later by an analysis of the way US American textbooks are structured in such a way as to exclude new approaches or challenges to existing theoretical frameworks (Lubek, 1993). Walkerdine (1990) includes reflections on the way the class structure of psychology impacts on working-class women, and there are a number of systematic studies of this issue in Walkerdine (1996); feminist studies that focus on racism in psychology are to be found in Bhavnani and Phoenix (1994), and there is a focus on heterosexism in Kitzinger and Wilkinson (1993) and on oppression of lesbian feminists by psychology, and clinical psychology in particular, in Kitzinger and Perkins (1993).

The Models Reflect the Methodological Procedures
Used to Investigate Them

Structural problems in the way research questions are posed, who they are posed by and who becomes the subject of the research turn the content of psychological theories into something that is profoundly affected by the form of the inquiry. When a study aims to measure an attitude along a dimension and the researcher asks the subject to tick a box saying how far they agree or disagree with a statement in a questionnaire, for example, the result reinforces the idea that our ideas are 'attitudes' that are organised along a dimension that has been predetermined by the researcher. Most studies get silly answers because they ask silly questions, but there is a deeper effect which is that the method by which the investigators ask the questions also leads them to a very limited model of the person.[16]

Experimental procedures require detailed constraints and manipulation

Compared with the stupid 'subjects', those who are made into something stupid in the process of the research, the psychological researcher setting up a laboratory experiment has to be the clever one. Not only do they have to outwit the 'subject' in the research, but they also unwittingly buy into the whole objectifying research process. What the psychologist fails to notice is that they have taken such care in ensuring there are no 'confounding variables' – extraneous things that will muddle up the results – that they end up measuring something that is entirely artificial, constructed by them. They try to avoid 'experimenter effects', screening out any human contact between themselves and their 'subjects' that might unduly influence behaviour. They also know that they must do their best to avoid 'demand characteristics', by which they mean that someone in an experiment usually tries to comply with what they think the experimenter wants of them. A 'subject' who tries to guess what the 'hypotheses' of the experiment might be is a

---

[16] On the way that psychology gets the answers it deserves to the silly questions it asks and the restrictions that are placed on those who fill in questionnaires, see Roiser (1974). However, Roiser and Willig (1996) show how Marx and Engels made use of questionnaires as part of their empirical (as opposed to empiricist) analysis of class society. A sustained argument against standard psychological theories of 'attitudes' which inform meaningless questionnaire studies is made by Potter and Wetherell (1987), in a book that launched an alternative 'discursive' tradition in British social psychology.

liability, as is someone who is too keen to help the researcher find what they want to find.[17]

Anyone who would like some insight into the ideological procedures psychology is based upon should volunteer to take part in an experiment; this kind of research into psychology – where there is conscious deliberate study of what the psychologists are actually doing – could thereby also challenge the traditional wisdom that differences between subjects can be reduced to 'volunteer characteristics'.[18] Psychologists have puzzled long and hard about 'ecological validity' – how the research situation corresponds to the real world – but every step they take to outwit their subjects leads them further into a world in which they anticipate and control the behaviour of others.

Behavioural change is treated as the basis for learning, and for education

The rather obvious drawback in most research is that psychologists cannot directly observe the mental processes that they pretend to study inside other people's heads. The problem cannot be easily solved by opening up the brain. That would tell us something about the structure of brains, but the connections between what the brain does and our actual everyday feeling and reasoning would still be a mystery.[19] The illusion that this mystery can be scientifically deciphered by turning psychology into a version of biology is a dead-end; it then mimics biology, but strips out what is already relational

---

[17] When 'subjects' do try to be helpful their activity is pathologised as 'demand characteristics' (Orne, 1962), and those who do offer to participate must already be treated with suspicion because there are certain 'volunteer characteristics' that the psychologist needs to beware of (see Rosenthal, 1965). In this twisted looking-glass world the 'hypotheses' the psychologist makes refer to guesses about what will happen when they change things that happen to their subjects; the things they change they call 'independent variables', and the things that they can measure as a consequence they term 'dependent variables' (because these are dependent on what the psychologist has done to their 'subject'). A peculiar aspect of laboratory-experimental paradigm research in psychology is that the researcher thinks that they must 'falsify' a hypothesis rather than show that their guess is correct; this, of course, leads to weird double-think in which they have to pretend to themselves they do not really want their guess about what will happen to turn out like that after all.

[18] Rosenthal and Rosnow (1975) argue that those who volunteer to take part in psychology experiments are more likely to be better educated, intelligent, of higher social status, more sociable and needing more approval from others (something you might like to bear in mind next time you are approached by a psychologist and want to help them out with their research).

[19] See Rose (2006) for a detailed discussion.

about it. Ecological and 'autopoetic' studies of biology are attempts within biological research, for example, to show how organisms develop and interact such that it makes no sense to rip them out of context to understand how they work.[20] The last thing these researchers need is a psychologist telling them what they are missing.

One of the strongest traditions in the US has preferred to guarantee the expertise of the psychologist by focusing only on the behaviour itself. This is the way of B. F. Skinner, and a peculiar kind of reduction of human action to 'contingencies of reinforcement'.[21] The studies of laws governing the connection between one bit of behaviour and another then leads to attempts to automate learning; the child in front of the screen is given rewards for their behaviour and will then be judged to 'learn' in much the way a pigeon in a 'Skinner box' pecks a button for food. Questions about who organises these 'contingencies of reinforcement' and what the place of the organiser is within the system are rarely asked. A neutral observation language that makes the agenda of the manager of behaviour invisible is in this way closely connected with administrative ideology, the ideology that assumes that those who administer other people have no stake in how things are arranged. This is a world of behaving organisms, behaving as if they had no thoughts about what was happening to them, and thinking that does occur is treated as an 'epiphenomenon' of the behaviour.[22] The impact of behaviourism in Western culture is quite powerful, and psychologists are into this power, up to their necks in it.

Cognition is treated as an abstracted process based on cause and effect

One of the important influences of behaviourism has been on psychologists' reasoning about what 'intelligence' is and how it should be measured. There are some researchers who would like to appeal once again to biological processes to explain why they get differences between different groups in their intelligence tests. They skip over the unfortunate discovery in the early days of test

---

[20] For this argument, which unravels claims that psychologists make about 'cognition', see Maturana and Varela (1980).

[21] See Skinner's (1969) book for the standard radical behaviourist account of 'contingencies of reinforcement'.

[22] For the Skinnerian argument that conscious awareness is a mere epiphenomenon, here applied to pigeons (which were not interviewed for their thoughts about the matter, of course), see Epstein et al. (1981).

development that women achieved higher scores than men, after which the test items were adjusted to bring them into line with what they 'know' to be really the case.[23] What is most important, though, is the way the tautology in definitions of intelligence was simply reframed as a virtue; thus it is concluded simply that 'intelligence' is what intelligence tests measure. Once it is 'operationalised' in this way it easily becomes part of the strange universe of 'operant conditioning' through which Skinner conjured away any reference to things inside the head. That way we have the method without all the messy experiential phenomena that might lead the psychologist to question what they are doing to others.

When non-behaviourist psychologists turn to study the 'cognitions' that are supposed to 'mediate' behaviour they actually compress all of the cause and effect relationships that structure the outside world, and they make the world inside the head look exactly like those relationships. If your ideal world is a giant office with arrows leading you from one cubicle to the next, then cognitive psychology is for you. Cognitive psychology treats the inside of your head as a being like a bureaucratic flow-diagram. In this way psychology abstracts the relationships from their real-world setting, wipes out the content of the relationships and works on them as abstract formal mechanisms. It is no surprise, then, that changes in the nature of work in Western culture are reflected in the cognitive models that psychologists work on. The increase in office-based work – the kind of work that academics are most comfortable with – encouraged them to see the mind as like a filing cabinet, and then the arrival of computers led them to produce models of 'artificial intelligence' that are just as artificial and culturally specific as computers themselves.[24]

---

[23] For an account of the development of intelligence tests in the US which showed that women initially did better than men, see Block and Dworkin (1977). For a recent critique of genetic explanations of differences between people, see Joseph (2003).

[24] For an account of the way cognitive psychology functions as a form of ideology, see Sampson (1981). For a feminist critique (that then also tries to salvage something from cognitive psychology), see Wilson (1999). For a Marxist (actually Maoist) critique of cognitive psychology, see Kvale (1975). It is then a short step from the filing cabinet metaphor to abstract boxes with arrows between them, and then to specifications for weapon systems; cognitive psychology has been one of the most amenable sub-specialities for the development of military technology. For a discussion of the connection between cognitive psychology and the military, see Bowers (1990); for a most bizarre account of the use of Deleuze and Guattari's (1977) work by the (Israeli) military, see Weizman (2006a) and, for an extended analysis, see Weizman (2006b).

Psychology Reinforces Dominant Western Ideas About
Who We Are, in Our Place

The images of the human being that circulate among psychologists as they describe behaviour seep into our everyday lives. The images are like 'permanent metaphors' that fix the things we do in place, and they serve to keep us in our place as well.[25] Once we have been reduced to a relation between things in psychology we will expect to relate to each other and our own creative abilities as if they are things. It is difficult to challenge this reification in a world where people are already taught in many other ways to relate to others instrumentally; psychology is so tempting because it is much of the time at one with commonsense, with ideology. Psychology also succeeds because even the moments where we experience ourselves as more active, when we are obviously more than mere objects, are also captured by limited disciplinary reasoning; this then limits us further, and betrays our abilities to make sense of the world.

Perception research assumes that the perceiving subject is static

Even the most basic psychological research into the way we perceive the world has smuggled into it assumptions about activity and passivity that then produce a culturally specific and limited view of what human perception is. First, the dominant paradigm for perception research once had the 'subject' being asked to view slides through a device called a 'tachistoscope'; in this device (and now in computer programmes that carry out the same function) images are flashed up for periods and in sequences that the experimenter decides upon in advance, but it is more than time that they control. Each moment of perception is treated as taking place inside someone who is in a fixed position, viewing the world from one definite fixed point. The first, methodological, problem here is that when we perceive the world most of the time we are moving around it.

---

[25] Sarbin (1986) provides an analysis of the way metaphors operate to fix certain images of the self in place in psychology, and Soyland (1994) follows this through with a more extended analysis of the way psychology as a discipline is held together by certain forms of metaphor. These analyses go so far, but not far enough, and need to be extended with a more detailed analysis of the way psychology operates as a form of ideology; see, e.g., Ingleby (1972) and Sedgwick (1974). The discussions of ideology in psychology since then – those which follow a more 'narrative' or 'discursive' line of work – have tended to sidestep the ideological role of psychology in favour of an account that sometimes drifts into being a reworked psychological study of ideology (e.g., Billig, 1982).

Perception research in psychology prevents movement, abstracts us from the world and fixes us in place, producing a false image of what we are as an active observer.[26]

The second problem is cultural and historical, for this kind of research reinforces a particular 'way of seeing'. It fits well enough with much Western art, which is produced so that there is one ideal point from which the viewer will look at the picture, but it thereby turns other kinds of art from other cultures into representations that are 'inaccurate' but perhaps quaint. Artistic representations outside the West are not always organised to show themselves to one fixed viewing point and so, if the Western psychologist is to be believed, they surely cannot be as sophisticated or 'realistic'. Perception is bound up with a certain kind of reality, and the particular kind of perception that psychology has been concerned with only fits this kind of reality, and makes it seem like it is the only reality worth taking seriously. This tradition of research not only privileges a certain kind of 'psychology', it privileges 'psychology' as such as a way of being that is assumed to be more civilised than that in other cultures.[27]

A defining experiential core is taken to be held in place by the individual's 'identity'

The fixed position from which the perceiving subject is expected to view the world in psychological research operates as a template for how the interior of the self is imagined to be. The concept of 'identity', for example, was actually adapted from one version of psychoanalytic theory that focused on the development of an internal core of the self that is itself adapted to society.[28] This concept was then absorbed within a more strictly psychological model of the self, and

[26] An alternative approach to perception that is in line with this critique was developed by Gibson (1966), and there is an impassioned defence of Gibson as providing the basis for a Marxist theory of perception by Reed (1996). Costall and Still's (1991) collection is a very useful resource on limitations of the cognitive psychological view of activity.

[27] See the account of assumptions made about the world in Western art by Berger (1990). Studies of 'indigenous psychologies' that are designed to challenge Western psychological conceptions of the human subject often use the term 'psychology' in a very loose way, and those studies which draw on social anthropology, for example, do provide useful ammunition against the limited 'psychological' model of the individual; see, for some good examples, Heelas and Lock (1981).

[28] Erikson's (1965) classic study was actually concerned with the specific cultural conditions that gave rise to different conceptions of identity, but the notion of 'identity' as such turned psychoanalytic theories of 'identification' into something that could be understood by psychologists. See K. McLaughlin (2003b) for an argument against 'identities' in social work.

so ambiguity and contradiction were wiped away leaving a core mechanism that is now assumed to organise perceptions, cognitions and behaviour. This core mechanism is structured very much like the fixed viewer in front of the old tachistoscope or computer screen, as if the real viewer was inside the head looking out.

Just as cause and effect relationships described by behaviourists are projected inside the head to produce 'cognitive' explanations, so the idea of static fixed relationships in cognitive-perceptual research produces a certain image of what the perceiving experiencing self is supposed to be like. The notion of 'identity' is now assumed to be the most important cognitive structure that holds the individual's sense of self in place, and this psychological notion then circulates in ideological representations of cultural and sexual differences; those who have been excluded and oppressed are supposed to draw comfort from being able to discover and celebrate their own particular 'identity'. Here the model that the psychologist uses to understand themselves as a subject, someone who is able to predict and control behaviour, is abstracted, reified and projected into the head of each and every individual.[29]

The corresponding sense of confidence and control that goes with identity is that of 'self-esteem', and so popular is this notion that it seems that only a spoilsport would say that there is something wrong with it. However, the use of self-esteem as the touchstone for understanding how people make themselves feel good about being individuals is part of the problem. Those with 'high' self-esteem are actually likely to be unhappy and defensive, more fragile than those with 'low' self-esteem.[30] The search for 'identity' and 'self-esteem' is a dead-end, a solution peddled by the psychologists and part of

[29] Tazi's (2004) edited book on 'identity' with contributors from different continents shows how provincial US American and European views are; see, in particular, Mamdani's (2004) account of the way the colonial powers in Africa insisted that their native subjects should have ethnic 'identities' (and so how 'fundamentalism' with respect to identity was an effect of colonialism).

[30] In the UK, Emler (2002) reviews evidence for 'self-esteem' and although his report is designed to reinforce the idea that low self-esteem is a bad thing (and in this sense he is writing as a good social psychologist delivering the message his sponsors wanted), he also shows along the way that high self-esteem can be debilitating. In the US, Baumeister and colleagues (see, e.g., Baumeister et al., 1996) have pointed to the dangers of high self-esteem, and, not surprisingly, this has come under attack from followers of Ayn Rand who value individual strength above all and see the individual as the fount and outcome of all that is best about capitalism (e.g., Campbell and Foddis, 2005). It is not surprising, then, to find such people – who call themselves 'objectivists' – enthusing about cognitive psychology (see, e.g., Campbell, 1999).

a process of psychologisation that might lead to some short-term 'happiness' but actually produces more intense alienation, separation from others and from oneself.

Alienation is seen as experiential, a shallow error-ridden version of false consciousness

There are profound political consequences of the reduction to the level of the individual, reduction to internal mechanisms that the psychologist assumes govern and drive healthy cognition and behaviour. An analysis of exploitation is liable to be turned from being a social historical account into an individualised one, and the focus then shifts to individual choices and experiences.[31] A question to do with the general 'alienation' of human creativity under capitalism is then psychologised, turned into something that is only taken seriously if it is directly experienced by the individual. This is good news for those who prefer psychological remedies to social change, but it shows us how psychology is part of the problem. Plenty of people are alienated but say that they are happy, and the drug companies are than happy to step in and cheer them up if they do not have good feelings about themselves.[32]

This psychologisation of exploitation and oppression then has further political consequences for the way we try to understand what ideology is and how it operates. Ideology – a representation of the world and our place in it that makes exploitation and oppression in capitalist society seem normal and natural – is reduced by psychology to being some idea you as an individual have about the world. Ideology is turned into something that is treated only as a set of beliefs about the world, and then those who make 'errors' are seen as suffering from 'false consciousness'. Instead of a social and historical account of how it is that certain conditions of life in capitalist society make it seem to people that there really could be no other way of living, the problem is seen as a psychological one.

[31] There is a tradition of academic research within Marxism that brought rational choice perspectives to bear on economic processes (e.g., Roemer, 1986), and it is not surprising that this attempt to psychologise Marxism eventually led those researchers away from Marxism altogether; for a critical analysis of this tradition, see Bensaïd (2002). For discussion of Marxist studies of alienation, and of the mistake of looking to individual experience to understand it, see Mandel and Novack (1970), and, for a Marxist definition of alienation, see Bottomore (1991).

[32] For a focus on the marketing of Prozac to enforce happiness, see Breggin (1995), and on the role of the pharmaceutical industry in research on depression, see Healy (2004).

Many people buy into the competitive ideology of capitalism, and their ideas correspond so perfectly to everyday commonsense that one can hardly say that they are making 'errors'. Their ideas and sense of themselves also, of course, correspond very well with what psychology tells us about ourselves.[33]

Globalisation Redistributes Dominant Ideas About What Psychology Should Be

Capitalism is, for the time being, triumphant as a world system, and the dominant ideas about human beings that have been so necessary for the smooth functioning of this economic system are relayed through all academic disciplines, including psychology. However, just as there have always been challenges and conflicts inside the imperialist countries, so the globalisation of capitalist ideology is riddled with contradictions and there are many sites of resistance to psychology. One key contradiction that is managed by the process of globalisation is that as capitalism spreads around the world it adapts itself, and it has to keep transforming itself so that it can function as part of a global system while also making itself acceptable to different local contexts.[34]

Developmental models assume correspondence between adulthood and civilisation

Psychology has played an important role in colonialism, and when Europeans constructed models of 'development' it was not surprising that the development of individuals was mapped in some way onto the development of nations. The sequence of ages and stages in Jean Piaget's account of development, for example, privileged the most 'civilised' people so that the highest stage of cognitive development – that of 'formal operations' – was assumed to be attained most easily by those living in Switzerland.[35] In the field of developmental psychology there is often a divide between researchers working in the Piagetian tradition and those following the work of the Russian psychologist Lev Vygotsky. Piaget was a Christian socialist working in Geneva, and Vygotsky wrote as a Marxist in Russia after the

---

[33] Even Marxists trapped in psychological reasoning make this mistake; see, e.g., Augoustinos (1999).

[34] For a discussion of the globalisation of capitalism, see Went (2000).

[35] Morss (1996) provides a critique of Piaget, part of a lovely vitriolic attack on the whole project of developmental psychology. For a specific discussion of problems with the notion of 'progress' in developmental psychology, see Vandenburg (1993).

Revolution, and so adherents of each of these developmental theories have tried to read progressive political consequences into Piaget's and Vygotsky's work.[36]

The problem for those who try to pretend that developmental psychology can be progressive is that Piaget, for example, can only be read as a progressive insofar as he was a 'genetic epistemologist' (a philosopher concerned with the way we gain knowledge about the world) rather than a psychologist. It is when we turn to his work in developmental psychology that we find the normalisation of certain kinds of development and pathologisation of those who do not fit that model. The same applies to Vygotsky; while he had some interesting things to say about the relationship between thought and language, his work on *psychological* development was still part of a process of pathologising peoples who were viewed as less civilised than those in the Russian heartland.[37]

Psychology as a discipline is here making some of the same mistakes that anthropology made, mistakes that were fostered by imperialist state agendas for the observation and control of 'native' populations overseas but mistakes that many anthropologists today try to distance themselves from. If social anthropology 'was the handmaiden of colonialism',[38] cross-cultural psychology is now the loyal manservant also produced by that colonial relationship. Studies of mentality outside the West were used to confirm the 'infantile' nature of those who were supposedly less developed. The colonial impact of the mapping of development of the individual onto the development of nations was explicit in psychological research that saw African 'natives' as being less developed. The agenda of those developing psychological methods was deliberately focused on work discipline and productivity.[39]

---

[36] On Piaget's Christian socialism, see Vandenburg (1993). For a defence of Piaget (despite the overall critical line of that review of different developmental theories), see Burman (1994), and for a defence of Vygotsky, see, e.g., Newman and Holzman (1993).

[37] See Vygotsky (1966); for a critique, see Morss (1996).

[38] Nadar (1997), p. 115. Nadar's chapter is a good study of the way anthropological research was used by the US military to understand and control foreign and native populations; it shows how disciplines adjacent to psychology can be just as dangerous, and provides a warning to those who think that a progressive solution is to do more interdisciplinary research.

[39] See, for example, the scathing review of African psychological research by Bulhan (1993) in a volume produced by radicals in the run-up to the first post-apartheid elections in South Africa; see also Bulhan (1981). On psychology and the 'third world', with reference to community psychology, see Sloan (1990) and with reference to developmental psychology, see Burman (1995).

Psychology reinforces the idea of 'separate development'

One of the most brutal expressions of the logic of development linked to psychology was in the construction of the apartheid system in South Africa. Hendrik Verwoerd, the first apartheid prime minister and architect of the 'separate development' of the races, was a professor of psychology at Stellenbosch University before putting ideas from psychology into political practice. The formation of the Psychological Institute of the Republic of South Africa was designed to exclude blacks, for example, and the presidential address in 1962 spoke of 'the natural need for protection against a worldwide hysterical mass-movement of equalization etc.'.[40]

The development of intelligence tests in South Africa is actually another lesson for radicals as to how ideological agendas determine psychological techniques. Just as women in the United States were originally shown to score better on tests, until the tests were adapted, so in South Africa the psychologists had to deal with the embarrassing discovery that 'poor whites' scored worse on the early tests than black subjects. Once again, the test items were changed so that the measure of intelligence would come into line with what the researchers knew must be the reality, and now white intelligence could assume its rightful place at the top of the cross-cultural league tables.[41]

Class stratification reproduces the 'centre' in distributed centres of power

The discipline has always been able to recruit local enthusiasts for psychological explanations, and in this way the imperialist centres are distributed around the world so that there can now be many centres. What we should notice about this distribution of power is that globalisation reconfigures each local context as if it were a mirror image of the wider global structure, and it needs to do this so that each local hierarchical structure organised around a 'centre' will nest neatly into imperialism. The ideal individual is then, of course, one who adapts themselves to this structure and operates as if they too have a 'centre' within themselves; discrete 'identities' and the attempt to boost 'self-esteem' follow as logical consequences for each local individual agent. Then the ideological system is quite

[40] A. J. la Grange, cited in Foster (1993), p. 70.
[41] See Hook and Eagle (2002) for a discussion of the various ways psychology was used to reinforce racial stereotypes and keep the black population in place under apartheid, and then the way the discipline continued in this vein in the New South Africa.

complete, for the psychologically minded individual will feel that it is quite normal and natural that the world is organised around hierarchical chains that run from the heights of the multinational companies all the way down into the depths of their soul.

What is most important is that each centre reinforces the idea that those who are 'non-psychological' are viewed as the barbarians. Those who are most 'civilised' will agree with what psychology textbooks from America and Europe tell them, or write their own versions of the textbooks that serve to reproduce the same kinds of ideas. One of the most pernicious effects of this logic of imperialism now underpinned by the discipline of psychology and pervasive psychologisation in contemporary capitalist society is that those who do not operate according to psychological categories are seen as less developed. When big glossy US American psychology textbooks staple in extra pages to provide 'local context' for students in different parts of the world, we can see the way that ideology operates as a material practice. Mental representations are not just faulty ideas inside people's heads, but operate to endorse and reshape relations of power so that when someone notices a problem they will conclude that it is an experience peculiar to them, that they are at fault.[42]

Psychology Is Tied into an Abnormal Distribution of Power

The image of the statistical 'normal distribution' in psychology and its appeal to the 'bell curve' to explain and justify inequalities between people should alert us to the fact that the apparatus of power that psychology is part of is actually very 'abnormal'.[43] The 'bell curve' is supposed to show how people are naturally distributed so that a small number fall on each side with the mass of 'normal' people in the middle. It is employed again and again in racist arguments that pretend that there are biological reasons for differences in intelligence and ability.[44] The bell curve distributes people along

[42] For analyses of the way professionalisation in neoliberalism corrodes activism in different parts of the world, see Laurie and Bondi (2003).

[43] Herrnstein and Murray (1994) use this notion of the 'bell curve' in an explicitly ideological way to justify inequalities of class, race and gender; there is a scathing review of the book by Kamin (1995).

[44] Herrnstein famously argued that nature had 'colour-coded' people of different races so that we could more easily detect who was bright and who was stupid. The Block and Dworkin (1977) collection contains lots of argument and evidence against Herrnstein's ideas on race and intelligence. Herrnstein's co-author on the bell curve book was Charles Murray, who is an old friend of the forces of social control; 'in the 1960s [he] was in Thailand working in counterinsurgency' (Nader, 1997, p. 129).

different dimensions to divide and sort the people of the world in a certain kind of way that, surprise surprise, corresponds to the distribution of wealth and economic resources.

The production and experience of psychology is uneven

Psychology has been slow-cooked in the academic research centres of US America and Europe, but it is also popularised so that it will sell around the world and seem nutritious at the same time. But it is not nutritious at all, and even the addition of a salad option to cater to niche markets will not make it more so. Psychology is the fast-food franchise master of the academic research world, and it has learnt to sell its product to different niche markets so that those who consume it believe that it will be good for them.[45]

Contemporary capitalist society is characterised by deregulation of education and welfare support, the privatisation of services so that each sector of the state operates as if it were a separate company. And each individual then becomes all the more separated from everyone else, with their success and wealth put down to their own ability or hard work and their failure and poverty down to their own stupidity or laziness. This new 'neoliberal' capitalism breeds competition and insecurity, and is the dominant form of globalisation.[46] It provides the perfect context for the discipline of psychology to thrive. In fact, more than ever, psychology is necessary to justify the operation of this unequal and unjust system to those who are subjected to it.

The differences are intimately combined in relation to one another

When psychology reflects upon itself in this neoliberal world it still does so through its own categories. The dimensions it uses are still the false categories that have served it so well in capitalist society, and it now keeps those categories alive in 'cross-cultural' research. It sets the measure by which people will understand themselves in

[45] Ritzer's (2004) analysis of 'McDonaldization' is relevant to the process of psychologisation because it concerns work processes and the material conditions in which people are schooled and graded, more so than the companion argument focusing on mass culture – analyses of 'Disneyization' – by Bryman (2004).

[46] For a discussion of this form of globalisation, see Went (2000) and Cammack (2003); and for an analysis of the politics of the anti-globalisation and anti-capitalist movement engaging with the new distribution of power and resistance under neoliberalism, see Hardt and Negri (2000, 2004) and Hollway (2002); see also Laurie and Bondi (2005) for feminist arguments from within geography and development studies against neoliberalism.

relation to those who produced psychology; when they are still trapped in psychology they are still seeped in ideology.

Although it is highly 'globalised', psychology is still very disparate, in which there are grounds for hope, and there is all the difference in the world between globalisation and the forging of international networks by which people can organise in solidarity with each other. Globalisation is the context for ideology in psychology, and the context for ideological research into 'cross-cultural' differences, but against this unequal internationalisation we can find sources of strength to build alternatives that include alternatives to psychology.

3

Psychology at Work:
Observation and Regulation
of Alienated Activity

Many graduates of psychology courses who initially planned to go into clinical psychology or educational psychology eventually end up in personnel or marketing. They are then able to put what they have learnt in psychology into practice as part of a large company managing 'human relations' to enable things to run smoothly and profitably. Alternatively, the more well paid option, they spend their time thinking up new ways of advertising and selling products to people to consume in their leisure time. Just as the psychologist's own career path is structured by the hopes and disappointments psychology provides, for they do not end up working where they expected they would, so psychology as a discipline comes to play a powerful role in structuring how other people – clients and consumers – relate to work. This chapter is about how psychology operates at work and at home, how it aims to make the workforce productive and the family efficient as a site of reproduction.

Psychology plays an important role in production,
in the extraction of surplus value

Psychology as a discipline endorses a crucial characteristic of work in capitalist society, which is that there is an intensification for each individual of the separation between manual labour and intellectual labour. This artificial separation already alienates what we do from what we know. Psychologisation then reinforces that alienation when it focuses on what we know and how we think; abstracting it from our own embodied activity.[1] Manual labour is creative

---

[1] Feminist politics has included a focus on this reclaiming of knowledge about women's bodies from male experts so that knowledge becomes once again embodied in those who live it, as the title of the influential self-help and information book (first published in 1971, and now in its eighth edition) *Our Bodies, Ourselves* indicates (Boston Women's Health Book Collective, 2005). The women's therapy complement to this book,

embodied engagement with things in the world that links understanding with change. Psychologists tend to study this kind of work very carefully and cautiously as a collection of measurable physical activities. The behaviourist tradition in psychology, particularly the so-called 'radical' US version, tried to wipe out the mental element, and so tried to dispense with the psychology as such; this is why some of the followers of Skinner now reject the label 'psychologist'.[2]

Psychologists are happier studying *intellectual* labour because that seems to be the real stuff of psychology, and they treat this kind of work, intellectual work, as the work of the mind. The cognitive research tradition emphasises this 'mental' activity over what they see as mere physical movements studied by behaviourists, and so the split between the two major traditions in Western twentieth-century psychology has been built on the separation of 'behaviour' from 'cognition', of manual from intellectual labour.[3] Personnel psychologists, those working in the 'human relations' departments of large companies, find this kind of activity much more interesting than having to deal with people going off sick due to accidents at work. The separation between manual and intellectual labour is thereby maintained by the psychologists, and there are then consequences for the way that surplus value is extracted from the workforce by their employer as profit.[4]

Psychology regulates reproduction of labour outside the workplace

Another characteristic of work that psychology endorses, alongside the separation of physical from intellectual work, is the separation

---

In Our Own Hands, has broadly the same ethos (Ernst and Goodison, 1981). A version of this attempts to surmount this problem (of the abstraction of knowledge so that 'knowing' becomes treated as if it is something separate and superior to activity) from within Marxist politics (though departing from orthodox Marxism in many respects) is to be found in the volume *The End of Knowing* (Newman and Holzman, 1997).

[2] One of the leaders of the 'behaviorologist' tendency is Skinner's daughter, Julie; opponents have claimed that his other daughter, Deborah, suffered mental problems after being raised by her father for a time in an apparatus known as an 'heir conditioner' (e.g., Slater, 2005).

[3] The 'third force' humanist movement, which emphasises personal growth, tries to transcend the divisions between behaviourist and cognitive traditions. For an edited volume which brings together some of the 'third force' arguments, see Wann (1964), and for a review of problems, see Parker (1999a). For a discussion of some contradictory aspects of Skinner's work which shows that he could not succeed in blotting out subjectivity altogether, see (Parker, 1995a), and for a Marxist defence of Skinner, see Ulman (1996).

[4] Sohn-Rethel (1978) provides the best historical and conceptual account of this separation and its function in capitalist society.

within intellectual labour of 'instrumental labour' from 'emotional labour'. Instrumental labour is the part of intellectual labour that is rational and ordered, directed to specific tasks; emotional labour is concerned with feelings and relationships experienced in the body, even if it is also treated as if it is something 'intellectual'. Academic psychologists still puzzle over the connection between 'motivation' and 'emotion' and observable behaviour, and so remain trapped in categories produced under alienated life conditions.[5]

The separation of intellectual labour into instrumental and emotional labour has become more and more important to the processes of production and reproduction that hold capitalist society together economically and politically. Here psychology really comes into its own, for it has been able to reconfigure itself as the discipline with expertise on intellectual activities and so on the way human beings balance rational and emotional aspects of their lives. The world of feelings and relationships is often assumed to be more important in women's lives, so this is also where psychology becomes important to the regulation of family life as well as life at work. Women's roles as care-givers then come under scrutiny by those psychologists who want to find a 'balance' between life at home and life at work.[6]

Psychology Plays a Key Role in Helping Us Learn to Labour for Others

Early industrial relations managers called upon psychology to ensure that manual labour was carried out as efficiently and profitably as possible. It was as intellectual labour became marked off as a different kind of activity, separated from manual labour, that psychology was also able to mark itself out as a discipline with a specific function. Psychology highlighted the importance of workers' attitudes and expectations, and it turned the study and regulation of these attitudes and expectations into its own specialist domain.

Psychology is rooted in the detailed measurement of work tasks

Early industrial psychology is indebted to the research of Frederick Taylor,[7] for his approach systematically broke work down into discrete

[5] Psychology textbooks then include sections on 'motivation' and 'emotion' as if these were separate pieces of the puzzle, and then they wonder why they have difficulty patching together all the different bits.

[6] Zaretsky (1976) shows how the personal and public spheres become separated out. For outlines of the psychological 'work-life balance' research and some limitations, see Gambles et al. (2006).

[7] Taylor's (1911) account provides a clear exposition of the rationale and method.

components. Taylor worked on the premise that each component in the production process could be analysed and timed so that an employer could determine exactly how long a worker should take on the tasks assigned them. 'Taylorism' then became the perfect model for observation and management of industrial enterprises, and was taken up throughout the United States. It has been pointed out that in class terms Taylorism was 'an ideology of the ascendant engineering profession rather than that of management'.[8] The number of engineers increased rapidly between 1880 and 1920 in the United States (from 7,000 to 136,000), and so Taylorism was a practice that these engineers could use to control the workforce and to curb the power of management.[9]

Lenin also urged factory managers in the Soviet Union to make use of Taylorism to increase efficiency. Lenin argued that the 'Taylor system' was 'the last word in progress',[10] and saw possibilities in the increased efficiency of production for the reduction of the working day. Taylorism was debated very soon after the 1917 October Revolution, way before the bureaucratisation of the state and the rise to power of Stalin, though enthusiastic reports to the 1918 economic councils were tempered by worries that Taylorism would 'divide the working class by creating a "labour aristocracy" out of those workers able to earn high wages through incentive schemes'.[11] The focus on 'industrialisation' and productivity was to feed into Stalin's claim that there could be 'socialism in one country' (that is, the Soviet Union), and that history proceeded through discrete economic 'stages'. The tidy mind of a bureaucrat is the ideal site for 'psychology' to appear, especially a form of psychology concerned with the prediction and control of behaviour and cognitive activity.

Psychology requires obsessional concern with order,
an image of order in the mind

Taylorism linked work and psychology in a new way. The link was apparent in Taylor's own approach to his tasks; one psychobiography shows him to be an amazingly obsessional person, wanting complete order.[12] He exemplified the connection between prediction and

  [8] Smith (1993), p. 12.
  [9] Smith (1993), p. 12.
  [10] Cited in Smith (1993), p. 13.
  [11] Smith (1993), p. 14.
  [12] Sudhir Kakar's (1974) biography of Taylor brings to his subject the perspective of an Indian psychoanalyst, and so he neatly pathologises Taylor and Taylorism. For critical perspectives on psychology and psychoanalysis in India, see Kumar (2006).

control at the level of capitalist production and prediction and control as the ethos of psychology at the level of the individual. Production schedules needed to be developed by the growing industrial enterprises in such a way that there could be accurate prediction of consumer demand; in this sense the 'five year plans' of the so-called 'socialist' states were merely making explicit the management of production targets under capitalism. The moulding of the individual in line with production targets has been most intensive in contemporary capitalist society, however, with the expectation that professional and middle-management should produce 'career plans' and aim to meet 'personal development' targets.

The link between work and psychology is also evident in Taylorism in the way it encouraged a certain view of mental processes as ordered into separate hierarchical systems. Cognitive conceptions of the mind as consisting of discrete modules have their origin in this way of thinking about the mind of each individual as operating like a little factory.[13] There is an assumption in this kind of model that the mind will only work efficiently if there are specialist 'supervisor' functions to monitor activity and ensure that each part of the mind is working as it should. The ideological circuit that comes into action here ties the individual worker all the more firmly into their workplace when each individual comes to believe that they will only be able to work efficiently if there is a specialist supervisor telling them what to do, and an owner of the enterprise who knows how to invest wisely in the future of the company.

Psychology reflects a labour process producing
a machinery of body and self

Industry in the early twentieth-century United States was the place where the psychology of work was tried and tested. A complete system of manufacture was developed that built upon Taylorism in the Ford factories in and around Detroit, for example, and 'Fordism' became the model form of advanced capitalism.[14] Henry Ford wanted the work regime in his factories to function as an environment that would turn immigrants from outside the US into good citizens. He took a keen interest in the 'Americanisation' of the workforce, and a special division of the company was charged with ensuring that systematic measures were kept of the progress of employees towards

[13] For some examples, see Richards (1996).
[14] For a critical analysis of Fordism that also points to the later emergence of 'post-Fordism', see Lipietz (1987).

total assimilation. Only when workers could speak good English and show a good enough knowledge of local dress codes, cultural mores and attitudes to work would they receive full pay.[15] There has always been a close link between capitalism and racism, and the employment of 'aliens' in the new industries during the early development of capitalism also inspired employers to use divide-and-rule tactics to separate workers from each other. This is why alienation always includes peculiar racial fantasies about those who are 'other' to Western selves.[16]

In the case of the Ford factories in Detroit it was the 'sociology' division where the nascent real psychology was being implemented, and one lesson of this aspect of organisational and management practice is that simply making psychology more 'social' will not make it more progressive.[17] We can also see in this industrial enterprise an early anticipation of the worst of 'community psychology'. To be accepted as a good worker you did really have to be part of a community, and this community was set against outsiders. Other more benevolent worker communities that were designed to ensure cohesion and loyalty were established at around the same time.[18] Work discipline in each of these 'community' workplaces was balanced with social care in different proportions depending on what the owners thought they could get away with or how benevolent they wanted be. The concern with manual labour did then include a concern with notions of adaptation and identity, intellectual matters, the stuff of the new discipline of psychology.

[15] Ford published his own rabidly anti-Semitic newspaper in the Dearborn district of Detroit, also published the notorious fabricated 'Jewish conspiracy' text *Protocols of the Learned Elders of Zion*, and received awards from the Nazis for his contribution to German industry in the lead-up to the Second World War (Baldwin, 2001).

[16] For a fascinating study of the development of capitalism in Manchester, and Engels' time there, a study which includes an analysis of the importance of women and 'aliens' (who in that case were mainly Irish people), see Marcus (1974).

[17] For a good analysis of organisational psychology, see Hollway (1991), and on the way psychology is used to deal with those facing unemployment, see Miller (1986).

[18] One example was at Port Sunlight in Britain, where workers were housed in the same complex as the factories and had to buy their food from company shops. The short-lived 'socialist' community experiments in New Lanark, Scotland organised by Robert Owen ran on the same principles, and the grateful workers, who did have better working conditions, were still expected to work to produce profit in a capitalist economy; this 'utopian socialism' failed to address the structural limits and exploitation necessary to capitalism, and they lacked psychologists to help persuade the workers that they should be content with their lot. For a Marxist response to 'utopian socialism', see Engels (1892).

Psychology searches for novelties in the production
process to stimulate more work

A breakthrough for psychology, one that became one of the founding myths of 'occupational psychology' repeated in textbooks, came in studies carried out at the Hawthorne works of the General Electric Company. Physical changes in the working environment that seemed at first sight to impact directly on the speed of production were not, it seemed, the most important thing. The actual changes were less important than the fact that there had been changes at all; the lesson drawn from this study was that workers felt that management was interested in them. This 'insight' gave psychology a perfect way in to persuade industrial enterprises that there was a particular aspect of the production process that they could work on.[19]

The attitudes and perceptions of employees were thereby transformed into the separate domain of psychology. This opened a space for an attention to intellectual aspects of labour, something that was to blossom later on in 'human relations' divisions of companies concerned with the emotional well-being of the workforce. The first steps in human relations were to convince the employers that they would get something more out of their workers – more surplus value – if some attention was given to what was going on inside their heads above and beyond the tasks they carried out. The next step was to target the motivations of workers, and then to encourage more focus on 'feelings'. Some of the later psychoanalytic studies of the workplace that explained industrial conflict as being down to 'splitting' and 'projection' had the function of drawing attention away from the exploitation of workers so that their resistance to this exploitation could be more thoroughly psychologised and so pathologised.[20]

Psychology in the Study of 'Human Relations' Occupies the Self

One of the peculiar things about psychology is that it corresponds most of the time with commonsense, but psychologists take what

[19] For an analysis of the way the Hawthorne study now operates in the mythological history psychology tells itself about its origins, see Bramel and Friend (1981).
[20] Jaques (1951) used the ideas of Melanie Klein (1986); her bizarre ideas, quite popular in the Tavistock Institute of Human Relations for many years, rested on the assumption that the mind was like a container in which all kinds of frightening objects spun around and were sometimes 'projected' out. For a Marxist defence of Klein's ideas, see Young (1996), and for attempts to connect her work with theories of alienation, see Hinshelwood (1996).

we know and sell it back to us as if they were the first ones to discover it. In this respect psychology is actually modelling itself on the 'deskilling' process that industrial workers have long been subjected to; their own creative activities are recorded and formalised and then they are taught to carry out the tasks as if they were not the original source of these practices, as if they did not really know what they were doing. This deskilling process – the separation of what we know from what we do so that we then feel stupid – is a key aspect of alienation in contemporary capitalist society.[21]

Notions of ability for different class-related tasks are
sedimented in 'intelligence'

In the overdeveloped countries children learn to labour at school, and here they are also inducted into the kinds of work they will be best suited for in adult life. The circular and vacuous notion of 'intelligence' is used by psychologists as a way of determining the fate of those who will be fit for intellectual labour (to include those who eventually go on to become trained as psychologists), and those who will be fit for manual labour. Tests of 'ability' or 'aptitude' for different kinds of education were more complex versions of the old tests of 'intelligence'; selection by the psychologist might seem like natural selection, but a lot of work had to be done by the early psychologists to get the tests to work; much of that work was so driven by an ideological agenda that the data had to be forced to fit, and in some cases entirely fabricated.

The first state-employed psychologist, Cyril Burt, worked for London County Council and devised educational tests that would sort children into those who would benefit from different kinds of schooling. His studies of class differences in intelligence purported to show that these differences were inherited, and so he confirmed that the British class system was something entirely natural. However, results were published in journals he himself edited, and research assistants who helped carry out the studies were later revealed to be fictional, as fictional as the notion of intelligence itself.[22] In this way

[21] Harry Braverman (1976) wrote the classic analysis of deskilling; for an extended, updated account, see Bellamy and Braverman (1998). Shotter (1987) provides an excellent analysis of the way cognitive psychology operates by deskilling people, taking what people already know about their activities and then telling them that there is a hidden mental process that only the psychologist can detect and understand properly. For an analysis of cognition as a practice rather than something going on inside the head, see Lave (1988).
[22] Hearnshaw (1979) realised that there was something seriously wrong with Burt's data when writing his biography. On attempts to rehabilitate Burt, see Samelson (1992).

models of schooling and models of mind became intertwined, and the idea that children must be prepared for the world of work was exported to other cultures where children have always worked from a young age. The debates over 'child labour' then become framed by a particular culture-bound separation between 'work' and 'play', and by Western conceptions of what a 'child' must be like.[23]

Personality differences reinforce class-stratification of productivity and obedience

Research into the inheritance of ability, measured by psychologists as the 'Intelligence Quotient' (IQ), was complemented by studies of personality differences. Hans Eysenck, a psychologist based at the Institute of Psychiatry in London, supported Cyril Burt even after it became clear that Burt had fiddled his results, and Eysenck became a well known proponent of the idea that innate personality differences were linked with class and with potential criminality.[24] The particular focus on the 'intellectual' aspect of labour in psychology was now taken further with studies of rationality and emotion, as if rationality and emotion could be treated as separate components of human activity.

Eysenck also linked various personality dimensions with brain activity, locating introversion and extraversion in the 'ascending reticular activating system' (and so psychologising aspects of brain function). Not only were social and political factors in crime turned into the domain of psychology but biological processes were also reinterpreted so that it would be the psychologist who would be the one with special abilities to discover who would be best suited for what kind of work and who might be best off in prison. Psychologisation of a certain ideological view of biology, and particularly biology of the brain, was thus intimately linked with psychologisation of a certain ideological view of society. From this poisonous combination, all kinds of racist and sexist ideas would sprout and be used to support the division of labour and the dividing of workers from one another.[25]

---

[23] For a useful international collection (translated from French) which explores these issues in a number of different countries, see Schlemmer (2000).

[24] See Eysenck (1977) on crime and personality (and the supposed inheritance of a disposition to criminality), and see Eysenck (1975) on the role of class.

[25] See Billig (1979) for a review of the connections between Eysenck's psychological theories and the activities of explicitly racist and fascist organisations. Kamin (1993) shows how images of sex are woven into racist imagery in this kind of psychology.

Psychological differentiation is reflected in the
study of executive 'stress'

There are many instances in the history of psychology that reveal
the class interests of the discipline. It sides with the employers
and the drive for the maximisation of profit, and against workers and
the possible democratic collective ownership of production. One
of the most striking examples is in the study of 'stress'. Stress was
assumed to be a psychological process with biological effects, and
psychologists believed deep down that only those who engage in
intellectual work could be doing things that bring psychological
processes into operation. When monkeys were subjected to
'stressors' – events over which they had no control and which made
them helpless – they developed stomach ulcers, and so what could be
more natural than to term these poor creatures 'executive monkeys'?[26]

What should be noticed about the later realisation by psychologists,
that it is not only executives that get stressed and that perhaps
assembly-line workers might really feel helpless, is that a whole new
field of research was opened up. Instead of questioning the ideological
assumptions of the initial research, psychologists shamelessly
expanded the scope of their work.[27] Middle-class experience – which
was always treated as more genuinely 'psychological' than that of
working-class brutes – was used as the template for investigating
psychology at work. Here was a perfect opportunity to broaden the
domain of psychology so that it would deal with the manual
workers as well as the intellectual workers, and to deepen it so that
'psychological' components of manual labour could be detected and
separated out from creative embodied activity. This is a process by
which the psychologisation of all spheres of life proceeds, from the
middle class that is assumed to think to the working class that
should be made to behave.[28]

Commitment to work is examined in depth in 'emotional labour'

Studies of stress at work also provided an opportunity for psychology
to work on the separation between instrumental and emotional labour.
They enabled psychologists to claim that feelings and relationships

[26] See Brady (1958) for the earliest study on ulcers in stressed 'executive monkeys'.
[27] See Newton (1999) for the argument that 'stress' is not a very useful concept, and
K. McLaughlin (2004) on the role of 'stress' in producing depoliticisation and vulnerability.
[28] For a grim example which makes explicit the link between stress and 'human
performance' at work, see Matthews et al. (2000).

should be studied and that employers would benefit if these specifically 'psychological' aspects of activity were taken seriously. This is a domain personnel psychologists are most interested in intervening in; an attention to feelings and relationships at work makes it seem as if what they are doing is deeper, more genuine, psychology than merely administering intelligence and personality tests. The rise of the service sector (such as shops, restaurants and leisure facilities) and the recruitment of more women into paid work also encouraged a focus on emotional labour and upon the way that performing for the customer will also eventually maximise profit for the employer.[29]

The expectation that the worker in service industries should perform their role for the customer persuasively, so that it does really seem that they also enjoy being there and are thoroughly committed to the quality of the product, entails an intensification of psychology at work. This performance has been well described as a form of 'deep acting' in which the worker is colonised at a level of emotional experience and ends up further separated from themselves; they are thereby fully immersed in the relationship with customers, expected to behave as if they really want to be there, and they are drained of their own response and alienated from themselves. This 'alienation' is not something that can be detected using a simple questionnaire; it only becomes apparent to the worker when they have broken from the 'deep acting', at times when they engage in another kind of collective activity against the company – in meetings, protests, strikes and occupations – and are then able to appreciate how deeply their lives have been colonised for the profit of others.

Psychology Reaches into the Heart of a Heartless World Outside Work

The entry of more women into the workplace has provided added impetus to psychology. As we have noted, intellectual labour under capitalism is separated out into instrumental labour and emotional labour. Stereotypical images of men and women treat men as more instrumental while the emotional side of life is supposed to be

---

[29] See Hochschild's (1983) work on emotional labour; for a more recent account, see Hochschild (2000). On the vacuous and ideologically loaded concept of 'emotional intelligence', see Goleman (1996), and for a feminist therapeutic take on 'emotional literacy', see Orbach (2001).

women's stuff.[30] This stereotypical view of men and women also depicts men as the ones who are suited to do manual labour, which is very peculiar given the high proportion of women involved in manual labour in the early days of Western capitalism and still in most parts of the world.[31] While there had already been increasing opportunities for psychology to work on intellectual labour, the emotional aspect was put onto the agenda more effectively when women needed to be dealt with and encouraged to give themselves over to the world of work. Although it has historically been a stereotypically masculine enterprise, concerned methodologically with the prediction and control of behaviour, the discipline has always been very interested in the relationship between rationality and the more stereotypically feminine world of the emotions. This also serves to intensify psychology's interest in the family.

Psychology examines and normalises forms of family function and dysfunction

Happy families make docile workers, and psychology set itself the task of examining what a happy family really is like and repairing it when things go wrong. The 'family' in psychology is treated as if it were a unit that can be observed, and it is psychologised through two conceptual moves. First, each individual member of the family is assumed to comprise a system of complementary, and sometimes competing, functions. This projection of the particular sets of social relations that obtain under capitalism into the individual is a process we have already described; hierarchical structures at work are also assumed to be at work inside the mind of the worker.[32]

The second move is where the conception of the individual as comprising different functions, separated into different components, is used as the template for what happens in the family unit. The psychologisation of the family thus treats the family unit as if it were a kind of individual, the particular kind of individual that psychology

---

[30] This characterisation of 'sex differences' is standard fare in psychology (for a good sceptical account, see Squire, 1989), and the stereotypes are recycled again and again in pop-psychological accounts of men and women as from Mars and Venus and suchlike (and for an analysis of that nonsense, see Crawford, 1995).

[31] See Marcus (1974) for the role of women in the development of capitalism, and Rowbotham (1973) on the role of women workers in the twentieth century.

[32] See Donzelot (1979) for an examination of the way the welfare state intervened in the family to reconstruct it as an apparatus that could be used to regulate each separate member. For a socialist feminist account of the family and a critique of some recent theories, including those offered by Donzelot, see Barrett and McIntosh (1982).

has already fabricated. We then have a circular definition of what social relations, individuals and families are like, and family therapy is not surprisingly concerned with functional systems in which there are healthy feedback systems. In this psychologised cybernetic image of the individual and their family, it is assumed that dysfunctional systems will then need to be fixed, patched up.[33]

Psychology produces a place for women in the home,
and for maternal attachment

The separation between men at work and women in the family as capitalism developed meant that the family is treated as a quintessentially feminine space. The family is the place of women's work, and child-bearing is thereby naturalised by psychologists through notions of the child's 'attachment' to the mother. According to one increasingly popular account in psychology, 'attachment' is the concept that would explain the link between family environment and individual experience. This concept combined observations from studies of animal behaviour with psychoanalysis,[34] and 'attachment theory' is now growing in influence again in psychoanalytic research as well as in academic psychology, this time linked to some very dubious brain-imaging studies.[35] John Bowlby's ideas about 'attachment' originally became popular after the Second World War in Britain; women who had worked in the factories while the men were fighting had to be encouraged back to their families, and the claim that they needed to be with their children – who had been evacuated from cities or placed in crèches during the war – was a useful ideological tool to persuade them to return home.[36] Problems in attachment will, according to this theory, give rise to problems in

[33] For an analysis of the role of family therapy as a practice that normalised the Western nuclear family and pathologised other forms of relationships, see Poster (1978). For alternatives that developed out of the family therapy tradition and attempted to 'deconstruct' the family and 'therapy' in order to address problems in the wider culture, see Parker (1999b). Monk et al. (1997) used 'narrative therapy' ideas in a similar way, and showed how questions of power and culture have been addressed by radical practitioners in New Zealand.

[34] Often Bowlby's work is seen as drawing on the ethological research of Konrad Lorenz, but Lorenz was actually already drawing on psychoanalytic notions of attachment of infants to mothers, and so research on 'aggression' in human nature circulates in a vicious ideological loop in academic research (see, e.g., Bacciagaluppi, 1989).

[35] For an example, see Fonagy and Target (2004). For other attempts to connect 'attachment theory' masquerading as psychoanalysis with neuroscience, see Green (2003).

[36] Riley (1983) provides the most thorough account of this process, and does so without falling into crass conspiracy theories; she shows how Bowlby's ideas functioned in postwar Britain to legitimise a certain view of the family and of the role of mothers.

later life, perhaps even to a criminal career, and this is where John Bowlby's work on attachment complements work that emphasises biology and inheritance.[37]

Psychology reinforces compulsory heterosexuality, and treats sexual activity as something that will glue the marital couple together. The ideal family, understood as a healthy functioning system, is assumed to rest on a natural psychology of men complementing a natural psychology of women. The harmonious relation between the husband and wife is thought to be what guarantees the health of the family, and here once again psychology has to make assumptions about the 'psychological' nature of biology.[38] A reduction down from the level of a society which is organised around the power of men over women and of older men over younger men is complemented by a reduction upwards from the level of the instincts that are assumed to channel sexual attraction from one sex across to the opposite sex and back again. Patriarchal society and heterosexual biology – an image of biology that will confirm heterosexuality as something 'natural' – then makes the family into the place where psychologists suppose that there must be sex, and only a certain kind of sex. In this way psychology reinforces 'compulsory heterosexuality', and those who want a way out from this little prison are seen as pathological.[39]

'Other' families are treated as models and mirrors of the normal reproductive unit

Psychologists take the patriarchal nuclear family in Western capitalist society as the natural, normal social unit within which new healthy workers will be produced. At the same time it is becoming more evident even to psychologists in the overdeveloped countries that the nuclear family is not the only setting for bringing up children. The rising divorce rate, incidence of single-parent families, and the influx of people from other parts of the world into the imperialist

[37] Bowlby's (1944) study preceded an influential report for the World Health Organisation (Bowlby, 1951). For contemporary British psychological perspectives on 'criminality' (in which there are no references to Bowlby, in line with the erasure of psychoanalysis from the history of psychology, but in which there is still a focus on 'parenting'), see Sutton et al. (2006).

[38] For a bizarre example of the construction of sexuality through psychological measurement of bodily differences, see Hegarty (2003).

[39] Adrienne Rich (1976) elaborated the argument against 'compulsory heterosexuality'. For arguments against heteronormative views of relationships in psychology, see the work of Celia Kitzinger (e.g., Kitzinger, 1987, 1990) and Wilkinson and Kitzinger (1993).

heartlands make the nuclear family less and less relevant. However, the nuclear family still functions as a very powerful ideological form, and in psychological research it is still the 'normal' template against which to compare and contrast 'other' forms of family.[40]

Psychologists hate to be left out of any sphere of life, and so there has been increasing interest in other forms of family. However, it should be noted that 'extended families' or family units where lesbians or gay men bring up children are still treated as 'extensions' or mutations of a basic taken-for-granted family structure. The nuclear family still functions as a powerful ideal model; increasingly influential religious fundamentalists are also very keen on it, for example, and much work needs to be done to challenge the idea that the 'other' types of family should be measured against this ideal standard form.[41]

Psychology Strikes a Balance Between Changes in Work and Changes at Home

The question of 'sex differences' is very much alive in the practice of psychologists studying the 'balance' between labour-time and leisure-time. The notion of 'work-life balance', for example, rests on the assumption that there are two spheres that complement each other, and it implies that psychology has something to say about each sphere.[42] Recent changes in working patterns have given a new twist to this, with an attention to 'integration' rather than balance.[43] The term 'integration' here merely tracks the more insidious processes by which people's lives are organised by the imperative to produce and consume in one continuous cycle in contemporary capitalism. The psychologists who focus on 'integration' are following the latest fashion and, yet again, demonstrating their loyalty to this economic system.

Psychology looks to new productive forces, turning to 'feminised' work

Women have always played a crucial role in the workplace, though they are still often marginalised as secretaries, sometimes servicing management and sometimes resisting,[44] but employers now need to

[40] On the ideology of the 'normal' family, see Poster (1978), and Barrett and McIntosh (1982).

[41] For a feminist critique of fundamentalist Christianity in US politics, see Morgan (2006).

[42] For an argument for 'work-life balance' and limitations, see Gambles et al. (2006).

[43] For case studies on 'work-life' integration, see Lewis and Cooper (2005).

[44] See Pringle (1989) for a study of secretaries and power in organisations; for a more extended study, see Pringle (1991).

draw on the more 'feminine' qualities that women are supposed to embody in order to increase efficiency. With an increasing psychologisation of work there is greater recognition that women can be useful. Now it is more expedient to view them as functioning as well as men and willing to take leadership roles as the new 'femocrats'.[45] They can be harnessed as a resource, bringing into the workplace an attention to feelings and relationships so that every employee will invest themselves at an even deeper level in the company.

At the same time, psychology ratifies home-working and the casualisation of labour in changing gender roles. New working practices mean that an increasing number of women are turned into workers as part of the productive process directly from home. Many people in Western countries now do not have to leave the home and come to work in the factory, for new technologies increase the possibilities for home-working, for men as well as women. This poses a puzzle for the 'nature' of work that psychologists are ideally placed to solve, and it is no surprise that they are most-times solving it in favour of the employers. The idealisation of 'women's work', the place where emotional labour is an aspect of intellectual labour, is the site where psychologists have always targeted their research, and when men are also working part-time they become part of this new 'feminised' workforce.[46]

Psychology reproduces leisure as a masculine sphere,
the prison of measured time

The changes in working practices to include more women have consequences for what the men do at work and at home. The rise of the service sector and greater 'leisure time' calls upon more human resources, and there are then also more opportunities for employment. The provision of activities to keep people busy during their leisure time is becoming increasingly important. This time then becomes a place for production, with the rise of service sector

[45] A 'femocrat' uses feminist rhetoric to step up the management ladder and adapts to stereotypically masculine norms, and so to patriarchy; the term was first used in Australian feminism by Sawer (1990). For a detailed analysis, see Eisenstein (1996).

[46] For studies of 'feminisation' and implications for feminist psychology, see Burman (2004).

entertainment industries being one of the most striking characteristics of 'late capitalism'.[47]

We also see an extension of research into 'sports psychology', for example, as a domain for which men can be prepared to participate more effectively, and in which women are also permitted to participate on condition that they behave as peculiar stereotypical versions of men. Sport in capitalist society is organised around competition, and is a stereotypically masculine activity which reproduces structures of working life. Far from being an escape from work, this kind of sport is a 'prison of measured time',[48] and psychology is one discipline that actively participates in the commodification of leisure time.

Psychology buys into the idea that 'leisure time' can be assessed and recorded, and detailed observations of how people spend their money on leisure pursuits can be useful for marketing campaigns. Marketing and advertising are perfect domains for psychologists to work on people as consumers, and so the double-life of the workforce under capitalism – in production and consumption – is finally tied together. Psychology as a discipline has always sought greater and greater responsibility for controlling people at work and predicting what they would buy with their wages.

The development of late capitalism and the increasing importance of service sector industries also entailed a transformation of old-style Taylorism. Taylor's strategy of increasing efficiency by careful measurement of individual tasks will not work so well in the kind of industry that relies on interaction between the worker and the customer. Taylorism worked well with Fordist production lines, but late capitalism relies on 'post-Fordist' kinds of work process in which teamwork, 'deep acting' and the more intensive psychologisation of everyday life become a priority. Psychology here should not be seen as a progressive intervention in the world of work; psychology has become more important precisely because current production processes demand it.[49]

---

[47] Mandel's (1974) analysis of the development of 'late capitalism' as a distinctive development of capitalism after the Second World War draws attention to the rise of the service sector, and the shift in sites of production. There are close connections between Mandel's Marxist analysis and academic sociological theories of 'post-Fordism' and the associated idea that modern society has mutated into a 'postmodern' culture. For one (not entirely accurate) account of the links between theories of changes in culture and Mandel's analysis, see Jameson (1984). For another Marxist analysis of postmodernism, more sceptical, see Callinicos (1989).

[48] Brohm (1989) argues that sport functions to separate and alienate 'leisure' activity under capitalism.

[49] See Hochschild (1983) for an analysis of the commercialisation of feelings and 'deep acting'.

Psychology Normalises the Unthinkable as Production Processes Change

The early years of industrial capitalism in Europe and America were organised according to the precepts of Taylor, and Fordism provided the template for how production should be organised. However, the breakdown of strict boundaries between work and play that has accompanied transformations in production and consumption has seen 'post-Fordist' patterns become more and more powerful. These post-Fordist patterns are an integral part of the neoliberal globalisation of capitalism and the incorporation not only of women into work but also of new sectors of production into what used to be called the 'third world'. These new forms of production and consumption require a good deal of plasticity, a flexible, more playful outlook, a new ideology that is sometimes seen as 'postmodern'.[50]

Psychology manages a world in which everything that is solid melts into air

The world is changing fast, with fast-paced neoliberal deregulation and privatisation of welfare services driven by Western-based 'international' agencies, but capitalism has always been about change; it is an economic system that constantly revolutionises production and demands innovation at such a speed that it does indeed seem as if 'everything that is solid melts into air'.[51] Rather than prompting psychologists to question whether the models they developed of the individual were ever worth elaborating, the reflexive awareness that we live in a world of rapid change is now yet another opening for psychology as a discipline to offer expertise. The work patterns that affect how manual labour is carried out are changing fast, but instrumental labour – and emotional labour as part of that intellectual labour – now demand even more attention to the domain of the individual, a domain that psychology has carved out as its own and that we need to seize back from it.

---

[50] See Rose (1999) for a discussion of neoliberalism and subjectivity, and Jameson (1991) for a discussion of postmodernism; for a discussion of neoliberalism, globalisation and anti-capitalism, see Went (2000). For discussion of the impact of neoliberalism on subjectivity, see Papadopoulos (2002, 2003), and for the argument that psychologists cannot do anything progressive for the anti-capitalist movement that has emerged in conditions of neoliberalism and globalisation, see Drury (2003).

[51] This phrase from Marx and Engels (1965) on the 'uninterrupted disturbance of all social conditions' is used by Berman (1983) as the key motif in his analysis of contemporary capitalism.

The separation between manual labour and intellectual labour remains whether psychologists focus on things going on inside the head or upon the 'discourse' that people use.[52] This also means that when psychologists try to solve the problem of what to do about the continued importance of manual labour by focusing on 'embodiment' they simply abstract that aspect of activity and turn it into something that can be examined by psychologists.

Psychology fixes people in place, in existing structures of production

The attempts by some psychologists to pretend that they can swim with the current and build a 'postmodern' psychology to suit a postmodern society miss the point of these changes. They conveniently sidestep questions of exploitation and oppression in a society that is still capitalist and which is still organised around patriarchal and colonialist power to alienate and divide the workforce against itself. Such a 'postmodern' psychology stays at the surface self-image of contemporary capitalism, and serves to cover over deeper structural problems.[53]

Psychology ratifies the capitalist system at each and every point so that the process of change becomes managed by the individual, and the individual is unable easily to question what is happening to society beyond what is happening to them personally or what is happening to their own family. Psychology is willing to adapt itself as capitalism changes, and then adapt individuals to new forms of production and consumption. The only way out of this circuit of production and consumption is through collective action, but we have to take care, because, as we shall see in the next chapter, psychology might have got there first, able to anticipate, pathologise and attempt to close off even that escape route.

---

[52] There are connections between the study of 'discourse' and theories of 'postmodernism' in recent idealist versions of psychology (see Parker, 2002).

[53] There are US American liberal versions of this 'postmodern' psychology (e.g., Gergen, 1991) and 'post-Marxist' versions (e.g., Holzman and Morss, 2000), and these writers all seem to believe that playing up what is positive about postmodernism will cause a cultural shift inside the discipline of psychology (see, e.g., Kvale, 1992). For critiques of this theoretical shift, see Parker (1998, 2000).

4
Pathologising Dissent:
Exploitation Isolated and Ratified

The world of psychologists is in some significant respects quite unlike the real world, and so approaches to social issues that are taken by different branches of the discipline are sometimes quite unexpected. A case in point is the way 'social psychologists' and 'political psychologists' deal with conflict and dissent. We might assume that those on the more 'social' side of the discipline would be more sympathetic to social explanations, but this is not the case. Paradoxically, some of the most reductionist and reactionary accounts of collective action are to be found here. The 'political' psychologists are, in addition, often among those most hostile to political explanations of social struggle. This chapter shows how a 'balanced' approach to social and political 'behaviour' leads psychologists to make group and collective activity seem abnormal.

Psychology defines itself by identifying dysfunctional and pathological characteristics

The discipline is very adept at identifying particular abnormalities in individual behaviour, and psychological descriptions unfortunately chime all too well with commonsensical views of who is 'mad' and who is 'bad'. Research psychologists aim at a 'scientific' description of behaviour, usually behaviour that they have played an active role in shaping. They assume that this description must be neutral, non-partisan. This neutral, supposedly scientific detached vantage point will then, they hope, serve to support their own particular pet theory of general patterns of human thinking and behaviour. Each general theory is also rooted in commonsense, and so thereby in the ideological forms of explanation that make life under contemporary capitalism seem so normal and natural to many people.

Here social and political psychology often excels in its task, a psychological task, for it has come up with no shortage of theories to explain why social activity and political action to change our lives is pathological. When social change *is* treated as something positive, it is limited by the assumption that there must be balance and consensus. At the level of personal change this means that psychologists want the individual concerned to be fully aware of all the options and consequences, and this assumption then provides the template for social change. At the level of small-scale group activity the social psychologist attempts to bring about consensus, but they are then haunted by the idea that too much consensus might be harmful. At the level of larger-scale social change in a 'community' the political psychologist wipes away wider contextual issues.[1]

Psychology always arrives, by default, at an image of
the 'normal' individual

The social sectors of the discipline compete with other areas of psychology, and so they are already hamstrung by assumptions the discipline makes about 'social' behaviour. As with other sub-areas of psychology, aspects of social activity are chopped out of the flow of life so they can be studied more easily, but then the overall picture that social and political psychology ends up with is even more peculiar.

By treating group and collective activity as something to be suspicious of, the researchers lead us to assumptions about the underlying universal nature of the normal happy and healthy person that many other psychologists would also sign up to. This normal individual, they assume, engages in rational decision-making and is not unduly influenced by others. Then, because other people are treated as a source of 'influence' these social researchers are halfway down the slippery slope to being fearful of a lack of balance or of political commitment of any kind.

The Psychologisation of Politics Focuses on Balance, to Equate the Left and the Right

Once politics is reduced to being a question of psychology, as a series of puzzles which psychologists have expertise in investigating, we are caught in a little trap from which it is then difficult to escape.

---

[1] The case of community psychological interventions in Venezuela is a case in point; otherwise radical political psychologists managed to describe a whole series of interventions in communities without once mentioning the deep conflicts in Venezuelan society over the role of the Chávez regime (Montero, 2004). For an analysis of class, racial and sexual divisions opened up in Venezuela, see Rodríguez Mora (2005), and on 'critical psychology' in Venezuela, see Montero and Montenegro (2006).

The trap works like this: psychologists believe that they are neutral scientific observers developing theories that are impartial; they then imagine that the people they study should be the same as them, that ordinary people should be neutral and impartial in judgements about the world. This means that when psychologists are faced with people who are steadfast in their opinions and willing to fight for them there is a threat to the discipline's view of the ideal rational individual, and there is also a threat to what psychologists imagine scientific investigation should be like. Those to the left and those to the right of the psychologist therefore pose a problem to the psychological view of the self. This is a problem that many social and political psychologists try to solve by taking a middle way and encouraging people to 'balance' two sides of an argument.

Models of flexibility and adaptation require that the person is seen as a little 'democracy'

The ideological assumption that structures a good deal of psychological research into social behaviour is that democracy will provide a balance between different competing political opinions. What this ideal 'democracy' should be like in practice is left vague, but it usually boils down to the idea that the way political debate is conducted in Western liberal society is best. So, the right to free speech and a vote for representatives every now and then is high up on the agenda, while the ability to collectively determine what happens to the fruits of our labour does not figure in this model of politics at all. This view of democracy privileges individual activity over collective activity, and once this individual-centred 'democracy' sets the rules of the game, all research on collective action that is defined by those rules will make collective action look undemocratic, if not pathological.[2]

Psychology goes one step further, and roots that view of liberal democracy inside the human mind; what could be better than to see each individual as weighing up the pros and cons of every argument, as if they were taking account of the different views being

---

[2] The intense debates within the anarchist and revolutionary Marxist traditions over the role of 'democracy', and the attempts to challenge the social democrats who take the moral high ground on this issue, provide a quite different set of coordinates for thinking about the limits of liberal bourgeois 'democracy'; see, Mandel (1979), and, for feminist discussion of anarchist politics, see Freeman (1996).

voiced in a debate?[3] In this way democracy is guaranteed; at least, a certain limited idea of what democracy is about. This psychologisation of political activity means that those individuals who do not think as if they were miniature walking, talking democracies must be treated with suspicion.

Abstract characterisation of 'political behaviour' evacuates political analysis

The ideological loop that ties individual patterns of thinking into dominant social structures is an example of reductionism working downwards – from society to the individual – to confirm and legitimate political behaviour. It mirrors reductionism that works upwards from the individual to society, the kind of mistaken view that treats nation states as if they were 'competitive' or 'jealous' and explains wars as the result of irrational psychological states.[4]

An assessment of each particular conflict is wiped away by reductionism; the social psychological approach evacuates political analysis and we are left with ridiculous explanations. Often these are psychological explanations that appeal to a view of 'human nature', explanations that psychologists bear some responsibility for keeping alive every time they frame research in terms of behavioural variables or political 'attitudes'. It looks neutral to subscribe to this view of political activity, but it is not; it is highly political; 'by their neglect of social analysis such researchers are in fact upholding a particular social analysis'.[5]

There is a right-wing agenda for the equation of left and right politics in psychology

The balancing out of left and right viewpoints to leave room for a supposedly neutral 'third way' that will simply concern itself with the most pragmatic management of society is a bourgeois politician's dream.[6]

---

[3] Billig's (1982) ambiguous social-psychological discussion of the motif of 'balance' sometimes portrays this balance as part of ideology and sometimes celebrates the posing of dilemmas as a universal process of human thinking; see also his argument in favour of polemic in social psychology (Billig, 1988). His later focus on the 'dilemmatic' nature of thought unfortunately fits with standard social-psychological assumptions about what is healthy and democratic (see Billig, 1987). For a review of some of the political problems in Billig's argument, see Reicher (1988). Billig was, before his turn to the study of discourse and rhetoric, one of the few Marxist social psychologists doing politically relevant research (see, e.g., Billig, 1976, 1978).

[4] For a good analysis of this problem in social psychology, see Billig (1976).

[5] Billig (1976), p. 222.

[6] See Giddens (1998) for an outline of this argument for a 'third way'.

This is why accounts of the 'end of ideology',[7] or even 'the end of history',[8] have been seized upon with such glee; such accounts are summoned to prove that those who really want to change the world must be mistaken and outdated. Many of the venerable old US American social psychologists were actually quite left-wing, and they did want to make the world a better place. This is why there was such attention given to 'prejudice', 'conformity' and positive inter-group alliances in the early work.[9] The discipline of psychology provided the wrong frame to investigate these issues though, and the researchers were eventually silenced. Now the radical politics of those researchers is hidden from view or made to seem quaint and unrealistic.[10]

Now psychologists are very popular in middle-of-the-road political management circles because they stir in the notion that those who depart from the middle of the road must also be deluded. It is not surprising that psychologists with right-wing political views have been keen to pretend that they are simply describing the world as it is. In some ways, of course, they are quite right; they do describe a political-economic system held in place by exploitation of isolated individuals as it is now, and then they depict those who struggle against this system as isolated individual crackpots. Opponents are pathologised, accused of having 'authoritarian' personalities, even though authoritarians usually love rules and regulations, which those who struggle do not. Anyone who refuses to accept the 'democratic' rules of the game is seen as hating democracy and loving power; real political disagreement is lumped together in one psychological category. If communists and fascists really are psychologically similar, then uncomfortable political arguments will be treated as

[7] Bell (1965) provides a classic restatement of this idea, a claim about ideology that is recycled by different writers every ten or fifteen years to try and shut the opposition up.

[8] Fukuyama (1992) ratcheted up the old end-of-ideology argument in an article and then a book that claimed that the victory of capitalism over the fake-socialist states showed that liberal democracy was now the only game in town; we are now, he claimed, at the 'end of history'.

[9] Condor (1997) makes this argument very clearly; for a discussion of the case of the leading experimental social psychologist Sherif, who had to leave Turkey for the US because of his membership of the communist party, see Batur and Aslıtürk (2006).

[10] The vacuous appeal to liberal-democratic values of openness to debate in place of political argument then leaves leftists in psychology completely at sea when explicitly right-wing psychologists join the debate and play them at their own game; see, for example, the intervention by Redding (2001).

expressions of pathology rather than taken seriously and debated and fought through.

There is a left-wing version that also ends up extolling the value of democracy

It is not good enough to treat the problem of reductionism as merely a psychological problem, as simply down to the spiteful wrong-doing of right-wing psychologists. There are material political conditions for the equation of left and right in Western bourgeois democracies. Political opposition rocks the boat, and the smooth running of society, which feels open enough for many law-abiding people, makes disruption and the prospect of radical social change feel threatening and a cause of uncertainty. It was once claimed that workers would unite to overthrow capitalism, and that they had nothing to lose but their chains.[11] Many workers do have more to lose than their chains now, and this is partly because they are also all the more strongly psychically invested in what capitalism offers them. It is not only because of the delights of consumer society available to the bloated middle class. The rise of psychology is closely connected with this process by which the 'chains' that tie people to patterns of relating to others that are damaging and miserable have become embedded in the way we think and relate to others, as if they have been 'internalised'.[12] It is understandable that what good things have been won in the liberal democracies should then be contrasted with what is on offer under left- and right-wing regimes that do often seem to be worse places to live.

Some of the most interesting studies of 'authoritarianism' carried out by Marxist social scientists in Germany in the 1930s, for example, were later developed by these same researchers in a quite different

[11] The 1848 Manifesto of the communist party concludes with the stirring claim that 'proletarians have nothing to lose but their chains. They have a world to win. Working Men of All Countries Unite!' (Marx and Engels, 1965, p. 77).
[12] Michel Foucault's (1977) history of the modern prison regimes and their place in modern society emphasises how physical chains were replaced with much more effective chains in the mind, and then people also learn to accept and love their own servitude. Foucault was a member of the French communist party in the early 1950s, and trained as a psychologist before turning to study systems of thought (see Parker, 1995b). Although some of his political writings have an uneasy relationship with Marxism, many of his analyses of discipline and confession are relevant to Marxist politics (see Foucault, 1991).

direction when they were forced into exile in the United States.[13] The work of the 'Frankfurt School' tradition is still very much alive in social and political theory, but in social and political psychology the empirical questionnaires and interview research in that tradition are not very enlightening. In the context of 'democratic' US society after the Second World War facing a Soviet regime that murdered members of the opposition, this later research emphasised 'psychology' more and more, eventually concluding that a 'democratic' personality was preferable.[14] Politics itself was reduced to the qualities of different personalities, and a Marxist account of fascism (as being a last-ditch attempt by the ruling class to save capitalism from communist revolution) disappeared altogether from academic study.[15]

Psychology Pathologises Collective Activity

Once political differences are cleared out of the way, psychology can then more easily reinforce the idea that any disagreements about policy should only be voiced by individuals. Collective activity raises the spectre of bad old 'political' arguments creeping in again. However, this does not mean that research is straightforward, and the very complexity of seeking out the opinions of different individuals is an opportunity for psychologists to make themselves seem useful. There are many factors that have to be attended to and carefully balanced in a psychological view of the world to make sure that people think and behave as they should. Social psychologists have been masters of balancing out the helpful and harmful 'influences' of other people on the individual.

---

[13] Adorno et al.'s (1950) study is often cited by social psychologists, but it is only the study of 'attitudes' that interests them; the psychoanalytic theory that Adorno et al. use is treated by social psychology with suspicion because it speculates about unconscious things that the positivist researcher cannot directly observe or measure. The title of an earlier paper by the researchers (bar Adorno), 'The antidemocratic personality', makes the shift to an endorsement of American society quite explicit (see Frenkel-Brunswik et al., 1947).

[14] There is a good discussion of this adaptation of Adorno et al.'s theoretical perspectives to US society by Billig (1978) in his study of the rise of fascism in 1970s Britain. For a general discussion of the way radical psychoanalytic researchers adapted to US society when they fled from Europe, see Jacoby (1975, 1983).

[15] On the Frankfurt School and a tradition of empirical survey research in Marxism, see Roiser and Willig (1996). For Marxist accounts of the rise of fascism, see Guerin (1973) and Trotsky (1975).

*A balance between 'social facilitation' and
inhibition governs social psychology*

The 'individual' in social psychology is already a rather abstracted and
minimalist concept, as can been in the studies of 'social facilitation'
in the US. The main studies in the 1960s were carried out not on
human beings but on cockroaches set off to scuttle down a little
runway either on their own or in the presence of their friends.[16] The
advantage of this experimental paradigm was that it purported to
show that one or two others would encourage the 'subject' to run
faster while a crowd would have the effect of slowing him down
again. What was even better was that a graph of the rise and fall in
performance showed a 'normal distribution' U-shaped curve.

Ridiculous though these studies were, they were faithful to the
logic of 'scientific' social psychological investigation. The actual
social and political circumstances in which people interact with others
was stripped away and a chosen 'variable' – here 'social facilitation' –
studied as if it were in its pure state. If this behaviour in its pure state
is to be measured, so the fake-scientific reasoning of the psychologist
goes, then it does not matter what kind of animal is doing the
behaving; studies of conditioning in pigeons, decision-making in
rats or stress in monkeys follow the same rocky logic. And then any
behaviour can be described to support the claim that a particular psychological explanation is valid. When men, rather than cockroaches,
were observed pissing in the presence of others, for example, a similar
'social facilitation' result was demonstrated.[17]

*Crowd behaviour, of 'women, savages and children',
anticipates evolutionary work*

Compared with such small changes in behaviour in the presence of
one or two fellows, the images of crowd behaviour in the real world
across the Atlantic Ocean that haunted the early years of US American
social psychology seemed really horrific and outrageous. The classic
study by Gustave Le Bon, *The Crowd: A Study of the Popular Mind*, was
inspired by the author's experiences as a medical aide during the

[16] Zajonc (1965) was responsible for this strand of research, and a study by Bond
and Titus (1983) provides a rather pointless 'meta-analysis' of what had been found
(in which it must be remembered that a 'meta-analysis' of pointless experiments merely
aggregates the ideological misrepresentation of social activity of each researcher into
one big mass of ideological misrepresentation).
[17] Middlemist et al. (1976) carried out this study; there is a discussion of this and
other studies in Parker (1989).

Paris Commune of 1871, and so translation of his book from the original French into English brought some dire warnings about irrationality from Europe to the Americas.

The first social psychology experiment in the 1890s was on the effect of the presence of others on the speed of the 'subject' turning fishing reels.[18] This experimental anticipation of the social facilitation paradigm was small beans compared to the mayhem that Le Bon described. A generation of US social psychologists was galvanised into research on how individuals in 'democratic' countries could be saved from the fate of the Europeans. The individual in the 'crowd', by which Le Bon meant a wide range of collective processes including 'criminal crowds', 'criminal juries' and 'parliamentary assemblies', lost all their critical faculties and regressed, he said, to the level of 'beings of inferior forms of evolution … women, savages, and children, for instance'.[19]

Collective activity is equated with irrationality,
as if it were 'deindividuation'

While Le Bon and his political co-thinkers clearly had in mind what those at advanced levels of evolution should be like – that is, the individual members of the European aristocracy and bourgeoisie – the US social psychologists were keen to make the message more 'democratic'. As long as people were able to make decisions individually then some degree of rationality would be assured. An experimental tradition concerned with 'deindividuation', for example, took one aspect of experience in crowds described in Le Bon's study and replicated it in the laboratory.

This tradition of research employed the then popular social-psychological experimental device of getting subjects to believe they were giving shocks to other people. The 'hypothesis' to be tested in the deindividuation experiments was that when individuals were completely anonymous they would lose their precious individuality

[18] This study was carried out by Triplett (1898) and sets the pattern for research in which psychological aspects are abstracted from context and then measured in different settings.
[19] Le Bon (1896), p. 36. For a review from deep within the 'European' tradition of social psychology of the role of the 'crowd' in conceptions of social action, which then also falls into some of the same assumptions Le Bon made, see Moscovici (1986). For a critique of Le Bon's description of crowd behaviour and ideological assumptions at work in it, see Reicher (1982); and for an elaboration of this critique with respect to later social psychological theories, see Reicher (1991); for good empirical studies of crowd action that take political context seriously, see Reicher (1984) and Drury (2002).

and then be more unpleasant to fellow human beings. The 'subjects' were nastier to others if they were dressed up in Ku Klux Klan hoods;[20] not only did they look stupid making decisions in fancy-dress but they showed that rational decision-making was associated with being a nice clear-thinking US American individual.

Individual activity is rational, bedevilled by error and false consciousness

The social-psychological studies of abnormal and irrational behaviour helped define what 'normal' and 'rational' social behaviour should be like. As any psychologist will tell you, however, it is always necessary to be on your guard because that normal and rational behaviour is liable to be subject to error. That is why you need a psychologist to make sure that the highest standards of behaviour are maintained and to act as an ethical role model for those ordinary folk who are less balanced. One of the founding studies of prejudice in the US, for example, purported to show that there was a discrepancy between the views that would be expressed in a questionnaire and an actual social encounter with someone from a different culture.[21]

What people thought about themselves was thus shown to be mistaken, their 'consciousness' about themselves was therefore 'false', and even everyday social interaction could not be ruled out as a cause of bad things. There is an inversion of the Marxist view of ideology here; for Marxists, the *isolation* of individuals from one another is the breeding ground for distrust and fear of collective action and social change. When Marxists talk about 'false consciousness', they do not mean that individuals are making some kind of cognitive errors, mistakes in their reasoning. It is rather that people are making conscious choices based on life conditions that are 'false' and every false option available to them serves to confirm their alienation and sense that nothing can be done to change those conditions.[22] The psychological view, in contrast, is that 'false consciousness' is

[20] Johnson and Downing (1979) conducted this study, basing it on a paradigm of research set up by Zimbardo (1969).

[21] The study was by LaPiere (1934), and the welcome he got for his Chinese travelling companions was very different from the racist attitudes expressed in questionnaires sent out later.

[22] This Marxist view of ideology and false consciousness as rooted in the material conditions in which people make choices within limited parameters is relevant to our understanding of obedience to authority at times of dictatorship and also to the rather more banal everyday role of bureaucracy in organisations that aim for another world (Mandel, 1992).

something that kicks in when people work together. Perhaps, we are invited to conclude, it is better to know nothing than to know something that might end up as pathological as that.[23]

Social Psychology Pathologises Group Activity

Social psychology functions as a series of short sharp shocks to anyone who thinks that it is the separation and isolation of people from each other that might be harmful. Over and again the false and self-limiting message is that groups are bad for you, but a lot of psychological work needs to be done to guard the sanctity of the individual and their good behaviour. At any moment, so the story goes, the individual might be tempted into striking up relationships with others, and misfortune is then soon sure to follow. Notions of 'group inhibition' and 'diffusion of responsibility' are then used to explain why people do not act to stop behaviour they know is wrong.[24]

Studies of group behaviour in the US are suspicious of the effects of others

One of the most well known social psychology experiments is Stanley Milgram's shocking demonstration that men in white coats could persuade good red-blooded US citizens (who had been screened to ensure that there were no mental health problems that might confound the results) to deliver lethal high-voltage punishments to other people.[25] It is not clear exactly what this study of 'obedience to authority' was supposed to show, and Milgram did not even have clear hypotheses before he ran the experiment, but it provided a highly psychologised, ideological explanation for why people obey others in authority. The hopeless and reactionary moral of the Milgram story is that resistance is futile, and it is very rare for people to point to the Milgram study to show that in these conditions there will always be people who will resist.

Milgram's study of obedience became associated with another notorious experiment that has had huge appeal outside the discipline,

[23] For an example of research in social psychology that reduces 'false consciousness' to errors made by individuals, see Jost (1995); then, even when this research is carried out by those sympathetic to Marxism, psychology leads them to puzzle away as to why talk about 'false' consciousness is mistaken (e.g., Augoustinos, 1999).

[24] The influential US social-psychological study by Latané and Darley (1970) is one of those explored by Cherry (1995) in her thoughtful critique of the way moral lessons from the history of social psychology wipe out political context.

[25] Milgram (1963); for a recent study of Milgram's work, including the obedience studies, see Blass (2004).

part of the popular diffusion of social psychological images of collective activity.[26] Philip Zimbardo carried out the notorious study at Stanford University which put volunteers into prisoner and guard roles, but it had to be abandoned after six days because of the levels of abuse and distress.[27] The Milgram and Zimbardo experiments are usually chained together in social psychology textbooks and popular accounts precisely because one gives sense to the other, the sense that social behaviour is bad for you and for others. What is often forgotten is that a number of participants in the Milgram studies broke down as they gave what they thought were electric shocks to other people, many people refused to play along and many partici-pants later said that they knew that the whole set-up was fake. Zimbardo's study allowed no space for people to collectively organise against his pretend prison system, and so options that are available in the real world were closed off in order to drum home the miserable message about the power of social roles over the individual.[28]

Politics is treated as subject to the influence of 'groupthink'

The war against the effects of group mentality has been conducted on different fronts. Often the message that political debate should avoid group effects is implicit, but sometimes social psychologists have tried to interpret political events using their own categories. Irving Janis' work on 'groupthink', for example, is a much cited demonstration that US foreign policy deliberations were clouded by group dynamics. The cases of decision-making afflicted by 'groupthink' included the US response to the attack on Pearl Harbour, conduct of the Vietnam War, and the attempted invasion of Cuba which resulted in the Bay of Pigs fiasco. Janis then makes some suggestions as to how checks and balances could have been introduced to ensure that decisions were made more rationally.[29]

[26] A German film, *The Experiment*, was released in 2001, and a BBC documentary (made in collaboration with social psychologists) was televised in May 2002. (For Zimbardo's prison-experiment website, see http://www.prisonexp.org/).

[27] See Haney et al. (1973) for a description of the experiment, and Zimbardo (1973) for a discussion of ethical issues. There is a good discussion of these studies and what they do and do not tell us about 'human nature' by the humanist psychoanalyst Erich Fromm (1974).

[28] Reicher and Haslam (2006) provide a different reading which does highlight resis-tance to authority and shows how that resistance must be collective activity in order to succeed (based on their replication of the Zimbardo study for the BBC documentary mentioned in note 26 above).

[29] See Janis (1972) for the definitive study of 'groupthink'.

What Janis does not spell out is exactly what alternative courses of action might have been taken, and it is difficult to see how he could have done so without providing a *political* assessment of the relationship between US imperialism and the rest of the world. From some vantage points the decisions would be seen as reasonable as US power and apple pie, whether there was 'groupthink' or not; from other vantage points the leaders would be tried as war criminals, and any psychologist who tried to help them decide that course of action more efficiently should then surely be put in the dock with them. The phenomenon of 'groupthink' is the crazy bit of equation left after we have agreed not to ask other more important questions about the rationality and irrationality of world politics and the struggle between those who profit and those who are oppressed.

Organised groups are treated as pathological,
crystallised in notions of sect and 'cult'

The work on 'groupthink' ends up with some proposals for political leaders as to how they might manage their affairs more sensibly. No such friendly advice is to hand for the real political target of this powerful strand of work in social psychology, those who are involved in alternative politics. Those who step out of the legitimate spectrum of debate are treated as off the edge mentally as well as politically. This social-psychological view of politics is then used to dub tightly organised groups 'cults'. The *reductio ad absurdum* logic of this cult-baiting is quite evident when researchers claim that 'Cults can consist of as few as two people, in which one person dominates the other and claims a position of privileged insight for himself or herself.'[30] This use of the label 'cult' imports highly ideological notions of 'brain-washing' that were first developed by the US security services to explain why some of their countrymen joined the communists during the Korean War.[31]

---

[30] Tourish and Wohlforth (2000a), p. 4. This volume is unfortunately representative of the worst of this use of psychology to smear political groups researchers disagree with. This is particularly distasteful when Wohlforth, a former Trotskyist, uses the occasion to settle scores with his previous comrades and concludes that 'It is difficult to avoid the conclusion that the "source code" for cultic practice must lie within Leninism itself' (p. 213).

[31] In the US, Lifton (1989) wrote the classic study on brain-washing by the Chinese. In Britain, a classic study first published in 1946 was *Battle for the Mind* (Sargant, 1959). The author, William Sargant, was a psychiatrist who described conversion experiences of evangelical Christians and communists. One obituary after his death in 1988 records that during 25 years in charge of psychological medicine at St Thomas' Hospital in London he was known as 'God'.

Social psychologists sometimes point out that in Jonestown, for example, a political agenda did actually incite members to commit mass suicide. And then, of course it could not possibly be conceivable that political reasons alone could be reason enough, could it? A psychological category that is already loaded with political consequences is wheeled in to explain away political choices that individuals or groups or larger collective forces might have made. Again, the awful choices that groups make are abstracted from the contradictory conditions in which they are forced to act, and the 'psychological' bit of the explanation makes it seem like the bad choice must be based on faulty reasoning or mental pathology.

European studies complement studies of individual identity, but within limits

US crass individualist social psychology is, perhaps, too easy a target, and the presuppositions of the laboratory-experimental studies on obedience and group behaviour are too easy for Europeans to sneer at. Are things so much better the other side of the Atlantic, home of Le Bon and of so many equally ridiculous ideas about the irrationality of the mob? Unfortunately, the false opposition between 'US American' and 'European' social psychology, with the Europeans presenting themselves as more authentically 'social',[32] has served to obscure the reductionism that still strongly underpins European studies of group psychology. The distinction between US American and European social psychology is itself a misleading one; the distinction carves up the world of social research into these two academic superpowers, and it makes those at the margins into dupes of bad US psychology whose only hope for something better is then, it seems, to be good Europeans.

The key defining studies of group categorisation carried out by Henri Tajfel, for example, showed that schoolboys in Bristol would distribute greater rewards to their own 'group' even if the basis for

[32] The volume edited by Israel and Tajfel (1972) indulges in this rather smug contrast between US American bad laboratory-experimental social psychology and good European social psychology. One of the prime movers in this rhetoric, Serge Moscovici, used the book as one of the launch-pads for his theory of 'social representations'; see, for an outline of the theory and other discussions, the volume by Farr and Moscovici (1984). The theory has spread from France to Latin America, and its supporters there overlook the fact that most of the social representations research is reductionist, even often taking the form of laboratory-experiments, as the American social psychology they were so anxious to escape.

the existence of that group was entirely artificial.[33] This inspired one of the most futile debates in social psychology, between those who emphasised the importance of 'individual identity' and those who emphasised 'social identity'. Either way, the lesson was still that your 'identity' led you to favour your own kind, and this motif of the conflict between 'us' and 'them' has exercised social psychologists in Europe in many banal studies.[34] The Europeans ended up conducting their own battle to reduce politics to social psychology, shoulder to shoulder with the Americans in the war against large-scale collective action.

Psychology Pathologises Opposition to the Premises of Individualised Democracy

If the communist threat during the twentieth century seemed bad enough because it was based on irrational group effects and because communists seemed to promote collective activity, then Islamic 'fundamentalism' has provided something worse, the latest, most salient threat to psychologically balanced life in the West. A degree of disciplinary double-think is necessary to shift the focus from militant atheists to religious fanatics, but so it goes. The presence of Christian fundamentalism in the West and the history of the Crusades are conveniently overlooked in order that the psychologists can once again take a balanced view of the problem, and position others as the ones with the problem.[35]

Psychology invokes its own notion of community in the response to 'terrorism'

The response of the American Psychological Association (APA) to '9/11' – the 11 September 2001 attacks on the World Trade Center in New York – is an instructive guide to the worldview of psychologists when faced with extreme threat. Zimbardo, well known for the

[33] Tajfel's (1970) experiments led to an interminable series of studies and models of 'social identity' that have been carried on after Tajfel's death by one of his former collaborators, ex-Maoist John Turner in Australia (e.g., Turner et al., 1987), and incorporated back into US laboratory-experimental social psychology (e.g., Worchel and Austin, 1986). For a critical response to this tradition of research, see Michael (1990).

[34] Billig (1995) tackled this head-on, to show that the categorisations that are repetitively used to set one national identity against another did, indeed, have a banal character, but this has not stopped many social psychologists tracking the same motif here, there and everywhere.

[35] For an account that does take the role of Western 'civilisation' seriously in the current drift to 'barbarism' in world politics, see Achcar (2006). On Christian fundamentalism in US politics, see Morgan (2006).

Stanford prison-studies, used his presidency of the APA after the attacks to urge psychologists to put aside their differences and pull together to face this common enemy, which included what he referred to as the 'cults of hatred'.[36] Now, it seems, a community of psychologists should come up with a solution, and a united front in the face of a common threat is assumed to be a good thing.

When other people – non-psychologists – are brought together in a group they are treated as objects of suspicion, prone to any number of troublesome phenomena – ranging from 'groupthink' to 'risky shift'[37] – with one exception; that exception is when they work together in a 'community' with a common purpose. The homely comfortable image of 'community' evokes the friendly democratic values that US American psychologists approve of. The sting in the tail is that there is then an exception to this, for when people in other cultures that might be hostile to Western 'democracy' gather together in a community, the old psychological suspicions of anything larger than the ideal-typical individual kick into action again. When those communities include close-knit groups closed to outsiders the problem is even worse as far as psychologists are concerned, for then any variety of sect and 'cult' processes might be triggered. The racist assumptions that riddle white Western psychology come to the surface when the West is under threat, and the old categories that are used to pathologise cultures that are organised differently come alive again.

Psychology strips away political rationality in a version of the clash of civilisations

The idea that a particular discipline might unite to fight an enemy characterised as an irrational barbaric threat reveals how closely the political agenda of psychology corresponds to that of the

---

[36] See Zimbardo (2002) for his reflections on the APA Annual Convention. The APA has since been so keen to keep the ear of government that it refuses to join the American Medical Association and American Psychiatric Association in barring members from participating in Guantánamo interrogations; instead the then APA President in October 2005 travelled to Guantánamo as guest of the Pentagon and announced afterwards that he saw the invitation 'as an important opportunity to continue to provide our expertise and guidance for how psychologists can play an appropriate and ethical role in national security investigations' (quoted in Levine, 2007).

[37] The 'risky shift' phenomenon – the observation that groups would be more likely to take extreme positions than individuals – disintegrated after researchers found that there could also be a 'conservative shift', and so another fine idea ended up going nowhere; for a first outline of the theory of 'risky shift', see Kogan and Wallach (1967).

US political elite and ruling class. One force – the good community of psychologists – is conjured into being in the combined energies of the APA against another force that is as yet incomprehensible but must be understood if it is to be defeated; here the political compass-points are provided by the idea that the civil wars in Iraq and Afghanistan boil down to a 'clash of civilisations' rather than a history of subjugation and then invasion by imperialist powers.[38]

The argument that the current rise of 'terrorism' can be explained by a 'clash of civilisations' is convenient for lazy academics and opportunist politicians. It is also a very tempting argument for psychologists. The 'clash' looks like old 'cross-cultural' psychology theories of the difference between ways of understanding the world and misunder-standings of communication as being the root of political conflict. This 'clash' of civilisations also smuggles in the racist implication that the other 'civilisation' is not really as civilised – suicide-bombers are obviously less civilised than helicopter gun-ships, for example – and so the cross-cultural research is conducted from a position in which the superiority of the researcher is never questioned. Once the political questions are out of the way, the pragmatic technical issue of how to deal with the violence can be explored, using such vacuous explanatory frameworks as 'Terror Management Theory'.[39]

Psychology pathologises collectively oriented cultures as 'dark, dim and backward'

What marks the other 'civilisation' as 'other' is that they are supposed to operate on fundamentally different principles that are alien to the Western way of life. The history of psychological 'cross-cultural' differ-ences between 'individualist' and 'collectivist' civilisations is brought into play once again. It is only at moments of stress that the underly-ing assumptions in this contrast are made clear; it is visible when the fight against evil-doers after '9/11' in New York was initially trumpeted as a new crusade, or when '7/7' suicide-bombers in London are described as having an ideology that is 'dark, dim and backward'.[40]

[38] Huntington (2002) started this hare racing in the US, and unleashed a series of studies of the mentality of 'other' cultures that are assumed in one way or another to be less advanced than that of the most civilised country on earth. For a Marxist response to Huntington, see Achcar (2006).
[39] The Pyszczynski et al. (2002) book elaborating 'Terror Management Theory' was published by the American Psychological Association.
[40] See Whitaker et al. (2005) for this story and Bush's comment on the 'dark, dim and backward'; in contrast, for an account of depression among Asians in the context of the racist backlash in Britain after the 2005 London bombings, see Sale (2006).

The 'prejudice' about other cultures that is voiced in the heat of the conflict is the least of the problem, and when psychologists try to get at the aspects of 'prejudice' that might inform judgements made by political leaders they are misplacing and reducing the problem. The structural conditions of exploitation and resistance, and of racism and identity, are not 'attitudes' inside the minds of the individuals involved that can then be detected using a questionnaire.

Psychology focuses political change on leaders, individualising and pathologising them

The emphasis on 'regime change', which identifies particular political leaders to be removed, perhaps the same ones that were parlayed with in lucrative arms-sales deals in the years just beforehand, makes the individualist worldview of Western leaders clear. Psychologists are always at hand to back up this worldview, and they actively participate in the reduction of political action to the level of the kind of small-group interaction or individual behaviour that can more easily, they think, be predicted and controlled.

Psychologists are implicated in this problem at the levels of representation and practice. At the level of representation, they feed the press with investigations of the childhood trauma suffered by dictators of different stripes and diagnoses of mental instability to explain why these people should hate democracy.[41] In practice, they encourage negotiations between leaders of different groups – small-group meetings held in secret that isolate the leaders from those they represent, treating them as individuals with whom relations of trust can be built – and then hail 'peace accords' that sell the hopes of oppressed peoples down the river as steps forward in 'conflict resolution'.

Psychology Is Based on the Wrong Material

Social psychologists and political psychologists have not simply made errors of judgement in various lines of research. They follow the political logic of the cultural ideological context in which they work. Their work is so 'false', and their justifications for why they

[41] For two typical examples, on the childhoods and personality structures of Slobodan Milošević and Saddam Hussein respectively, see Immelman (1999, 2003). There is a long tradition of psychological investigation of the childhood and inner motivations of dictators that serves to obscure the political conditions in which dictatorships emerge.

focus on the wrong questions so deeply embedded in their 'false consciousness' appropriate to the reductionist ideology of their discipline, that simply trying to persuade them where they have gone wrong is a lost cause. Their work is very 'rational' and very mistaken at the same time. The shame is that they have not been prepared to grant to their opponents the same degree of rationality.

Psychology compounds its own errors by treating the material as psychological

Psychologists imagine themselves to be free-thinking individuals who have chosen to adopt a particular perspective, and the final twist is that they assume that everyone else has made the same kind of choice about how they see the world. Unless, of course, the psychologist wants to be really generous, in which case they will explain the bad choices that non-psychologists make as being the pathological effects of faulty reasoning or the influence of other people.[42]

Those who carry out research and give psychological advice to other people have to overlook the political conditions that structure how they see the world. The illusion that policy-makers will take a social psychologist or political psychologist more seriously if the advice is untainted by any particular standpoint leads this ostensibly more 'social' research into a dead-end. The attempt to be balanced, and to make that balance function as the sign to their leaders that they are detached scientific observers of social and political behaviour, just leads them to speak a language to power that power will appreciate. Balance in research alongside the search for consensus in social change psychologises politics and turns the 'radicals' in psychology into agents of social control.

There is a material basis for political choices and errors

The class, gender and racial composition of psychology is reason enough for why we might expect to find the discipline overall pursuing a liberal-to-right-wing political agenda. The funding opportunities that frame research and the tough tenure-track system in the US which demands that psychologists publish or perish in mainstream journals to get a career are further powerful inducements for them to keep shy of political controversy.

---

[42] For reflections on the gendered and class composition of psychology, see Walkerdine (1990, 1996), and for an acute sociological analysis of 'academic gangs', see Scheff (1995).

The best way of avoiding any entanglement in politics, of course, is to ensure that 'social psychology' and 'political psychology' are evacuated of any social or political content, so that questions of power, conflict and change are turned into questions only of psychology.

5
Material Interests:
the Manufacture of Distress

Some psychologists believe that the consciousness we have of our actions is no more than sea-froth, that this little bit extra that makes us feel human is a mere 'epiphenomenon' of the real stuff which is behaviour that can be measured and reinforced. This view of ourselves fits quite neatly with alienated life under capitalism, where we may feel our bodies to be lifeless machines in which we think but over which we have little control. Our psychology and what the psychologists say about it are important precisely because these things are interwoven with physical reality. The discipline of psychology is embedded in the material organisation of the world, and the decisions psychologists make have consequences for our space to act and to think. This chapter shows how psychology is part of a network of practices structured by political and economic interests. To understand the stuff of psychology we need to take seriously how the discipline operates to physically limit us, with effects that go well beyond some strange ideas about what individuals should be like.

Psychological processes are grounded in biology

Once 'psychology' has been carved out as a distinct domain of study a weird unsolvable puzzle drives the psychologists to try and find out where 'it' – the psychology they measure and speculate about – really is. One desperate short-circuit is to study the 'biological bases of behaviour' and try and find psychology there. Another move in this bizarre dance is to patch together what we know about biology with some data about 'social influences' and imagine that our psychology will reappear somewhere in the middle. The 'bio-psycho-social' models operate in this kind of way.[1]

---

[1] Most research in psychology on 'mental illness', for example, claims to operate with a 'bio-psycho-social' model, but actually ends up with a 'bio-bio-bio' model (Read, 2005). The best that can be hoped for if one adopts a 'bio-psycho-social' model is that one arrives at an account somewhere in the middle, with psychology, but the worst, most

It is true that our thinking and acting are embodied and as dependent on the evolutionary history of the human species as our breathing and digestion are. This biological nature is transformed when we ourselves struggle to understand ourselves and others, and the historical social relationships through which we carry out that struggle produce a 'second nature'. This second nature comprises needs, demands and desires that are peculiarly human, becoming human at the moment we articulate them to others and ourselves. This second nature, only possible because of the evolutionary biology of the human species, is profoundly affected by what the psychologists say and what they do to us.[2]

There is a pecking order between psychiatry and psychology

What the psychologists say and do is also grounded in something else other than biology. The historical relationship between different institutions concerned with good behaviour and the detection of abnormality makes psychology as a discipline dependent on others, and dependent in a peculiar way upon knowledge of biological processes. Psychologists know this, and that is why they anxiously search for approval and legitimation from their colleagues in the natural sciences. The laboratory-experimental paradigm in psychology mimics how psychologists imagine natural scientists carry out their work, and clinical psychological models of distress then remain awestruck by what they think of as big hard science, psychiatry.[3]

Psychologists are below psychiatrists in the scientific and professional pecking order, and while some psychologists are very loyal and willing to know their place and lowly status this does give rise to some resentment.[4] Psychiatry itself has battled for status among other medical professions, and that battle has encouraged the shift

prevalent outcome is that the research builds everything on what psychologists imagine biology to be. See Fonagy et al. (2004) for an example of an approach that oscillates between the bad and worst options.

[2] Young (1992) discusses the concept of 'second nature' and the way it operates in the work of Donna Haraway (1989, 1991).

[3] For an analysis of the mistaken view that psychology holds of the natural sciences, see Harré and Secord (1972). Hedges (1987) questions the image that psychology holds of what 'hard' and 'soft' science are; for a recent argument that qualitative research in psychology is actually more scientific than quantitative research, see Harré (2004).

[4] For an account of the way this operated in the development of clinical psychology in Britain, see Pilgrim and Treacher (1992); for brave attempts within the field of psychiatric nursing to beat back the influence of medical psychiatry, see Barker and Davidson (1998).

to medical models of distress; more time is now spent diagnosing mental 'illnesses' and prescribing medication than any other activity. The kingpins now are those working for the pharmaceutical industries, and so 'psychopharmacology' as a medical speciality has become the site for what appears to be real knowledge about the 'biological bases' of behaviour. Material institutional relationships that psychologists are tied into then function as relays for the prescribing of psychiatric drugs. These drugs have powerful effects not only on our 'second nature' as human beings, but also on underlying biological processes that makes it possible for us to think and act.[5]

Pharmacology Constructs Psychology in Its Own Image

Modern medicine is driven by the development of new drugs produced by the gigantic pharmaceutical companies, and these companies spend trillions of dollars on research and advertising to encourage doctors to prescribe them. The pharmaceutical industry has come to define what the research agendas are for psychiatry. The focus on certain kinds of 'problem', and on what can be cooked up to make the problem disappear, has also come to define what normal and abnormal 'psychology' is expected to look like. In recent years the drug companies have managed to persuade doctors that an increasing number of 'disorders' can be targeted and managed with their own special medication; Pfizer markets Viagra as if it could now operate as therapy for every man, Lilly targets mood swings as 'bipolar disorder' and has medication ready for this, and GlaxoSmithKline has approval for drugs to treat 'Restless Legs Syndrome'.[6]

Diagnostic systems have a material history

The International Classification of Diseases (ICD) provides one powerful and explicitly medical framework for identifying different kinds of mental disorder.[7] This is usually used by psychiatrists and psychologists alongside the even more influential handbook, the *Diagnostic and Statistical Manual of Mental Disorders* (DSM), which, like the ICD, has been through a number of different editions and

[5] For a powerful analysis of contemporary developments in pharmacology, see Healy (2002), and on 'side effects' of psychiatric drugs, see Breggin (1993).

[6] See Moynihan and Henry (2006) for an edited collection on these cases. For critical responses from within psychiatry to the way the drug companies guide psychiatric research, see Healy and Cattell (2003) and Moncrieff (2006).

[7] The 2006 ICD is available online, see World Health Organization (2006).

various revisions.[8] The DSM categories, the number of which increases exponentially with each version, are elaborated by committees of psychiatrists and psychologists. Definitions reflect the committee structure; the presence of a particular disorder is to be decided by a certain number of relevant symptoms out of a list.

Psychological disorders are rooted in medicine and in the particular mistaken application of medical ideas to mental distress by the discipline of psychiatry. The existence of each of the particular 'illnesses' that psychiatry claimed to have identified is contested, but this does not stop psychologists from taking up those categories and turning them into categories they can work with.[9] Far from simply applying medicine to a new domain, however, the DSM and ICD categories mimic medicine; the peculiar formulation of 'symptoms' and 'disorders' reflects the influence of the pharmaceutical companies and the committee structure that sifts and simplifies descriptions of 'abnormal' behaviour given by representatives of different disciplines. The DSM was once a fairly amateurish enterprise influenced by the particular personalities of those running the committees, but now it has become big business, structured accordingly.[10]

Categories of disorder carry the weight of medical knowledge

The DSM and the ICD were transformed by the success of drug treatments in the 1950s. The influence of psychoanalytic notions started to wane, and the number of categories of disorder that would be defined in relation to the medication that was given to treat it started to increase rapidly. The battle inside psychiatry between the psychoanalytic and more hard-line medical practitioners was tilted further in favour of medicine, and psychologists then found themselves further squeezed. At this point psychology fell back on

[8] The fourth edition (text revision) of the DSM was published in 2000; see American Psychiatric Association (2000). This is not available online, partly because the APA relies on sales and updates of the DSM to pay the mortgage on its headquarters building. For a good overall account of the development and marketing of the DSM, see Kirk and Kutchins (1992). There are other specific responses to assumptions made about psychology in the DSM by Schacht (1985).

[9] See Parker et al. (1995) for a review and 'deconstruction' of categories of psychopathology, and for two excellent collections that bring together activists working against the dominant models in psychiatry, psychology and the psychiatry system survivor movement, see Newnes et al. (1991, 2001).

[10] See Spiegel (2005) for an entertaining account of the role of Robert Spitzer in DSM committee work.

what it knew best; since it had little to offer in terms of explanation or treatment it put its energies into categorisation and measurement.

The technical process by which the categories in the diagnostic systems are arrived at once again reflects the primary function of psychology as a *method*. Any number of theories and speculations about the nature of the mind are permitted to slosh around inside psychology; what is crucial to those who uphold psychology as a 'science of mental life' is that it should follow a scientific methodology. In this way the process of categorisation as such is more important to psychology than any particular category. Diagnoses of discrete disorders may be taken up and dropped out – with homosexuality voted off the list in 1973 as one of the most famous instances – as long as the process of inventing and applying labels can continue apace. The incredible increase in the number of categories from one edition of the DSM to the next is evidence of this methodological imperative in psychology, and reflects the increasing influence of psychologists in the committees.[11]

Everyday neurotic miseries are treated as if they are on a continuum with madness

Medical definitions of really serious disorders, the 'psychoses', and the success that new drugs had in dampening down symptoms and keeping the patients quiet, have had a number of consequences for the more common 'neurotic' complaints. These complaints – of anxiety and depression that the psychologists had been left to deal with – now started to be treated with drugs as well. The category of 'depression', for example, started to come into common usage, and the medical definition of the problem put more pressure on the psychologists.

It is sometimes difficult to appreciate how new 'depression' is in Western culture, for the vocabulary of depression, and even of 'depressive illness', has circulated through the culture so rapidly and become part of the dominant system of self-talk in everyday life.[12] In this way 'depression' becomes one of the everyday disorders, often to be treated with medication, and there are then also calls for

[11] For the argument that psychology is defined by method rather than theory, see Rose (1985); see also Danziger (1985). For a critique of 'evidence-based medicine' as a rationale for rationing services, see Saarni and Gylling (2004). The argument that the rise of 'evidence-based' studies then rebounds on methodology itself, closing down developments in qualitative methodology, is made by Lincoln and Cannella (2004).

[12] For a history of the development of the category of depression, see Healy (1997), and on the role of the pharmaceutical industry in this, see Healy (2004).

the mass training of clinical psychologists to get the depressed unemployed workforce back to work.[13] This is then the 'psychological' complement to more serious disorders like 'schizophrenia'. The argument that so-called 'schizophrenia' is a construction within medical discourse is crucial to finding ways of addressing distress; the distress is so serious that medical models that intensify it and turn the diagnosis into a life sentence need to be questioned, *and* psychological alternatives should also be treated with caution.[14]

The drug industry constructs its categories of disorder around effects of medication

The main selling point of a new drug is that it will remove symptoms, but the definition of the symptom concerned is itself constructed around the behaviour or experience that a particular drug will remove. The emergence of new categories of disorder has been driven by the pharmaceutical industry being able to persuade doctors that they have discovered how certain chemicals will remove a certain kind of problem and then branding that problem as a psychiatric disorder. Different systems of control have focused on different aspects of behaviour that they would like to suppress; in the Soviet Union there was particular concern with those who refused to work or voiced dissident opinions;[15] in the Western world there has been a growing obsession with erratic or unstable behaviour that is unsettling to those around the person who is targeted and labelled.

Again, it is crucial that we take seriously the physical effects of the drugs. The most horrible physical 'side effects' can be permanent, and tardive dyskinesia – involuntary movements and failures of muscle groups – are then viewed as evidence that the individual has a problem and needs medication, rather than that the psychiatric drugs are the cause of those physical problems.[16] Diagnosis and

[13] The medical view of depression is still dominant (see Healy, 2002), but recent studies in the UK have enthusiastically called for those trained in 'cognitive' treatments to be put to work on the unemployed and so to save the government the money paid out in disability benefits (Layard, 2006).

[14] Boyle (2002) shows that the construct 'schizophrenia' lacks any credibility when the historical and clinical literature is examined; some clinical psychologists claim that it is better to treat the symptoms (e.g., Bentall, 1990), but they then, of course, often take the descriptions of each symptom at face value.

[15] Cohen (1989) gives an account of Soviet psychiatry, following up an earlier book in which he shows how it operates alongside equally grim stories of psychiatry in 'democratic' countries (Cohen, 1988).

[16] See Breggin (1993) for a discussion of the way drugs for depression and psychotic disorders cause tardive dyskinesia.

prescription have material effects on the ability of people to think and act, and to think and act about the problems that led them to ask for help or be referred to a psychiatrist or psychologist in the first place. Psychiatrists who have noticed an increase in the incidence of 'mental disorders' and examined the connection between political economy – the structure and dynamics of capitalist society – and individual distress have come to the conclusion that 'schizophrenia' and other supposed 'illnesses' are a function of a sick society.[17] Some psychologists have also come to that conclusion, but the majority show obeisance to psychiatry and aim to be accepted by those they still view as their superiors so that they can better manage those beneath them who have failed to live a 'normal' life.

Psychiatry Constructs the Normal, in Which Psychology has a Function

The diagnostic systems that have been constructed by the pharmaceutical industry in alliance with medical psychiatry provide psychologists with certain limited room for manoeuvre. Though there is some space for movement, the psychologist is hemmed in now by medical terminology used to describe the 'serious' disorders and by the increasing influence of medicine on everyday problems of living defined as psychological problems that could be removed with the right medication. When psychologists carve out their own sphere of influence, however, things are not much better.

Health is relocated from the body into the mind

One response by psychology has been to redefine medical areas of expertise as lying within its own discipline and pretend-expertise. One example is 'health psychology', and this gives some space for psychologists to contest medical power. The problem is that questions about what makes people define themselves as 'sick' are put aside in favour of good advice about a healthy lifestyle or moral ideals about the importance of 'well-being'.

It is worth noticing at this point that psychologists are here bravely battling against one dominant assumption that many individuals in Western culture have about their bodies, an alienated conception of their minds as separate and helpless passengers inside biological organisms. However, the corner they are arguing for – the active self taking charge of their body and working to keep it

[17] See Hill (1983) and Warner (1994) for analyses of the political economy of mental health and illness.

healthy – is itself just as deeply framed by a peculiarly Western assumption about the split between body and mind. The search for 'health' and the concern with making people responsible for their own health (if they have the right guidance from the psychologist) is now deeply embedded in the neoliberal deregulation and privatisation of health services. In this sense, 'health psychology' is neoliberal self-management. It arises from a culturally specific separation of mind and body and now takes root in an economic system that makes each individual responsible for managing their mind and body.[18]

Embodiment is relocated into body image, and normalised images of the body

The most typical move that psychology makes in relation to the other disciplines – those it parasitises on and aims to displace – is to shift attention onto the way that people perceive their problems. The normative dimension, what is taken to be good and right, is smuggled back in by way of ideological systems that define how people could be and how they imagine they should be in order to fit in with what others expect of them. Studies of 'body image' are a case in point, and the psychologist who simply describes how people see themselves thereby seems to sidestep criticism that they are actually reinforcing dominant ideas. They are still working with culturally normative images of the body, but in an indirect and more insidious way.[19]

The moral advice that psychology has traditionally given to women, for example, is now supplemented by the injunction for the woman to reflect on her own values and to come to see that it would be better for her own health if she were to take responsibility. The intimate relationship between moral advice, self-governance, gender and class can be seen in the attempts to instil healthy attitudes about weight. The panic about obesity in the West thus serves as an exercise in class contempt, with middle-class psychologists lining up with the other professions and media pundits to emphasise the importance of 'self-image' and 'self-control'; it also operates to confirm the importance of psychology as such, for those who have

[18] The split here is classically Cartesian; that is, it works with the assumption that the 'mind' can be treated as something separate. This is a state of affairs that is examined by the US American critical psychologist Ed Sampson in a series of articles in relation to assumptions about identity (Sampson, 1985), indigenous psychologies (Sampson, 1988), the 'self' (Sampson, 1989) and social control (Sampson, 1990).

[19] For studies of women's and men's self-body image and a commentary on the norms of beauty and health in Western culture, see Grogan (1998).

failed are those who do not speak the same language about their 'selves' and 'identity' and 'self-esteem' as everyone else.[20]

Sex differences are relocated into gender identity

While traditionally psychologists used to be obsessed with sex differences, they have been quick to learn that there is a difference between 'sex' and 'gender'.[21] Sex differences are biological differences between 'males' and 'females', but even these differences are determined by interpretations of what these two categories are like and how boys and girls should be assigned to them. Gender differences are mapped onto what seem to be real physical sex differences, but a masculine or feminine sense of oneself does not necessarily correspond to what sex one actually is.[22]

However, while many psychologists now study 'gender' instead of 'sex', they still treat these categories as given, and they still tend to buy into the gender-identity definitions that are elaborated in the psychiatric diagnostic systems. This is very clear in the conception of 'identity' that is used to understand sex-change operations, and in the advice that is given to those who manage the transition from one 'sex' to another.[23] Psychology merely repeats in a different key, then, the standard psychiatric images of women as closer to madness; femininity as such was historically seen as something more unstable, pathological and closer to nature, as can be seen in the classic nineteenth-century conceptions of 'hysteria'. Women cannot win within these theoretical coordinates, and the practice of psychiatry

[20] There is also, of course, a cultural dimension here, for it is white middle-class norms about weight and self-responsibility that are being assumed and advertised to everyone else. For feminist 'constructionist' analyses of images of women and weight, see Malson (1997) and Hepworth (1999).

[21] The focus on 'gender' was important for many years in sociology in the English-speaking world before making its way into psychology as a crucial starting point for feminist analyses of the way 'sex' was usually treated as a given in research on and treatment of women; there is a good overview of these developments, which includes attention to a range of alternative psychoanalytic arguments, by Sayers (1986). In US American psychology the notion of 'gender' became treated as a cognitive process, and here the notion of balance between 'masculine' and 'feminine' cognitive qualities sat uneasily with the feminist project. The work of Sandra Bem is indicative of the way feminist psychology became another version of psychology as such; see, for example, discussions of 'androgeny' and 'gender schema theory' by Bem (1976, 1983).

[22] There have been conceptual advances in the question of the relationship between culturally constructed 'gender', and what we imagine to be the real 'sex' to be that corresponds to it, by Butler (1990, 1993).

[23] Raymond (1980) shows how the sex-change industry is underpinned by conservative images of what 'masculine' and 'feminine' psychology are like, and psychologists end up enforcing certain norms of behaviour and experience for 'men' and 'women'.

and psychology has ensured that 'normal femininity' is itself a trap which will serve to alienate the woman from herself at the very moment that she is supposed to be cured.[24]

Psychology Models Itself upon and Then Competes with Medical Psychiatry

Evaluation is closely linked to 'evidence' – a particular empiricist and pragmatic idea of what 'evidence' is – and this has been the field within which psychology has become most successful in providing an alternative to medical psychiatry. However, the 'evidence-based treatments' that it provides merely mimic the 'evidence-based medicine' that the drug companies and the medical profession are together using to redefine psychiatry. Evaluation of treatment has then been claimed by psychologists as a speciality that their discipline, which has always been defined by method rather than particular theoretical content, excels in. Psychology builds its own account of what is important from its own field of expertise, which is close observation and measurement of how people think and feel about themselves. Most of the time this way of approaching a problem effectively recycles commonsense rather than offering particular distinctive models of the mind.[25]

'Evidence-based treatment' warrants the distribution of disorder and physical treatment

The concern with 'evidence' is now an expression of a distinctively psychological approach used to define how a range of psycho-therapeutic treatments should be evaluated.[26] In this sense, the cultural shift to 'focus group' politics in which representatives try to ensure that their policies merely reflect what people say they want is an ideal climate for the triumph of psychology over the old medical

[24] The analyses by Chesler (1973) and Millett (2000) in the US and by Ussher (1991, 2005) in the UK and Australia underscore the way that women are already, culturally speaking, 'mad' and how thus to be 'normal' is already to be confined in certain alienating conditions of existence. Waterhouse (1993) extends this critique of the way psychological treatments normalise certain kinds of behaviour for women to the more humanistic 'person-centred' approaches. See also Kitzinger and Perkins (1993) on the fate of lesbians at the hands of clinical psychology.

[25] For an analysis of cultural assumptions in the development of Western medicine, see Turner (1987).

[26] See Westen et al. (2004) for an example of this kind of logic applied to support psychotherapy. See Strathern (2000) for an analysis of the assumptions made about 'transparency' in this kind of framework; see Lincoln and Cannella (2004) for a discussion of the way this reinforces certain ideas about methodology; and see Shore and Wright (1999) for critical reflections on the connections between 'audit culture' and neoliberalism.

psychiatry. People are encouraged to define for themselves what ideals they take from the representations of health and efficiency around them, and then tell the psychologist how far they believe they match up to these ideals.

The drive to conform to 'evidence' in treatment of medical and psychological problems rests on assumptions about the nature of the thing that will be measured and assessed. One must be able to define it clearly, which is problematic enough with respect to physical symptoms and extremely misleading when it comes to our experience of unease or distress. And one must be able to compare the effects of the different treatments, ideally in randomised controlled trials in which the participants do not know whether they have been given the real treatment or have been assigned to the 'control group'.[27] This comparison is, again, difficult enough in the field of drug treatments because placebos themselves have been shown to have beneficial effects for nearly every complaint.[28]

There is an experiential aspect to the taking of medicines that already has effects on physical symptoms. Comparison becomes nearly impossible with psychological treatments unless we screen out the experiential aspect, and so the very aspect that the psychologist wanted to study in the first place has to be wiped away so that the mechanical procedure can be defined and effects observed. The appeal to 'evidence' then ensures that the psychologist may hand their clients over to other professionals who claim to have expertise in a particular area. The psychologist may be one of the many professionals that legitimise the use of physical treatments such as electroshock, for example, if the psychiatrist insists that it really is necessary. Ethical judgement which would challenge such abusive practices is replaced by adherence to diagnostic categories that have been agreed between psychologists and psychiatrists.[29]

[27] See Bracken and Thomas (2001) for an attempt to move beyond these assumptions in British psychiatry; see Bracken (1995) for an argument for why Michel Foucault's work is relevant to critical psychiatry now.

[28] See French (2001) for an acknowledgement of the pervasiveness of the 'placebo' effect in psychology (and of hopes to tame it). For a detailed account from within medical anthropology, see Moerman (2002).

[29] For arguments against electroshock and drug treatments, see Breggin (1993), and for strategies for coming off psychiatric drugs, see Breggin and Cohen (2000); see also Lynch (2004). The classic study by Rosenhan (1973), which showed that those who have a label of mental illness will have every aspect of their behaviour monitored in such a way as to confirm the diagnosis, is further explored in Rosenhan (1975). There is an argument against diagnosis in clinical settings, on the grounds that it will not only pathologise the patient but also hand over power to the psychiatrists to determine treatment in what they judge to be 'serious' cases, in Parker (1999c).

Cognitive behaviour therapy reproduces certain notions of evidence

Psychology is led into a dead-end when it has to develop treatments that will be amenable to 'evaluation'; those that will meet the peculiar requirements of those conducting 'evidence-based treatment' studies. The reductive and mechanical contender that fits the bill now is Cognitive Behaviour Therapy (CBT).[30] The ambiguous and diffuse sense of difficulty that someone may have is now fixed, treated as existing only in strictly defined problem categories, and then it is only those categories that are measured at the beginning and end of the treatment. The focus is on making the individual imagine that they are thinking clearly and rationally about their lives and able to address problems effectively. In this way they become a little model psychologist.

Apart from the limited focus of CBT, there are also dangerous 'side effects' that may only become apparent to the patient well after they have filled out the assessment that tells the psychologist (and the insurance company, perhaps) how well the treatment has worked. When unpredictable and uncontrollable events happen later on which cannot be easily interpreted, the person's newly strengthened 'cognitive' abilities can collapse, leaving them more helpless and desperate than before. The way to prevent this happening, of course, is to ensure that people lead very limited lives in which they will not encounter anything unexpected, where they will not be given any opportunity to change how they live their lives or who they think they are. In this way, clinical psychologists using CBT must enforce a system of social control in which people only have limited room for manoeuvre and in which they should never have the opportunity to discover what alienation is so that it can be combated and transcended in the collective activity of interpreting and changing the world.

Notions of 'trauma' are taken from medicine and adapted to regimes of evidence

Cognitive Behaviour Therapy also reinforces the focus on the 'here and now' at the expense of historical and social factors. Not only is

[30] This approach was developed by Aaron Beck (1976), who turned from psychoanalysis when he was disappointed with the speed of recovery of his patients; the cognitive notions he developed in Cognitive Behaviour Therapy actually continue a track of clinical work in US American psychoanalysis after the assumption had been adopted that the aim of the treatment should be to strengthen the ego (Hartmann, 1958). For a critique of the way a certain notion of 'evaluation' flows from this tradition in psychoanalysis, from an alternative tradition, see Jonckheere (2005).

the exploitation and oppression that the person suffers bracketed out, because the psychologist is only concerned with how their 'patient' or 'client' thinks and feels about it during the assessment, but history is bracketed out. Personal history is even treated as something that may be misleading to the person, a source of error.

Studies of 'false memories' of sexual abuse, memories supposedly implanted by crooked psychotherapists, serve as a lever for cognitive psychologists to overturn the privilege that was once given to psychoanalytic theories. The irony here is that psychoanalysis was itself accused for many years of refusing to take actual child sexual abuse seriously, and this was indeed a problem in forms of psychoanalysis concerned only with infantile 'fantasy'.[31] The accusations that psychotherapists were inducing their clients to remember things that never happened began as a reaction to the perceived influence of feminist ideas, and so cognitive psychology now stepped in with CBT, which would completely sidestep the questions of fantasy, memory and history. The diagnostic category of 'post-traumatic stress disorder' (PTSD) has then been used to group together and reify the variety of different responses that someone may have to distressing events. This diagnosis also sets out a normal pathway that people are expected to take to overcome these responses.[32]

Advice and education in psychology enable individuals to school themselves

Much of the advice and education that psychologists offer comprise home-spun truths about living a healthy and rational life, with an insistence that people should take responsibility for addressing their problems. In this way some of the worst of old psychoanalytic

---

[31] Miller (1998) gives an impassioned account of the way children are disbelieved and betrayed by adult professionals.

[32] Feminists have argued that each of these shifts in clinical treatment – from the emphasis on infantile 'fantasy' to the panic about 'false memories' to the attempt to conduct treatment without addressing history at all – have served to silently introduce a political perspective which blames the victims (Burman, 1997). The idea that there should be a 'normal' reaction to 'trauma' and that those suffering abuse should show a certain range of reactions that can then permit a diagnosis actually serves to pathologise those women who show other kinds of reactions (Levett, 1995), and there are serious implications here for the way that cultural assumptions about the nature of 'trauma' repeat the colonial history of psychological theory and treatment (Levett, 1994). The assumption that there are specific ways of expressing distress particular to men and women or to people from particular cultures also serves to pathologise those who do not fit with what the expert on 'gender' or 'culture' expects; for a discussion of this problem in relation to 'transcultural' psychiatry, see Mercer (1986). See Bracken (2002) for a critical account of work on 'trauma'.

practice is repackaged and used to blame the victims. Complaints are now more neatly dealt with, though; rather than interpreting them as being due to long-standing grudges against parents (popular with some psychoanalytic types), the psychologist simply repeats the message that the individual can take charge of things now themselves.

The overriding message is that the client is the kind of person for whom psychology works, and once they have learnt that then all other forms of happiness that are really important will follow. This message is also drummed home to those who are positioned as 'users' or 'consumers' of psychology services, and those who are recruited as professional 'users' or 'consumers' on the committees that are supposed to operate as open democratic 'consultative' bodies. There is a distribution of responsibility in which the assumptions about mental functioning that the cognitive psychologist makes are relayed through to the way they run their consultative committees. At one level they assume that thoughts represent and manage behaviour, and that those thoughts can be engineered to enable the individual to live a more effective and healthy life; at the other level they imagine they can appoint people as 'representatives' and then tell those they represent that all is well, and that things are being done in everyone's best interests.[33]

Psychology Requires That We Be Schooled into Life, and into What Psychology Is

The psychologists operate in a limited space, and they then become committed to making their clients come to terms with the limitations operating in their own lives. The ideal client of a psychologist is expected to become like a psychologist themselves, and the expectations of an ideal client must be trimmed to size for psychology to be useful for them. Psychological techniques can sometimes be useful, but only if they are used in a tactical way rather than as a lesson about how people really are and how they should be. However, the room for manoeuvre has to be fought for because psychologists

---

[33] The advocacy movement in mental health has been struggling to find ways to get round these problems of 'representation', either by handing control directly to those affected so they can make decisions in advance about the kind of treatment they would and would not accept (see, e.g., Cohen and Jacobs, 1998), or by working collectively so that one individual is not picked out to 'represent' everyone else. For an excellent account of the collective struggle for better conditions and alternative practices, a struggle born from within the 'therapeutic communities' in the UK and which gave rise to organisations like the Mental Patients Union, see Spandler (2006).

do have a great deal of power to make decisions that will materially limit their clients' possibilities for movement.

We learn to labour, with schooling functioning as anticipation of work roles

Educational psychologists are responsible for carrying out assessments that will determine the trajectory of a child through school. The advice they give may decide whether a child stays in a particular class or whether they should be excluded from the school altogether. The issue here, once again, is not whether the educational psychologist is a nice person or not, though someone acting as an educational psychologist may be able to interpret the tests flexibly so as to be able to challenge the school.[34]

The key issue concerns the pathways and choices that are set out for the psychologist and the definitions of the psychologist's responsibilities that the discipline has constructed for them in struggles for psychology to define itself as a profession against the other competing disciplines in the school.

Inclusion operates on the basis of more detailed exclusion of those unable to fit

Definitions of ability and 'disability' serve to segregate children so that those with 'learning difficulties' assessed by the psychologist may be excluded and put in a place of 'special education'.[35] The logic of segregation in an educational system aiming to meet assessment targets is to remove those who are difficult to handle, and the 'special' label is then a euphemism for being 'abnormal' (one that 'normal' children understand all too well).[36] Government initiatives to ensure that schools function effectively then have the effect of making it all the more difficult for children who do not fit in.[37]

---

[34] Billington (2000) explores how an educational psychologist working in the school system in the UK can find ways of turning the tables on those who label and pathologise children's behaviour. Timimi (2002) explores this issue from the standpoint of a child psychiatrist.

[35] For a study of the way that such children are constructed as 'other' in teacher training ostensibly concerned with 'inclusion', see Evans (2002).

[36] Newnes and Radcliffe (2005) bring together radical psychologists, psychotherapists and psychiatrists who refuse to accept this pathologising of children's behaviour; a number of different progressive alternatives are discussed in the book.

[37] The UK government's 'Healthy Schools' initiative, for example, is mostly focused on what can be done to change children who do not fit into the 'healthy school'; it follows programmes from the United States, South Africa and Australia.

Children are increasingly pathologised for too much childish behaviour. As schools come under more and more pressure to meet educational targets, the children who are disruptive come under more pressure to be well behaved. If exclusion of the child is not an option, then medication is used. This is where the educational psychologist will be expected to make diagnoses of 'attention deficit and hyper-activity disorder' (ADHD), and then it is a short step once again to the world of psychiatric medication.[38]

Decisions are made about how children should fit into the family

The assessment of 'risk' is supposed to be used to protect the child, but this assessment also involves the use of notions of what is and what is not a healthy happy family. Forensic psychology then inter-meshes with developmental and educational psychology to deter-mine degrees of criminality and identify the guilty parties. Levels of 'attachment' of the single mother to her child (derived from the work of Bowlby and reinforced with animal behaviour studies) are then brought into the equation, with the supposedly 'scientific' evidence being that functional magnetic resonance imaging (fMRI) scans show that bits of the brain that should light up do not do so among these sorry inadequate creatures.[39]

This logic of adaptation is then reinforced by practices which aim to identify and 'reintegrate' those who have broken the norms of a group or 'community', and attempts to bring about 'reconciliation' between offenders and victims are then psychologised such that there is an expectation that a certain degree of 'shame' will be felt by those who are displaying remorse for their wrong-doing.[40] In strategies of 'reintegrative shaming' that have become popular among some criminologists, for example, the person who feels 'shame' is

[38] On the role of the DSM in pathologising children's behaviour, see Mitchell (2003). For an analysis of the way that 'emotional' and 'behavioural' difficulties are constructed, see Jones (2003). There is a detailed analysis of the way that the label 'ADHD' pathologises boys and those from outside the dominant culture in the West in Timimi (2005). For a narrative therapy approach to ADHD that treats the label as the problem rather than the behaviour of those labelled with it, see Law (1998).

[39] See, for example, the chapter by Fonagy and Target (2004); the theoretical framework for this grim research is set out in Fonagy et al. (2004).

[40] For discussion of reconciliation within the restorative justice tradition in New Zealand, see Monk et al. (1997); there is already a risk of psychologisation in these practices, though some narrative therapists are concerned with the way that psychology operates as a system of social control and try to find ways of 'externalising' the problems identified by psychologists (see, e.g., the papers in Parker, 1999b).

reinforcing dominant ideas about what emotions are inappropriate and what it is normal to feel.[41]

Psychology Creates a Niche for Itself As the Science of the Individual

The battles that psychology undertakes against other professionals, in medicine, the schools and courts, determine the shape of psychology as a discipline, and the shape of the individual that they operate on. The adjacent disciplines – medical, educational, legal – have historically been more powerful than psychology, and they set the ground on which psychology has to fight for itself. Those other disciplines also determine to a great degree how far the clients of the psychologist feel they can go in making demands for help, and what options are open to them. Some psychologists take them further and open up new possibilities, but this is not because they are doing good psychology. One of the crimes that psychology commits day after day is that it endorses those limits and encourages people to adapt to them.[42]

The 'bio-psycho-social' dimension is a cover for subordination to psychiatry

The dependence of psychology on psychiatry incites some psychologists all the more to try and study brain processes and the effects of medication themselves, to short-circuit the annoying relationship with the psychiatrists. Instead of questioning the role of medication, for example, psychologists have been eager to have prescribing rights themselves.

Psychologists once had to fight for their particular role to be taken seriously against rival professions, but they now have the ascendancy in many academic and clinical departments and the power to determine what research is conducted, and, most importantly, how it is conducted. While the particular content of psychological theory has

[41] Braithwaite's (1989) model of 'reintegrative shaming', for example, supposes that certain communities will be strengthened by the process; for an explicit example of this assumption played out in different 'ethnic' contexts, see Zhang (1995). When this 'shaming' is applied to expressions of white racism, it may then have the effect of reinforcing a loop of prejudice and self-congratulation by the racist in as much as they have been able to tell everyone how racist they are as they make amends for what they have said (for this argument, see Ahmed, 2004a).

[42] For an analysis of neoliberalism and the massive profits made by pharmaceutical companies with the increasing individualisation of distress and psychiatric responses, see Moncrieff (in press).

shifted year by year, and the role of political struggle by those who are subjected to labels that pathologise their behaviour has been incredibly important in reshaping what we take to be normality and 'pathology', the rise of the discipline of psychology has more insidious effects. Along with the psychologisation of problems of life in capitalist society – the increasing tendency for people to blame themselves for social problems and to try and find personal solutions to economic injustice – the methodology of psychology as a discipline has reinforced the mistaken idea that it is only what can be directly observed and measured that counts. The turn to 'evidence' in 'treatment' tightens the circuits of social control and closes down spaces for those who want to find new ways of living, new ways of being.

Psychology operates within a powerful 'personal-political-economic' complex

We need to understand the competing interests of the different groups that claim expertise in 'mental' problems and offer different ways of managing them. The notion of a 'cure' is appropriate to something that really is an 'illness', but even the drug companies and their agents inside the psychiatric system no longer promise cure. The traditional psychiatric wisdom that someone who has the label of 'schizophrenic' will always be a schizophrenic, and that the most they can hope for is to manage that identity with the appropriate medication, has now been given a psychological twist. In psychological culture everyone is encouraged to feel that they are vulnerable, that they are 'at risk', and that any glimmering of unhappiness must be a sign that something is wrong with them. In this society even the moments of unhappiness that could lead us to reflect on what is wrong with the world are turned into signs of pathology that must be blotted out; alienation in psychological culture is thus reinforced and any awareness of it is suppressed.

Medication and physical treatments are already adapted to function among the array of techniques that are offered by the different specialised branches concerned with mental health. Psychology unfortunately knows its place in this complex of practices; it reduces the sphere of personal life to that of 'health' and it deliberately rules out an engagement with politics. In the process, the discipline maintains the economic interests that feed off the very distress it played a part in manufacturing.

6

Spiritless Conditions: Regulating Therapeutic Alternatives

It is easy enough to complain about how dehumanising psychology is and to show that the mechanist paradigm of laboratory-experiments turns people into things. This kind of complaint resonates with increasingly influential strands of contemporary commonsense, particularly with new age and spiritual alternatives to modern science. Psychology as a discipline did once present itself as the scientific rationalist study of human behaviour, and this is why it adopted an experimental approach, even if that turned out to be a parody of science. Now, however, there are many psychologists who look to alternative 'participatory', 'qualitative' and 'transpersonal' ways of carrying out research and understanding people. This chapter shows why this new, apparently more cuddly, 'softer' side of psychology is just as dangerous and demeaning of human beings as the old 'hard' fake science.

Psychology feeds on what lies outside itself

Psychology early on proved itself to be a faithful ally of the ruling class, coming up with new ways of increasing efficiency and enabling the extraction of more surplus value. However, capitalism is a complex political-economic system; the bourgeoisie as the new ruling class – the class that replaced the aristocratic class dominating feudal society – is not only interested in benefiting from capitalism as a rationalist machine pursuing profit in the most effective way. Scientific knowledge has been extremely useful, but romantic and irrational ideas linger on, and they have often been attractive to those who always believed in deep inherited qualities and differences between classes and racial groups; at times of economic crisis mystical fantasies about blood-ties, spirituality and suchlike erupt to the surface.[1]

---

[1] One needs only to tot up the number of peers of the realm involved in new age spiritualist practices in the UK, for example, to see how the aristocracy remains besotted with mysticism; such ideas were then taken up by some members of the new ruling class in capitalist society, and were then even used by working-class activists trying to

The turn in psychological research toward everyday reasoning, 'ordinary language' and respect for the psychology of people outside the laboratory is but a new twist in the discipline's relationship to outsiders.[2] There would be no discipline of psychology without the intense individualisation of human experience brought about by modern capitalism. This has always meant that the discipline to an extent drew upon and endorsed the image that people had of themselves.

Psychology thus participates in an ideological process by which the alienated life conditions of 'individuals' are psychologised, and images of mental processes are formalised and sold back to them.[3] While 'scientific psychology' has usually guarded itself against the fads and fashions of the entrepreneurs and their comfort zone of middle-class chatter – dabbling in everything from mesmerism to theosophy – it has always attended closely to these ideas from outside. Now it feeds upon them more avidly as a way of updating and ingratiating itself with the general public.

The discipline filters and regulates what it will recognise as real psychology

There are certain historical conditions for the existence of psychology, and psychology always sets certain conditions for new ideas to become part of the discipline. The hoops and hurdles that turn popular prejudices and superstitions into tightly defined 'intervening variables' and 'hypothetical constructs' transform new ideas into things that can be more easily digested by the discipline.[4]

Now some of the restrictions have been relaxed, and some non-psychologists have been welcomed into the fold. Now 'participation'

---

understand and combat alienation; for a detailed analysis of the way that fascism then calls upon pre-Christian superstition to mobilise the masses against imagined enemies, see Trotsky (1975).

[2] The interest in 'ordinary language' was actually originally derived from the refined reflections of Oxford philosophers on the distinctions that everyday folk make without realising it (e.g., Ryle, 1949; Austin, 1962, and for a collection of essays in this strand of 'analytic philosophy', see Chappell, 1981); psychology has enthusiastically taken up the 'ordinariness' of everyday explanations of behaviour as part of its own 'turn to language' (e.g., Antaki, 1981, 1988), and then notions of 'dialogue' and 'rhetoric' are studied as part of the celebration of what people already know and there is a consequent liberal queasiness about talking of 'ideology' as disrespectful to these ordinary folk (e.g., Blackman and Walkerdine, 2001).

[3] A process nicely teased out by Shotter (1987).

[4] For a good account of the way that psychology developed its own particular vocabulary for mental processes, see Danziger (1997).

has become one of the watchwords, and people are invited and expected to participate in research, whether they like it or not.[5] Qualitative research is then designed to attend to the meanings that people attribute to behaviours rather than measuring the behaviours as such.[6] And 'transpersonal' psychology is supposed to be an attempt to explore and validate the different spiritual beliefs that people hold (we will examine some of the problems with this option in the course of this chapter).[7] However, the price to be paid is that these new ideas, whether they are useless quack remedies or valuable alternative views of the human subject, must turn into psychology. This means that certain rules of good behaviour must be followed, and certain assumptions about the self accepted.

Psychology Presumes the Middle-Class Individual As the Ideal Standard

When psychology purports to take 'ordinary' reasoning seriously, we need to ask who the 'ordinary' people are. Psychology has the same skewed class distribution as most academic specialities, and professional psychologists are recruited from nice middle-class families and they cultivate people who aspire to such a status. Working-class people and those from subordinate cultures are disparaged in the bourgeois press, and stereotypes paraded and ridiculed on television every day. A whole genre of confessional day-time television is devoted to giving advice to people about how they should dress and speak and live their lives like their social betters. Little wonder that there are so many anxious attempts to join the middle class, and attempts to show that you are really a 'psychological-minded' person, sensitive and thoughtful in the way the white middle class likes you to be.[8]

[5] For a review of problems with this drive to 'participation' in development research in different countries that has implications for the way psychologists are trying to invite ordinary people to participate, see Cooke and Kothari (2001).

[6] See Billig (1977) for a discussion of how qualitative psychology can be a liability for political analysis and intervention. For a review of problems with popular models of qualitative research in psychology, see Parker (2005a).

[7] It is symptomatic of the turn to respect for everyday commonsensical ideas people have in some strands of 'critical psychology' that 'spirituality' has now been put on the agenda (see, e.g., Walkerdine, 2002; Blackman, 2003).

[8] This is an issue that is described and analysed by Sennett and Cobb (1972). For a discussion of class issues in British psychotherapy that draws on Sennett and Cobb's work, see Richards (1995); see also Hannon et al. (2001) for a discussion of class in counsellor education in the US. There are instructive explorations of the contradictory nature of commonsense and the way it is riddled with class-hatred, sexism and racism in Walkerdine's articles (1986, 1987); the struggle to re-articulate 'pathology', and in particular what it might mean to 'hear voices', is tackled sympathetically by Blackman (2001) and James (2001).

Psychological assessment for therapy rests on the notion of 'psychological-mindedness'

One way the insidious standards of psychology are enforced is in the assessment of people to see if they will really benefit from counselling or psychotherapy. Those who are deemed to be 'psychological-minded' may be lucky enough to escape the fate of the 'physical treatments'.[9] These treatments include medication for anxiety and depression with the risk of serious 'side effects' and electroshock that are likely to lead to memory-impairment. No surprise that people of colour, for example, are much more likely to be given these physical treatments, and no surprise that working-class people generally are less likely to be offered psychotherapy. There is a grim reality to the characterisation of the bourgeoisie and petit-bourgeoisie as the 'chattering classes', and there are material consequences for those who seek help and who do not chatter in the same way.

The client in therapy is expected to be able to speak a certain kind of language. This means that admission to counselling and psychotherapy is to the marvellous world of the 'talking cure', but the trick is that the 'client' or 'patient' should be able to talk about themselves in the right kind of way. The criterion of 'psychological-mindedness' is not employed by the psychologist using telepathy or directly reading the prospective client's mind; instead, assessment is of a certain way of talking, using a certain vocabulary to show that one has a notion of the unconscious and will be able to talk more about painful memories and reflect on the defences that they use to keep these memories at bay.[10]

The realm of thought and emotion are separated so that each can be accessed for change

The way of speaking about the self that a psychologist likes to hear will include a certain vocabulary for referring to thoughts and feelings. The 'thoughts' are separated from the 'feelings', turned into distinct domains of individual mental life, and this separation has become

[9] Coltart (1988) provides the classic and still influential argument for focusing on 'psychological-mindedness', one that informs the assessment process in many UK National Health Service psychotherapy clinics.

[10] Forrester (1980) shows how the development of psychoanalysis was predicated on what one of the early patients (of Breuer, Freud's mentor) called her 'talking cure', and although psychoanalytic practice in the English-speaking world has been heavily influenced by research concerned with observable behaviour and child development, it still relies on the medium of speech (which always threatens to turn the process into one in which the analyst determines what it means to 'speak well').

one of the defining characteristics of alienation in capitalist society. Psychology in its ostensibly 'softer', more therapeutic mode, along with much counselling and psychotherapy practice, reinforces this alienation at the very moment that it promises to help people. Partly this is because 'psychological-mindedness' is assumed to be a quality of self-reflection and openness to change and it precisely operates on that separation.

It presumes that the 'feelings' are under the surface and 'thoughts' are a layer on top that keeps the feelings at bay, a layer that needs to be opened up. This is not merely a theoretical supposition; the problem is that in the practice of psychotherapy, psychoanalytic or otherwise, this assumption is reinforced and even drummed in as a moral lesson to the client.[11]

This dualist conception of mind is one that philosophy has worried away at for many years, but psychology broke away from philosophy toward the end of the nineteenth century and has done its best not to learn anything from conceptual debates since. The separation into thoughts and feelings is also a reflection of the compartmentalisation of psychology into different specialist areas; the 'cognitive' and 'behavioural' therapists focusing on thoughts or behaviours compete with the 'psychodynamic' and 'humanistic' psychologists who are more into the feelings and stuff. This means that the prospective client will have to work their way through a minefield of disciplinary conflicts as well as class and cultural assumptions in order to get treatment.[12]

The regulation of emotion is governed by certain notions about how it functions

The process of speaking about oneself and accessing emotions requires a theoretical framework that divides thinking from feeling, and different 'emotions' are also reified, turned into things. The basic building-blocks of psychological therapies have been shaped by observations of people in strange situations in which they have been deceived and manipulated. Psychological descriptions of what an 'emotion' is and what differences obtain between different kinds of emotion are thus not only closely bound up with the culture in

[11] For an outline of the way that 'therapeutic discourse' draws upon and reproduces certain assumptions about how we should speak about what lies inside ourselves, see Parker (2003).
[12] There are attempts to show people how to navigate this minefield in Hansen et al. (2003), and proposals for doing something better in Bates (2006).

which psychology developed but also with the artificial conditions in which they were 'discovered'.[13]

The building-blocks are then cobbled together with equally dubious and culture-bound notions of 'repression' and 'release'; in psychological culture it is thought that keeping emotions hidden will cause problems and letting them out will make you feel good. The 'therapeutic' side of the old mechanistic psychology thus functions as the flip-side of the same disciplinary practice; while the overly 'rationalist' tradition in psychology tried to ward off anything in human experience that could not be observed and measured, it always, in that very process of prohibiting what should be studied, prepared the ground for the opposite. Rationalist psychology constituted a divide between reason and feeling, and the feeling that it now tries to attend to is still constructed within a certain image of what human psychology should be like. Psychologisation in the wider culture outside the psychology departments then proceeds through practices in which people are required to speak about these 'feelings' to experts.[14]

Psychology Adopts and Adapts Certain Notions of the Self from Psychoanalysis

Psychology does not like to be reminded that it is dependent on the culture in which emerged, and it reassures itself that it is 'scientific' and neutral with respect to influences from outside. The old philosophy it broke away from is thus often treated as unscientific 'speculation', and some of the friends it met along the road and that it learnt so much from are now shunned.[15] Psychology textbooks will nowadays not mention the strong associations between some of its founding fathers and psychoanalysis. But this old ally cast by the wayside has been quite influential in popular culture, and psychology in the field of counselling and psychotherapy cannot shake it off.[16]

---

[13] See the collection by Harré (1986) on the social construction of emotion; see Littlewood (1992) on 'therapy' as culturally specific.

[14] See Cloud (1998) for a review of ideological problems with therapeutic discourse, and Dineen (2001) on the production of 'victims'; for a 'narrative' attempt to take these issues seriously and sidestep them in therapeutic practice, see Guilfoyle (2005). The history of the incitement to speak about one's self as the necessary flip-side of processes of social control is analysed in Michel Foucault's marvellous studies of confession (1981) and discipline (1977).

[15] Newman and Holzman (1996) give a good account of the way that psychology separated itself off from, and then tried to forget its origins in, philosophy.

[16] See Parker (1997) for a discussion of these connections.

The history of diagnostic systems wipes away psychoanalysis,
but the traces remain

Traditional diagnoses of 'neurosis' and 'psychosis' have been replaced by an ever-expanding list of disorders put together by the committees that update the ICD and the DSM. What psychologists want to know is exactly how the different 'neurotic' disorders can be categorised and the symptoms removed. For a while psychologists were content to leave 'psychotic' disorders to be dealt with by the psychiatrists; but it eventually dawned on them that if the many well founded critiques of the category of 'schizophrenia' were taken on board, psychology could pitch its own alternative approach. This would be one that broke this unwieldy category into discrete symptoms and tackled them one by one.[17] Impatience with the long and expensive psychoanalytic process led many psychoanalysts to adapt psychoanalysis to fit with a psychological approach, and then to formulate 'cognitive' approaches that psychologists would lap up.[18]

Versions of psychoanalysis are extracted so they can be co-opted into psychology. However, far from dispensing with psychoanalysis, the concepts that did make it through into psychology are themselves distortions of psychoanalysis that already make a strict separation between thoughts and feelings. Notions of 'competence' and 'burn-out', for example, are part of the heritage of US American psychoanalysis.[19]

That US American tradition of 'ego psychology' is a form of the theory that many psychoanalysts outside the English-speaking world would not recognise at all, and it buys into the worst of reductionist psychology.[20] It can then more easily be adapted to the needs of insurance companies and cash-strapped welfare services. It is quicker and it is more cheap and cheerful, but this then turns

[17] Boyle (2002) provides a definitive demolition of the category of 'schizophrenia', and Bentall (1990) outlines a way that psychologists might tackle the separate 'symptoms' that comprise it.
[18] Beck (1976) has been the most popular figure in psychology; but a number of psychoanalysts from the US American tradition developed their own home-spun cognitive educational approaches (e.g., Eric Berne, Albert Ellis).
[19] There is a discussion of the terminology of competence and 'burn-out' in the empirical studies by Vanheule and Verhaeghe (2004), and polemical responses to the way that 'evaluation' in psychotherapy distorts psychoanalysis by Jonckheere (2005).
[20] On the connections between this tradition in psychoanalysis and the reduction to psychology in the context of the US mental health system, see Kovel (2004).

people into the collections of mechanisms that psychologists think science should be concerned with.[21]

Psychoanalytic theories are translated so that
they become more 'scientific'

The translation of psychoanalytic theory into the English language already turned it into something that more closely approximated US American psychology. Freud's discussion of the 'I', the 'Above-I' and the 'It' is translated from everyday German terms into bizarrely named entities, as the 'ego', 'superego' and 'id'. The use of everyday terminology in the early years of psychoanalysis was a practice that prepared the way for the development of a 'science' that could then be considered as part of psychology. In the process some distortions of everyday meanings, and even of psychoanalysis itself, became inevitable.

The mind as a 'mental apparatus' in the English edition of Freud's writings, for example, translates the German word '*Seele*', which is 'soul'.[22] A psychological definition of what a scientific investigator would understand a 'soul' to be thus replaced everyday usage; once again, however, the way was prepared for spiritually inclined psychoanalysts to break with Freud's evolutionary, atheist and decidedly materialist approach and embrace different forms of religion, aiming to psychologise both religion and psychoanalysis in the process.[23]

Of all the problems of psychoanalysis, the translation of it into psychology is one of the worst. So influential has been the English 'Standard Edition' translation of Freud's writings that the added notes designed to introduce and 'clarify' concepts have been translated into German and are incorporated into the new German texts.[24] Western psychology and versions of psychology inside psychoanalysis are

[21] The classic studies reviewed by Eysenck and Wilson (1973) and, more sympathetically, by Kline (1972), press psychoanalysis into a methodological paradigm that will ensure that it fails to meet the 'scientific' standards used for evidence; or they distort it so that what gets through the hoops is unrecognisable to practising psychoanalysts; see Masling (1983) for an even more pro-psychoanalytic attempt to back up the discipline experimentally.

[22] See Bettelheim (1986) for the argument that the translations from Freud's German text into English have distorted fundamental ideas in psychoanalysis, and turned it into something that pretends to be a 'natural science'.

[23] For attempts to make psychoanalysis compatible with Roman Catholicism, see Symington (1990), and for psychoanalysis linked to a version of Buddhism treated as a religious system of thought, see Coltart (2000).

[24] See the collection by Timms and Segal (1988) for discussion of these issues.

colonising the world, and some of the routes by which it weaves itself into the fabric of other cultures are most insidious and peculiar.

Notions of 'stages' and 'personality types' are then built into psychology

The poetic and tentative formulations of the early psychoanalysts are turned into something more scientific-sounding by the psychologists who are keen to give respectability to descriptions of 'hysteria' and 'obsessional neurosis' and the possible relation to 'oedipal' conflicts. Psychoanalytic exploration of the way people make sense of the past is thus psychologised, and the psychoanalytic descriptions that draw on Greek myth to make sense of the relationships that structure experience are turned into 'hypotheses' about behaviour that should be empirically investigated.[25] Psychoanalysts trained in that US American and British psychologised version of psychoanalysis are thus schooled to think they can actually observe normal and pathological processes taking place between infants and their care-givers.[26] When psychoanalysis, for all its faults, is turned into psychology, the uncertain shifting accounts that Freud and his followers offered are turned into descriptions that pretend to be true; what we imagine our past to be like is thus turned into 'developmental psychology'.[27]

With friends like these, psychoanalysis has not had much chance in keeping open the idea that certain personality formations might be connected with events in childhood and with the way they are puzzled over.[28] Psychology ties the descriptions down, but the trick in therapy obedient to the discipline is still to make sure that the client will talk about them in the right kind of way, and that requirement for correct speech enforces Western middle-class psychology as the ideal standard.

[25] The hugely influential work of Daniel Stern (1985) is the template for this experimental study of mother–infant interaction; for a critique of the ideological effects of this research, see Cushman (1991).

[26] See, for example, Miller et al. (1989) for an account of infant observation as part of psychoanalytic training in the UK.

[27] See Burman (1994) for the argument that psychoanalysis operates as the 'repressed other' of psychology, and for a critique of the way that psychoanalytic descriptions are also incorporated into developmental psychology, as if the phenomena it is concerned with can actually be observed.

[28] For the psychoanalytic argument that memories are often reconstructions of experiences that we could not make sense of, a theory that is very different from psychological conceptions of memory, see Laplanche (1989). For a socialist-feminist analysis of these debates over memory and experience, see Haaken (1998), and for an analysis of the way 'memory' is dealt with in political debate (with specific reference to the Truth and Reconciliation Commission in South Africa), see Hayes (1998).

Psychology Takes What Is Acceptable from Spiritual Approaches

While the discipline used to distance itself from spirituality, some psychologists have been tempted by new notions of spirituality and spiritual interconnectedness. These recent takes on spirituality are associated with some of the environmental movements, and they do pose a challenge to traditional individualistic psychological ways of seeing the world.[29] This yearning for some way of making sense of the separation of people from each other is a perfect modern example of how spiritual ideas come to fill a void, the heart of a heartless world that capitalism has created for so many of us. The emergence of 'transpersonal psychology' has been an expression of the impact of these new movements, but the discipline still expects those interested in spirituality to play by the rules, its own rules. Psychology as a discipline was a child of the Western Enlightenment tradition, but it split reason from feeling, and psychological culture revolves around and tries to heal that split.[30] That split has had profound repercussions for the way that we fantasise about what lies outside, and 'other' to our individual selves.

Rationality and irrationality are split in psychological research

Superstition functions as the 'dark' underside of scientific rationality in the Western Enlightenment tradition, so dark that many scientists refuse to acknowledge the irrational hunches and prejudice that draw them to what they cling to as a 'rational' understanding of the world. As we will see, the underside and 'other' of the European white Enlightenment tradition have often been refused, explicitly or implicitly, as something dark. In the case of psychologists this refusal is especially dangerous, because the objects they are so determined to predict and control are other human beings. In psychological research, this subjectivity necessary to puzzle about any phenomenon

[29] New (1996) develops this argument from a socialist-feminist standpoint (but one that still gives too much of a role to psychology and psychotherapy).

[30] Adorno (1967) argued that the separation of the individual from social relations under capitalism, and the corresponding split between psychology and sociology, create two alienated aspects of the human condition that cannot just be patched together again; rather, 'Both are torn halves of an integral freedom, to which however they do not add up'. This observation identifies the problem that lies at the heart of the host of ridiculous studies of 'social psychology' that presume that the two halves can be patched together. For a discussion of this problem and its consequences in psychological research on discourse, see Parker (2002).

is treated as something merely 'subjective', as if it is a matter of individual bias that should really be avoided.[31]

The split between rationality and irrationality then operates so that attempts to bring 'subjectivity' into the research reconfigure this subjectivity as if it must be an attempt to bring in personal beliefs, feelings or intuitions.[32] The way is thus prepared for the development of 'action research' alternatives that start by treating 'subjectivity' as something that is constituted in the research process, but then end up appealing to personal experience as the touchstone for what is authentic about the phenomena that have been described. There is thus a fateful slide from one perspective – in which an experience is historically constructed and in which an explanation can be developed as to how it came about – into the 'transpersonal' approach to an underlying spirituality that searches for a likewise underlying experience that the psychologist assumes must exist so that they can busy themselves finding it.[33]

Transpersonal dimensions of parapsychology are abolished so that it can be tested

Psychology is now supposed to be a broad church, but it will only embrace the flocks of different denominations on certain conditions, and how these conditions are spelt out will depend on who is in charge at the different entry-points. The key issue here is not so much how the tests for who is allowed to enter this church are constructed, as how the phenomena that are to be taken seriously are represented, how they are codified by psychology.

Predictably, perhaps, some of the psychologists most interested in parapsychology, for example, have been those most committed to a scientific worldview. Scientific studies of astrology conducted by 'scientific' psychologists, for example, were designed to conclude in a balanced scientific way that star signs had little to do with personality.[34] While it is indeed implausible that a twelfth of the

[31] This problem, of the way that psychological researchers who realise that they always play a part in the phenomena they construct and describe, then think that they are being 'merely subjective', is discussed in Parker (1999d, 2005a).
[32] Feminist discussions of science and subjectivity in research have drawn attention to this problem; see, e.g., Hollway (1989) and, with an extension of these considerations to questions of race and racism, see Mama (1995).
[33] For a methodological approach which takes experience seriously but aims to show how it is historically constructed, see the Marxist-feminist tradition of 'memory work' linked to German 'critical psychology' (e.g., Haug, 1987, 2000). For the easier option which wallows in psychologised 'spirituality', see the 'transpersonal' approach in Rowan (2005).
[34] See, for example, the hard-nosed collection by Roberts and Groome (2001).

population of the world belonging to one particular star sign could be predicted to have the same kind of luck or misfortune on a particular day, what the 'scientific' studies do is to extract different aspects of parapsychology – the experience that people have that there is something more than the alienated separation of each individual from everyone else – from context.

This 'scientific' research has a double-effect. On the one hand it serves to ridicule believers, as well as overlooking the cultural and political functions that are served by different forms of religious belief. On the other hand, because of the utterly unreasonable way that experiences are invalidated and prohibited from the psychological court of reason, it incites those who remain alienated outside to search for something more than the 'science' that psychology has offered them. Psychology thus serves to keep alive the idea that there is something spiritual out there to which people can turn and must turn as the only alternative to a ridiculous psychology that pretends to provide scientific accounts of what human beings are and how they can change. Psychology as a parody of science does virtually no one any favours, neither the scientists nor those who search for mystical alternatives to it.

Spirituality, sexuality and racial difference in psychology

Fantasies about what authentic natural experience is like outside the rational frames of reference in which we have become trapped in psychological culture have entailed images of what the difference between men and women are, with the man of reason divided from the emotional woman. The development of psychologised rational man and psychologised emotional woman in a Western world that depended on the colonisation of other countries and the 'under-development' of other cultures also entailed that what we Western subjects imagine to lie outside reason always calls upon certain fantasies of racial difference, of what seems to be 'other' to us.[35] This means that when psychology turns to 'spirituality' to try and heal the split between reason and what is pushed outside reason, it necessarily has implications for how 'race' and racial difference are represented.

It is symptomatic of the turn to 'spirituality' in psychology that questions about 'race' and 'racism' in psychology have been displaced,

---

[35] For an analysis of Western 'orientalist' images of those constructed as 'other' to the West, see Said (1978), and for an analysis of colonial images of masculinity and femininity infused with fantasies of racial difference, see McClintock (1995).

transformed into questions of religious belief and attitudes to religion. In this way the attention to 'spirituality' functions as an individualised relationship with religion that fits perfectly with neoliberalism, and, as psychologised religion, spiritual experience and 'identity' turn questions of race and racism into questions of religious faith.

The responses to political violence from the 'Islamic world' (itself a reductive and latently psychologising category), for example, entail a psychologisation of political problems – colonial occupation, enforced secularism and imperialist exploitation – and these responses represent the political problems as something that emanates from the minds of fanatics who hold too firmly to their religious beliefs.[36] The very term 'fundamentalism' is an aspect of this psychologisation of political conflict, and it also serves to obscure the real effects of Western racism; one set of 'orientalist' images of those 'other' to the West is replaced by another set of images that just as effectively turns those who are 'other' into the problem.

Jungian notions of personality and integration are rendered compatible with psychology

The pervasive unacknowledged influence of the irrational shadow-side of rational science is perhaps a reason why Jung often appears to offer something to the psychologist searching for meaningful alternatives. On the one hand, Jung is writing within the tradition of dualistic representations of 'mind' and 'body' so pervasive in Western culture. On the other hand, he offers a conception of the psyche that can be treated as a unity, in which the alienated life conditions of human beings in capitalist society can be healed. This is one reason why Jung's mystical and essentialist view of the self is so appealing to those who have been suffocated, and think that what they are missing is their 'spirituality'.

As a shadow-side of scientific psychology Jung also offers a kaleidoscope of archetypes into which the psychologist can project their desire for discovering something deep and universal.[37] One of the

[36] For a discussion of Western images of what it is too convenient to think of as the 'Islamic world', see Mamdani (2005).

[37] This is why approaches that promise that they will address the 'politics' of psychotherapy are often so disappointing, for what they put in the place of politics is a Jungian or quasi-Jungian conception of a full spiritually rich life that they think will plug the gap between reason and feeling that capitalist society creates; see, for example, the contrast between the quite good conceptual overview of the relationships between politics and psychotherapy by Totton (2000) and the spiritually oriented collection in Totton (2006).

main problems with the Jungian tradition is that spiritual resources of non-Western cultures are treated as exotic partial truths. The Jungian 'collective unconscious' serves as a point of harmonious bringing together of the different cultural categories that psychology has played such a powerful part in constructing. There is also an unpleasant 'shadow-side' of Jung lurking in the background here, for he held to an essentialist and implicitly racist conception of different separate forms of 'racial unconscious'.[38] The way Jung functions in present-day psychology, however, is to bolster the long-standing attempt to find the 'truth' of the human condition in exotic far-away cultures. US American imperialism and dominant white psychology at home go hand-in-hand with Eurocentrism, but they are also occasionally given a fillip by a good dose of orientalism.[39]

The lesson is that the celebration of 'spirituality', as if it is something exotic that those in the West have lost and need now to reclaim, can simply repeat the racist images of 'other' cultures when they were reviled by the Western powers. This 'celebration of the Other' in spiritually oriented psychology can serve to drum home an image of what our underlying psychology is that is more convincing and thus more dangerous than the old rationalist psychology.[40] In both cases, it is the psychologist who will tell us what it is to be authentically human and will limit what we are permitted to experience; the discipline still functions, then, as an apparatus of social control that ratifies certain social arrangements and conceptions of self.

Psychology Produces Its Own Limited Humanistic Alternative in Counselling

At home, its home, psychology has its own little version of the holistic balanced guru figure that usually lives overseas and offers

[38] See Dalal (1988) for an excellent review of the racist elements of Jung's work, and see Samuels (1992, 1993) for a 'post-Jungian' appraisal of this problem and legacy of Jung's work. Jung was one of the figures in psychotherapy who was in favour with the Nazis after Freud's books were burnt (Cocks, 1985); for a study of the fate of psychoanalysis when it was treated as a 'Jewish science' in the Third Reich, see Frosh (2005).

[39] The Jungian search for essential underlying archetypical contents to the mind that are assumed to reflect the unified and homogeneous psychology of a national community has also informed the work of the psychologist Kawai Hayao, an influential figure in the formalisation of training in educational and clinical psychology in Japan. Here, psychology, underpinned by Jungian quasi-spiritualist conceptions of racial distinctiveness, is turned from being a discipline defined by methodology, as it is in the Western tradition, into a discipline defined by its religious content (see, e.g., Kawai, 1995).

[40] For the argument that we can solve racism by 'celebrating the Other', see Sampson (1993); for a politically acute reading of the way Western 'civilisation' secretes its own forms of barbarism which it inflicts on its 'others', see Achcar (2006). For recent attempts to make Rogers more congruent with radical politics, see Proctor et al. (2006).

enlightenment to followers and visitors. Western psychology came up with its own white wise man in the form of Carl Rogers; as nice as Mahatma Ghandi, and with empathy for the plight of others that makes him seem like a latter-day saint. However, there are serious problems with this 'humanistic' psychology that really does function as a psychologised spirituality within the Western psychological tradition, and within adjacent counselling and psychotherapy approaches that psychology has tried to trademark as its own.[41]

Rogers is valued as a clinical psychologist
focusing on individual insight

Rogers did not train as a psychoanalyst first and then defect to psychology, as many of the other leaders of US American pragmatic cognitive therapies did, but trained first as a clinical psychologist. Rogers is the perfect complement to mainstream psychology, for he takes the individualised separate person and finds a way of treating that isolated state of being as a virtue. The early dependence of this individual on a single care-giver in the nuclear family is also a thing to be celebrated, for the mother is the one who will provide the point of security and self-worth from which the individual will travel, go out into the world and find recognition from others.[42]

Rogers sets out a developmental trajectory that leads from a state of initial grace – 'unconditional positive regard' from the mother – to a state of 'incongruence' and unhappiness, until the individual realises that the answers lie inside themself. The psychologist trained in Rogerian humanistic principles will thus provide that 'unconditional positive regard' as a core condition of the therapy through which the client will once again find themselves. The 'unconditional positive regard' that Rogers and the Rogerian therapist promise thus serves to normalise certain kinds of development.[43] This is the most limited fairy-story of individualistic Western society, and while it tells us that our relationships with others are crucial to being our true selves, it reassures us that we can find enlightenment without challenging the socially structured nature of those relationships.

[41] The development of counselling psychology in the US has been more closely tied to mainstream psychology than in the UK; in the UK, while there are problems with the practice of counselling psychology, some of the conceptual discussions have actually been quite radical (e.g., Woolfe et al., 2003).
[42] There is an optimistic transformation of the ideas of Hegel here, and Rogers is a prime example of the psychologisation of philosophical ideas (see Pinkard, 2000).
[43] See Chantler (2004, 2005) for attempts to tackle racism in therapy through a reflection on the limitations of a strictly Rogerian approach, and see Chantler (2006) for a consideration of questions of power in this approach.

Core conditions of therapy require an impossible abstraction
from power relations

Laboratory-based methodologies in psychology required explicit deception and manipulation of subjects. There was a good deal of agonising about how that deception could be justified so that the level of 'self-esteem' of the 'subject' would be the same at the end as at the beginning of the experiment. The Rogerian counsellor or therapist, who is often a psychologist in disguise, and is for sure someone who has psychologised our sense of what it is to be human, is drawn into an even more peculiar position. They must show genuineness, warmth and empathy in the face of every deluded and malicious thing the client says in the hope that they, the client, will eventually arrive at insight that is more genuine, warmer and more empathic to others.[44]

Such a therapeutic technique can only be fake, and draw the Rogerian therapist into both being hypocritical – they cannot in all good faith agree with everything that a client says – and collusive with oppression, if they appear to be endorsing racist or sexist statements by the client. It is a therapeutic process that is impossible but politically expedient, for this limited 'humanism' must keep things personal and individual.

The attempt to extrapolate the approach to political contexts also reveals the limitations of Rogers' work. One of the tests of the Rogerian saintly approach to real-life problems came when he was invited to go to South Africa during the apartheid years. So important was the work he wanted to do in bringing black and white youth together that he was willing to break the boycott that aimed to isolate the regime, an isolation that did eventually bring results, alongside sustained mass protests and armed struggle. By all accounts, the Rogerian intervention did not go down too well, and we should conclude from this that the power relations that psychology has spent such a great deal of energy in buttressing cannot be dissolved by sitting together with the victims and smiling warmly at them.[45]

---

[44] Masson (1990) makes these points about the political problems with Rogerian therapy. For arguments from within the community psychology tradition that psychotherapy is 'futile', see Albee (1990); for a Marxist discussion of psychotherapy, see Cohen (1986).

[45] See Swartz (1986) for a discussion of this from within South Africa; and for discussion of links between US American psychology and apartheid, see Lambley (1973).

Psychology Often Functions As a Protection Racket

The discipline appears to open its arms to other cultures when it shows an interest in exotic 'transpersonal' psychologies. Instead, it actually fails to learn any lessons about the racism that made those forms of psychology so different, so 'other' to the standard psychology of the West. The discipline has also in this process tried to reconfigure itself as more feminine-friendly, finding a way to incorporate rather than dismiss the realm of feelings. It incorporates a few more women into psychology, and it also finds a way of giving more men expertise in what men and women really want.

Psychology guards certain titles to keep out those it labels as charlatans

Psychology claims to want to 'protect' the public, and the speed with which the discipline has moved into the domains of counselling and psychotherapy, setting up its own registers of practitioners to 'protect' other people, is breathtaking in its arrogant appropriation of what 'psychology' is from everyday life. However much psychology in its new spiritually friendly guises pretends that it is more open to what non-psychologists say about themselves, it cannot really trust the non-psychologists to look after themselves, still less anyone who is not accredited by the discipline to have the right to call themselves a 'psychologist'.[46]

A discipline that has been based on deeply unethical practices is now supposed to be the guardian of ethical conduct, and one of the signs of good conduct will be that someone has a certificate saying that the counsellor or psychotherapist is certified, a psychologist. There is now a serious turf-war going on between the different professional groups that want to keep out the 'charlatans'. But we need to look very closely at the nature of psychology to understand what charlatanry really is.

Psychology distorts and reproduces its own version of charlatanry, as worse

The turn to 'spirituality' by some psychologists pretends to be more in tune with what people really want, and so it feeds the sense that there is something missing in contemporary life. It is actually in tune with neoliberal deregulation and fragmentation of collective life.

---

[46] See Mowbray (1995) and House and Totton (1997) for good reviews and critiques of the drive to register psychotherapists in the hope that this will protect the public.

There is an emphasis on personal self-responsibility that reduces racism to harmful beliefs, and turns the experience of each individual into something that psychology can do business with.

Through all this the discipline of psychology maintains a profession that is intent on displaying the superiority of middle-class values and ways of being in the world; 'Are you thinking what we're thinking?'. This slogan, used by the Conservative Party during a general election campaign in the UK, is quite telling. It was a warrant for recycling all manner of racist images of immigrants and asylum-seekers, and using the ploy of making it seem as if, because we all secretly think these things that we are no longer allowed to talk about, deep down we must be right. The slogan, then, actually worked against the background of a deeply psychologised culture in which each individual experiences themself as having hidden thoughts that it would be ideally healthy but not always possible to share with others. Professional psychologists protect their own status, and are then torn when they try to protect others, caught in an impossible task of making their discipline relevant to anyone other than themselves.

7

Professional Empowerment: Good Citizens

There are many psychologists who are ready to acknowledge that there is something deeply wrong with their discipline, and some of them are prepared to put time into trying to figure out what went wrong. Some of them are radicals, even activists who want to find ways of using psychology in constructive ways. However, the discipline is a maze of debates over the nature of the objects and subjects that psychologists study and how we should come to know more, and there are interminable internecine disputes between those who want to find progressive alternatives. The good people then often get lost in some really useless pursuits, or worse. This chapter reviews some dead-ends and pseudo alternatives that consume the energies of those who think things can be fixed in the discipline. Psychology as an apparatus of social control cannot 'empower' people outside, and the attempts to offer alternatives inside the discipline often end up only empowering the psychologists.

There is a tempting shift inside US American psychology to accentuate the positive

Even mainstream psychologists will admit that there are problems with the discipline so far, and they are usually liberal and democratic enough to give the alternative voices a hearing. There is an increasingly popular view in liberal US American psychology, for example, that the discipline has been overly negative about people, and that it should now accentuate the positive.[1] The turn from negative to

---

[1] This is in the context of a shift inside the American Psychological Association from academic research to applied work, in which the 'scientist–practitioner split' has yawned open further and further and the 'practitioners' now drive the profession (see, e.g., Rice, 1997). They avidly seek prescribing rights over medication for psychological problems, for example, and want to sell psychology in a way that will encourage more people to take psychologists seriously; for an argument against this trend, see Holzman (1999).

positive does not, however, mean that psychology will now stop pathologising certain categories of people. Now the focus turns to those who are not 'emotionally literate', for example, those who refuse to speak the positive thoughtful reflective language that a psychologist likes to speak and hear others speak.[2]

Psychologists have often thought that the world would be a better place if they could spread their knowledge about people further, and the idea that the discipline should 'give psychology away' has never actually meant demystifying that knowledge.[3] Now the new 'positive psychology' emphasises the way the discipline can promote health and well-being.[4] By talking up the capacity of people to improve themselves though, these psychologists are once again encouraging individuals to make the best of destructive social conditions. This might make the psychologists feel better about themselves, but this is an intensely ideological move on the part of the discipline.

There are even more tempting alternatives inside
European psychology and the colonies

Those who draw attention to how bad the discipline is are usually seen by the US American 'positive' psychologists as destructive and unhelpful, and there is now a series of more balanced responses to the shortcomings of psychology. It would seem that these attempts to point out what is mistaken in the old psychology while offering constructive suggestions for what might be done instead is the healthy option. This might be healthy for the psychologists, but the alternative versions of psychology promise more than they deliver; they are very limited, carrying their own particular dangers for those outside.

Alongside rather crass feel-good 'positive psychology', new methodological and conceptual approaches in the discipline have appeared that also claim to offer something different and more progressive. Interpretative, discursive, critical and 'action research' perspectives certainly multiply the options available to

---

[2] For enthusiastic endorsement of 'emotional literacy' in schools, see, e.g., Sharp (2001); for a critique of the emphasis on 'emotional literacy' in education on the grounds that it reinforces gender roles, see Burman (2006).

[3] George Miller (1969) argued in the 1960s that psychology should be concerned with 'human welfare', and that he had to make this argument at all indicates how bad things were in the discipline.

[4] Seligman (1998) used his presidential message to members of the American Psychological Association to call for a turn to 'positive psychology'. There has then been a rash of publications inside and outside the US that have taken up the call.

someone going into psychology as an academic speciality, and they are appealing to practitioners who want to be nicer psychologists. These approaches effectively function as the left-flank of the discipline, assuring sceptics that there are serious attempts to put the house in order. We need to examine these approaches and see whether they are really up to the task; we will see that they are not.

Interpretative Approaches Appear to Go Deeper, But into Their Own Models

Methodological debates in psychology are most-times self-referential, with one fashion in the discipline posing questions in a certain way; these are questions that are attractive to some researchers but unsatisfying to others, who then respond with counter-claims and alternative approaches, and so it goes. The emergence of qualitative research out of 'new paradigm' debates is one example.[5] The recent turn to 'interpretation' is another recent expression of this attempt to carry out research in a different manner from the old mechanistic laboratory-experimental tradition. When mainstream 'old paradigm' psychologists insisted that we should only focus on behaviour and refuse to speculate about what is going on inside the head or that we should build computer models of 'cognitions' to explain how we think, the more decent humanist-inclined interpretative psychologists took fright. However, when these interpretative psychologists now insist that 'ordinary people' have intentions that can be discovered and laid bare they are also just as much caught in the grip of psychological reasoning. It looks very generous, but in practice it does not usually work out that way. The concern with 'interpretation' in the discipline is a mixed blessing; in mainstream psychology it has usually been a curse, and when it has drawn on psychoanalytic theory it has continued dividing those who interpret from those who speak.

Interpretative researchers attempt to discover real intentions behind what people say

There is a benign and a malign aspect to the search for underlying intentions steering behaviour, but the slide from one to the other is

---

[5] Harré and Secord (1972) argued for a 'new paradigm' in psychology, and drew parallels between the state of psychology and the progress of natural sciences, taking heart from the work of the historian of science Thomas Kuhn (1962). Kuhn had shown how astronomy, for example, had to undergo a 'paradigm revolution' to shift from an old assumption that the sun went round the earth to a different starting point that would make sense of anomalies in the data; this scientific revolution had a political aspect, and Galileo had to persuade those who looked through his telescopes that they could actually see something more (see Feyerabend, 1975).

so slippery that it is best not to leave the decision about an interpretation to a psychologist. The way someone describes what they do and why they do it is bound up with the kind of audience they are addressing. The interpretative researchers too quickly forget that we need to know what the *context* is for the account and what resources the speaker has to make sense of themselves to another person. There is a danger in even the most democratically conducted psychological interviews that these issues of audience, context and resource are ignored, so keen is the researcher to get to what the individual really meant.[6]

The more malign approaches lead the researcher to search for an 'emotional logic' which only they will be able to divine, and then interpretation really is an exercise in expertise and power. The search for hidden mental processes that are supposed to lie inside the mind of the person interviewed, and be only completely understood by the analyst, in many cases draws on some of the most bizarre psychoanalytic theories. Even when that psychoanalytic language is not used explicitly in describing what people really think, it underpins the conception that the researcher has of the mind as some kind of container from which the contents can be extracted and made visible to those reading the specialist journals in which they publish their 'findings'. The 'free association' that is claimed in the approach is not actually something undertaken by the person who is interviewed; insofar as there really is any kind of free association in this approach it is an activity the researcher engages in to help them connect what they read in their interview transcripts with psychoanalytic theory.[7]

Interpretative researchers tend to produce explanations that individualise

Interpretative researchers often like to think that they really value and respect what someone says to them. This, they imagine, is what an 'inside' perspective enables them to do; a deep empathic understanding of what is said to them will lead them to a truer account of

---

[6] The attempt to develop the approach known as 'Interpretative Phenomenological Analysis' is indicative (see, e.g., Smith, 2004). In practice this approach actually ends up describing what people think in psychological language, searches for real motivations for their behaviour and fails to locate accounts in context to discover how they have been constructed; apart from the problems that attend making 'interpretations', in many of the studies carried out in its name it is neither 'interpretative', nor 'phenomenological', nor 'analysis'.

[7] The claim by Hollway and Jefferson (2000) to use 'free association', for example, only serves to warrant them drawing on the theories of Melanie Klein (1986).

what was meant. It should be noted that 'true' here is still used with the sense of being more 'accurate', rather than with the sense of something that is true for someone about their experience or of discovering how they have come to be the person they are. This 'truer account' is still rooted in the empiricist tradition of research in which the scientist tries to find the objectively real reasons for behaviour. Furthermore, the extent to which the researcher aims to get an 'inside' perspective serves to obscure the collective and relational aspects of 'thinking' and 'meaning', making it seem as if these things only go on inside an individual head waiting to be disclosed to another person.[8]

This aspect of interpretative psychology becomes even worse when the researcher aims to link together 'themes' in the talk and build up a 'profile' of the person which will connect what they are saying now to their past experiences. Social explanations are thereby dissolved into a collection of individual accounts; interpretations made by the psychologist of individual life histories. The 'narrative' accounts that claim to value the sense that an individual gives to their life are still framed by a normative notion of 'narrative' and what it should look like to be given value by the researcher.[9]

Interpretative researchers seek pathological background causes for experience

Therapeutic interpretation in a clinical setting can, even in the worst of cases, be contested by the person whose account is being reframed and offered back to them. In the best of cases there is space for the client to see how useful the interpretation is or to come up with their own interpretations. Interpretative psychology that draws on psychoanalytic ideas in research, however, is the very worst of scenarios, for there is no opportunity for the expert account to be contested. When a psychologist is let loose on the internal life of another person, the picture that is given in a 'psychosocial case

[8] For an account of theories of 'communication' in mainstream psychology that work on the assumption that ideas are wrapped up in words so they can be conveyed to another person who then unwraps them, see Easthope (1990). This theory of communication is something that was tackled by those influenced by 'post-structuralist' ideas in British psychology (e.g., Henriques et al., 1984), though there were still some significant differences from the way these ideas were articulated by the original writers (for a critique, see Easthope, 1988).

[9] See, for example, Crossley (2000), and for what is meant to be a defence against critics that simply repeats the argument, Crossley (2003); the psychoanalytic approaches have even firmer ideas about what normal and abnormal narratives look like (see, e.g., Hollway and Jefferson, 2001).

study' too often proceeds by identifying pathological causes for the things that were told to them in their capacity as a trusted researcher.[10]

Interpretative researchers often make no attempt to empower those they work with. Sometimes there is an attempt in social research to equalise the power relation between researcher and researched, but the structural position of the researcher usually sabotages this attempt.[11] The interpretative approaches that draw on psychoanalytic theory construct a particular model of the 'defended subject' that makes the researcher unwilling to share their interpretations. Research might be carried out with an ethics of sharing interpretations, or it may be carried out in a 'free-association narrative interview' which refuses to share interpretations for 'ethical reasons'.[12] One way of finding out which is which is to insist, if you are a participant in research, that you have the right to see the transcripts of the interview and a copy of every published paper that includes interpretations made of your account.

The Turn to 'Discourse' in Psychology Is Another Distraction

The 'new paradigm' debates drew attention to the importance of language in psychology. Many psychologists up to then had treated what people said as mere 'verbal behaviour', and tried to deal with it by measuring it along with everything else.[13] The turn to language gave rise to a specialist area of work called 'discursive psychology', and this strand of research often ends up producing studies that are effectively studies of 'discursive behaviour'.[14] This work is worth

---

[10] See, for example, the study by Crossley (2004). This research was conducted within the tradition of interpretative 'narrative psychology' but then attempted to include some psychoanalytic perspectives. On the outrageous interpretations and pathologising of gay sex in the Crossley study, see Barker et al. (in press).

[11] See Parker (2005a) for a discussion of the position of the researcher and questions of power. For an attempt to find alternative research strategies to subvert this privileged position of the researcher, see Lather (1995); it should be noted that Lather (1994) is working from within a tradition of radical education research, not psychology.

[12] See Hollway and Jefferson (2000) for this 'defensive' argument.

[13] The classic argument for this approach, of course, was made by the behaviourist psychologist, Skinner (1957). For Marxist defences of Skinner, see Burton and Kagan (1994) and Ulman (1991, 1996).

[14] One of the earliest texts in 'discursive psychology', and still the best introduction to the approach, appeared in 1980s British social psychology (Potter and Wetherell, 1987); there were some later interesting studies of racism, which included discussion of the role of ideology (Wetherell and Potter, 1992), but the concern with language as constitutive of reality (Potter, 1996) led the approach to its rather-self enclosed current status (see, for a clear statement, Potter, 1998). For discussion of the way strands of discourse analysis in psychology that draw on Foucault's work often misread it to play up the role of language, see Hook (2001). For illustrations of how discourse research can be used for political critique in psychology, see Burman et al. (1996) and Hansen et al. (2003).

taking seriously because some of the early studies of discourse did turn around and treat the discipline of psychology as comprising 'discourses' about people rather than 'facts' about their behaviour or cognitive processes. However, even in that critical work the study of 'discourse' tended to be disconnected from what was actually done to people, how they were materially affected by psychology as a discipline. As 'discursive psychology' has grown it has most-times only been interested in studying what people say.[15]

Discursive psychology declares that there is nothing outside the text

The 'discursive psychologists' now guard their own domain of study very carefully, stipulating exactly how speech should be transcribed and, most importantly, how the researcher should avoid straying into talking about anything else. In this way discursive psychology buys into the worst of academic specialisation in which each compartmentalised area of work refuses to have anything to do with other areas. Discursive psychology thus appears to pose a challenge to other kinds of psychology but only insofar as it redescribes phenomena of memory or decision-making as taking place in language; it thus ends up simply providing its own 'discursive' description that can then jostle alongside the other mainstream accounts.[16]

Discursive psychology declares that nothing is outside the text and refuses to study power.[17] One of the ways hard-line self-enclosed 'discourse analysis' fits neatly into psychology is in its methodological assumptions about observation and description. British psychology – the heartland of discourse analysis – has been guided by 'empiricism', in which only that which can be recorded by the scientist is worth taking seriously. In that tradition measurements of connections and

[15] For the view that the turn to language and to discourse may have been a 'necessary mistake' to open up a space for radical work, see Papadopoulos and Schraube (2004). For a critical account of this reduction to language in the discursive tradition, see Nightingale and Cromby (1999), and for an attempt to extend the analysis of discourse to other semiotically structured social phenomena, see Parker and the Bolton Discourse Network (1999).

[16] See Edwards (1992) for an account that goes only halfway toward a critique of cognitive psychology (that is, the step which redescribes cognitive processes in language). Compare this with political analyses of the use of cognitive psychology twenty years earlier (Shallice, 1984); see also Prilleltensky (1990).

[17] This insistence that there is 'nothing outside the text' worth talking about also leads to some weird misreadings of theory on 'deconstruction' outside psychology, and that theory is then used to underpin discursive psychology (see, e.g., Hepburn, 2000). For an example of discursive psychological objections to talking about 'politics' in such research on language, see Widdicombe (1995), and for a defence (in the same volume) of (feminist) politics, see Gill (1995).

regularities give rise to causal laws about human behaviour, and other necessary bits and pieces that are necessary for constructing theories – intervening variables and hypothetical constructs – are handled with care, even embarrassment. This is where discursive psychology has the edge on the traditional psychologists, because when they examine texts of conversations in great detail they are faithful to this old British prejudice about not talking about things you cannot see. Some discursive psychologists try and keep power on the agenda, but here they are going beyond the strict 'textual empiricism' that defines and limits this approach.[18]

Discursive psychology redescribes the 'social construction' of phenomena

Some discursive approaches take a psychological phenomenon and describe how it is spoken or written about in different contexts, and the conclusion is then repeated that this phenomenon is a 'social construction'. Roadways and prisons and political-economic systems are 'social constructions', of course; critical historical study by Marxists and feminists shows how they are constructed so we can better understand how to deconstruct them and collectively construct something else. The best social constructionist work shows through detailed historical study how objects and systems of objects have come to be the way they are; this treats the everyday world as problematic so that the activity of investigation is simultaneously an activity which challenges that everyday world and changes it.[19]

Discursive psychology, on the other hand, wipes away historical analysis and even the social context for the bits of text it analyses. What people say about something is pedantically repeated, and the functions of the talk spelled out to the reader; often the exercise is as pointless as it is mind-numbingly unilluminating. Where there is a concern with 'reflexivity' in this psychological version of discourse analysis it is not designed to facilitate the critical reflections of those who produce the texts – whether interview transcripts or 'naturally occurring interaction' – but of those who conduct the analysis. As with the use of 'free association' in the interpretative traditions, an activity that we would expect to be facilitated by the psychologist is

---

[18] For an exploration of 'Englishness' which serves to throw light on some of the assumptions about empirical research made by discursive psychologists, see Easthope (1999); and for a history of the development of discursive psychology that takes up these themes, see Parker (2004).

[19] From within feminist sociology, see Smith (1988, 1990).

actually reserved for the psychologists themselves. In discursive psychology this gives rise to all kinds of playful 'reflexive' studies that are academic exercises completely detached from the real world.[20]

Discursive psychology requires that adherents use a particular jargon

The battle to show that it is a legitimate part of the discipline rather than a critique has led discursive psychology to resort to its own quasi-scientific jargon, which it has borrowed from 'conversation analysis' in sociology.[21] The sociological conversation analysts are sometimes willing to provide training to their acolytes in psychology, on condition that there is no talk about politics; ideology and power are treated as too-abstract macro-political concepts that should not be used in their micro-analysis of conversation. Even so, there is often puzzlement on the part of these sociologists when they observe what an easy ride conversation analysis and discourse analysis are getting in psychology as compared to their own discipline.

One answer to this apparent puzzle is that the discipline of psychology has always liked its different component parts to distinguish themselves by the peculiar language they use. Now different discursive psychologists are showing themselves to be good, well behaved scientific researchers, recycling ordinary language into descriptions of 'adjacency pairs' (the sequence in which one person says 'hi' and the other says 'hi' back, for example) and 'extreme case formulations' (in which a point is exaggerated in order to better distance the speaker from it, for example). The analysis of discourse is thus reduced to a game of spotting different rhetorical devices. In this way discursive psychology becomes one of the recent procedures of 'verbal hygiene' in Western culture, in which language is attended to and clarified so that those who use it feel happy that they know exactly what is meant by it.[22]

[20] For one initially amusing but eventually tedious and pointless example, see Ashmore (1989); this is then the model for other discursive psychological discussions of reflexivity, and leads to its authors treating references to the Holocaust as a rhetorical argument designed to make life difficult for relativists in social science (see Edwards et al., 1995); for a critique and response, see Parker (1999e, 2002). For alternative views of 'reflexivity' in research, see Finlay and Gough (2003).

[21] For an example of sociological 'conversation analysis' turned to politics, see Atkinson's (1984) study of contrasts and three-part lists in conference speeches.

[22] A critical study of discourse is concerned with the ideological functions of 'verbal hygiene', rather than simply participating in it as the discursive psychologists do; on 'verbal hygiene', see Cameron (1995), and for further analyses of the role accorded to 'communication' today, see Cameron (2000).

The New Form of 'Critical Psychology' Only Appears
to Provide Something Radical

There have always been internal critiques of psychology, with fierce internal battles by women and people of colour against the way the discipline normalises human behaviour around a masculine white norm. Lesbian and gay psychologists as well as people with disabilities and diagnostic labels of 'mental illness' have challenged the theories and practices of academics and professionals. Sometimes they have mobilised under the banner of 'radical psychology',[23] and often they have been ignored, burnt out or tamed by the discipline. One of the latest manifestations of unease at what the discipline does to people is 'critical psychology'. Meanwhile, alternative 'qualitative' methods of the new-paradigm researchers have been taken on board bit by bit as part of the armoury of the discipline. Qualitative researchers make a virtue out of interviewing people and giving them more space to talk than the old laboratory methods, and in the process they overlook the fact that some of the experimental approaches were used by radicals and were effectively already 'critical' psychology.[24]

Critical psychology disturbs the traditional psychologists

Those who call themselves 'critical psychologists' now come in different varieties, some more radical than others, but someone looking for help is unlikely to come across a 'critical psychologist' as such. This is because critical psychology is an academic pursuit, engaging in historical study of the assumptions made by the discipline or promoting alternative accounts of subjectivity. Sometimes the 'critical psychologists' will draw on Marxism or feminism, but they are happiest with newer shinier 'theory' which they can use to provoke and annoy the traditional psychologists.

The theory sometimes amounts to little more than a recycling of obscure continental philosophy, jargonised psychoanalysis or mind-boggling talk of 'rhizomes' and 'lines of flight' that deliberately refuses

[23] See, for example, Brown (1973), for an example from the US, and Heather (1976) for a UK text; for an argument for 'critical social psychology' before the current wave of interest in this speciality in the English-speaking world, see Wexler (1983).

[24] See, for example, the argument that laboratory-experiments reproduce a certain form of power, critical analysis of which can tell us about the nature of power in capitalist society (Reicher, 1997); for critical uses of behaviourist 'experimental' procedures in 'constructing' behaviour, see Cullen et al. (1981), and for 'planning' of community care which includes a discussion of the Skinnerian-Marxist 'Comunidad Los Horcones' in Mexico, see Cullen (1991).

to explain exactly what it is about. It does not make sense to ask of many of these academic parlour games whether they will actually be of any use to people.[25] When 'deconstruction' has been taken up as a buzz-word from philosophy via literary theory it has sometimes served as a way of introducing some radical perspectives into psychology, but this has then incited some psychologists to argue that politics should really be prohibited if one is to be faithful to what deconstruction really is in its 'original' state.[26]

Critical psychology often amounts to the formation of a new 'sub-discipline'

Since the wave of protests against psychology in the 1960s that was based in the anti-capitalist and anti-psychiatry movements, psychology has massively expanded. In the US, for example, it is possible for every weird and wonderful speciality to find adherents and push for membership of the American Psychological Association (APA) in a particular designated division to keep them occupied. The 'critical psychologists' have not yet made their mark in this way in the APA, but they have a presence in many countries outside the US, and they sometimes like to think of themselves as constituting a 'sub-discipline' of psychology.[27]

Many academic departments are run like seaside zoos, and there is sometimes now a hope that at least one, and preferably no more than one, 'critical psychologist' will be attracted and hired. The label has actually served to marginalise feminist psychologists who were already developing a more sustained critique of the discipline.[28] Critical psychology increasingly operates as a catch-all label to

[25] See Deleuze and Guattari (1977) for an account and celebration of 'rhizomatic' horizontal connections. For an interesting use of these ideas to critique traditional social psychology, see Brown and Lunt (2002).
[26] The flurry of books 'deconstructing' this and that in psychology was part of a fashionable co-option of theory from outside psychology (see, e.g., in chronological order: Parker and Shotter, 1990; Burman, 1994; Parker et al., 1995; Burman, 1998; Parker, 1999b), and the attempt to depoliticise it is evident in Hepburn's (1999) response; this perspective then mars Hepburn's (2003) text on 'critical psychology' (a text which caricatures and dismisses Marxist approaches).
[27] For critical perspectives on, and alternatives to, psychology around the world, see Dafermos et al. (2006).
[28] The spate of studies concerned with feminism and discourse in psychology was symptomatic of this (see, e.g., Wilkinson and Kitzinger, 1995); later on feminist research in psychology was often treated as a subset of 'critical psychology'; for an argument for feminist psychology as such in this context, see Wilkinson (1997), and for an argument that lesbian and gay psychology is already 'critical psychology', see Kitzinger (1999).

mean anyone who does something different from mainstream laboratory-experimental psychology.[29]

Positive alternatives chime with positive psychology in pragmatic postmodernism

Theories of 'postmodernism' have been a boon for critical psychologists, for they are able to move on from the claim to be bringing about a scientific paradigm revolution in the discipline to something much more grandiose. Arguments about the supposed transformation of contemporary society into a 'postmodern condition' of culture have been packaged in many different ways, and psychologists have tended to make the most optimistic reading of postmodernism.[30] For them, old traditional psychology was rooted in a 'modern' political-economic system that lasted from about the beginning of the nineteenth century up to the late twentieth century. With postmodernism, the story goes, we have moved beyond the search for scientific or personal 'truth' or 'progress'.[31] Some critical psychologists use postmodern ideas to argue that the modern age is now finished, and finished with it, of course, is modern psychology.

The risk is that the 'postmodern condition' of culture is then seen as one in which scientific talk is just another language game. Postmodernity is seen as a kind of culture where everything is a 'social construction' and then we are back to discourse and discursive psychology is the only game in town. Postmodern psychologists would want to see many stories about psychology flourish without any particular stories being privileged over the others, and they argue that postmodern culture encourages us to enjoy the multiplicity of experience that these many stories permit.

It is true that postmodern ideas do corrode scientific psychology from within, and these arguments undermine everything the

[29] There are, at the same time, attempts to use the banner of 'critical psychology' to open a space for radical political arguments; see, for example, Fox and Prilleltensky (1997), Sloan (2000) and Hook (2004); in 'critical social psychology', see Gough and McFadden (2001), Hepburn (2003) and Tuffin (2004).

[30] Lyotard (1984) provided one of the most systematic arguments for a 'postmodern condition', and Gergen (1991) responded with one of the most enthusiastic liberal pragmatist arguments for this new postmodern culture; for a (post-)Marxist version of this argument, see Newman and Holzman (1997). For a Marxist account of postmodernism as the 'cultural logic of late capitalism', see Jameson (1991), and for a critical analysis of the notion, see Callinicos (1989).

[31] Parker (1989) makes this argument, and seems at the time to have been rather besotted with 'postmodernism' as a radical alternative to 'modern' psychology. For an edited collection on the relationship between psychology and postmodernism, see Kvale (1992).

discipline aimed for. However, psychologists are just as canny as postmodernists, and now they are able to play them at their own game. The 'postmodern' critical psychologists say that everything is a language game and that we should just be concerned with how things work, and the positive psychologists reply that they are happy to just make things work well too.[32] These ideas have been helpful sometimes, but they can also lead to a hopelessly idealist view of the possibilities for change at an individual level, making it seem as if people can become different if only they speak differently about themselves. The lesson is that we do need to draw upon accounts of cultural change, but we need to actively participate in those debates instead of just borrowing ideas from sociology and importing them to try and solve problems in such a way as to reinforce the secure boundaries around the discipline of psychology.

'Action Research' in Community Psychology Is Not Always Radical Politics

It is quite understandable that some radicals in psychology who are committed to social action are impatient with interpretative, discursive and critical psychologies; these seem to them to be overly theoretical, elitist frameworks that interpret the world rather than change it. Action research, in contrast, appeals to them because it appears to be concerned with grass-roots organising and it promises to 'empower' people to work together in communities. Action research-oriented community psychologists have a lot of sympathy with the attempt to build something more constructive than the 'deconstructive' critical work seems to do. However, we have to ask what it means to do something 'constructive' that will be acceptable to psychology; the emphasis on 'community' can end up as a practice that is clap-happy and coercive.[33]

'Action research' often reinforces an existing 'community structure'

Before any 'action research' with a 'community' can begin, the academic or professional psychologist has to deal with the fact that funding agendas of the researchers lead to attempts to monitor and control communities. The community psychologist has to work within the constraints of an agenda that is defined outside of the

---

[32] For a detailed critical account of the role of postmodernism in psychology, see Parker (1998a), and for responses and further discussion, see Parker (2002).

[33] For interventions in community psychology that have raised questions of political violence, see Duckett (2005).

particular community they choose to work with. It is, of course, possible that a psychologist may spend time carrying out 'action research' that is not part of a funded project, but this is the exception rather than the rule. In those cases the 'psychologist' is effectively operating as a community activist, which is fine. What we are concerned with here is what happens when they operate as a *psychologist*; in this way the funding agendas lead to a closer monitoring and reporting of what a community is up to that is nearer to social control than to 'empowerment'.[34]

Down this road class politics is prohibited because it will upset the cosy relationship the action researcher wants to strike up with representatives of the community, and class struggle disrupts the ideological self-image that a community or society uses to assure itself that all is well. Anti-racist politics similarly draws attention to axes of oppression and privilege, but when a community psychologist attempts to intervene they can only do so by trying to identify different 'communities'. In this way the problem is simply reproduced as each of those 'communities' is reinforced in such a way as to suffocate dissent. The politics of gender and sexuality is then rendered difficult because the researcher threatens to draw attention to patterns of violence that usually remain hidden.[35] At some point a 'community psychologist' must face the charge of being a traitor; either the 'action research' will end up betraying those who suffer in the community the researcher has contracted to work with, or they will betray the community representatives who let them into the community in the first place.[36]

Good citizens are identified who will engage in projects and building of 'social capital'

'Action research' was once a favourite with colonial powers because observation, interference and control were much more efficient when it was possible to better understand local 'native' perceptions of the colonising power.[37] As important as the explicit colonial relations between the observers and those they want to study are, internal

---

[34] For discussions of ideological dimensions of 'empowerment', see Bhavnani (1990), Kagan and Burton (1996) and Riger (1993).
[35] See Burman (2005) for a discussion of 'minoritisation' as a process rather than an identity, and Burman and Chantler (2002) for a discussion of research on this process and violence against women.
[36] For a discussion of 'action research' perspectives in relation to critical psychological research and those who are 'disabled' by a community, see Goodley and Parker (2000).
[37] For a discussion of the historical connections between social anthropology, ethnographic research and colonialism, see Clifford and Marcus (1986).

power relations also hold an oppressed community in place. Colonial power tended to cultivate a layer of obedient servants who would be granted special privileges and encouraged to think they were better than the rest of their community, perhaps even coming to believe that they were nearly as worthy as those who controlled them.

The notion of 'community' entails an assessment of who is a good, genuine member of the community and who is not. Those who participate in the community are then viewed as the good citizens who should be supported, and the way to deal with those who do not participate is to bring them into the community. The neoliberal agenda of privatising services and forcing people to fall back on their own resources thus fits very neatly into the ethos of 'action research'. Both government and community psychologists are keen to help people build up networks and 'social capital', by which they mean forms of informal welfare support and entrepreneurial opportunities that are all that those without any real 'capital' have access to.[38]

Those who do not fit, who refuse to appreciate the inquiry,
are pathologised

There is an uncanny correspondence between the agendas of the community psychologists and pragmatic 'positive' psychologists. They are so keen to be 'constructive' that they emphasise questions about what 'works' rather than what problems people actually face. The narrative-based 'appreciative inquiry' techniques that encourage people to speak about their lives in more positive ways are pernicious examples of this trend.[39] Those who will not play this game because they already have a political critique and wish to link theory and practice to change social conditions are thus at risk of being treated as bad-tempered destructive types.

The notion of 'community' is always to some degree suffocating for those who would like to think and act differently, and community leaders are usually respected worthy types who think that they have the right to speak for everyone. The community psychologist is very quickly caught in the trap of ratifying existing power structures in a community, and they have to keep the leaders sweet if they want cooperation in their research. Those who are happy to work with the researchers thus maintain the silence and oppression of those who

---

[38] See Cooke and Kothari (2001) for an international collection that shows the way that 'participation' demanded of communities by 'action researchers' can be oppressive and reproduce colonial control.
[39] See Cooperrrider and Whitney (2005) for an appreciative account.

might cause trouble for the notion that they are really a 'community'. The situation of those who are 'disabled' by existing social arrangements is a case in point, and some of the most radical developments have come from disability 'action research'.[40] That research had to develop outside psychology, however, and the only way to keep contradiction, struggle and change on the agenda is to keep clear of psychology or of the psychologisation of communities.

'Community psychology', then, often glues together the two terms 'community' and 'psychology' in such a way as to psychologise what a community is – to treat the community as something that can be conceptualised and studied by psychologists on their own terms – and then to use that psychologised image of the community to understand the individuals that comprise it. Many well-meaning community psychologists make exactly this mistake in a bizarre double-move that betrays all of the good things they hope to do with a community. Some of them do not, but when they do not they have to abandon dominant images of psychology and community and find something better.[41]

Each Alternative Is Still Trapped Within the Disciplinary Agendas of Psychology

Psychologists nowadays want to be liked and they want people to like their colleagues in academic inquiry, but they are caught up in a discipline that is reactionary and unpleasant and which people should be suspicious of. While people outside psychology are often already suspicious of the rather ridiculous laboratory-experimental studies that break up behaviour so that it can be measured and integrated into a psychological theory, they are sometimes impressed when new methodologies that promise to respect their own experience are described. It is all the more necessary to examine these new methodologies very closely, and to show how interpretation, discourse, critical perspectives and action research still remain mired in psychology and in the process of psychologisation in capitalist society.

---

[40] See Goodley and Lawthom (2004).

[41] On the temptation to dissolve oneself in a 'community' and lose any critical distance from the political structure and contradictions that constitute a community, see Jiménez-Domínguez (1996). For the argument that the naming of a 'community' always functions to close down distinctions, see Badiou (2001); and for a discussion of Badiou's ideas in relation to psychology, see Parker (2005b).

The psychologists need to be empowered, interpreted,
read and politicised

Many of the new ideas in psychology come from other disciplines, but they are carefully filtered so that they will be acceptable to psychological conceptions of the 'individual' and 'society'. Political perspectives that would show the way to challenge that separation between the individual and society are prohibited, for they throw the project of psychology as a discipline of social control into question.

A psychologist who says that they are different from the rest of their colleagues and who promises to do something different does need some help. It is useful to examine the discipline that frames how they speak and act in order to encourage them to find the strength to break from psychology. Their actions need to be interpreted very closely, and the texts they produce should be read with care and discussed with them. In this way it might be possible to politicise them.

The task is to reconnect with historical
political changes in psychology

The concern with turning the dumb non-psychologists into good citizens who would be grateful to those in the discipline who have given away their knowledge is a conservative response to political problems in psychology. It not only betrays the hopes of those outside the discipline who thought that psychology would have something interesting and useful to say about alienation, it also betrays the activities of those who have really tried to put politics on the agenda.

Radical psychologists have occasionally been active in political struggle, and while they have usually tried to bring psychological knowledge to bear on the movements for change that they have participated in, they have sometimes also tried to prioritise social change over psychological interpretation.[42] There is a history of struggle in psychology for something better than the reductionist models and practices that reinforce alienation; this struggle has been inspired by revolutions outside psychology. We look at the impact of these revolutions on radical theory and practice inside psychology next.

[42] See, e.g., Finison (1976) on US American psychologists' responses to unemployment in the 1930s, and Finison (1977) for mobilisation in support of the Republicans during the Spanish Civil War.

8

Historical, Personal and Political: Psychology and Revolution

The development of psychology has often been interrupted by events beyond its control, and these historical events still mark the discipline today. Rather than simply treat revolutions as historical traces of times past, we can turn to them as key elements in the collective memory of psychology, attending to them as part of a 'history of the present'. The standard history of psychology is a partial view elaborated from a particular standpoint, and the way we retell it from the standpoint of the oppressed has consequences for how we think about ourselves. This chapter is about revolutions that forced psychologists to rethink what they were up to, and about how radical ideas that once affected the discipline survive today.

Internal critiques inside psychology mirror dominant debates

Each of the revolutionary shocks to the discipline we will describe in this chapter had the effect of breaking down the compartmentalisation of the discipline into separate areas of study. Such areas as developmental psychology, the psychology of language, social psychology and psychoanalytic psychology are usually treated as if they could be sealed off from each other. Psychology of women, biological psychology, cognitive psychology and theories of consciousness are divided off into competing specialities. The connections that are made in 'interdisciplinary' research usually serve to reinforce dominant ideological views of what people are.

Challenges to the dominant ideology that occurred during revolutions have also necessarily been challenges to psychology. Revolution shakes up the categories that we use to make sense of experience; it shows how artificial but compelling is the separation between the 'individual' and the 'social' under capitalism, and the activity of changing while interpreting the world reveals that our individuality is social through and through. The challenge to

147

psychology's alienating separation of people from each other and of our sense of our selves from our creative capacities also entails a challenge to the image of mind and behaviour as compartmentalised into separate areas of study. Simple 'interdisciplinary' research that tries to patch together the separate components is no longer good enough, and neither is 'intradisciplinary' research that respects the existence of academic sub-divisions in psychology.[1]

Alternatives appear when there are political crises that force psychologists to change

Revolutions turn received wisdoms on their head, but a revolution is not only a time of chaotic upheaval. It is not a nihilistic abolition of everything that went before, and that mistaken image of a revolution is an ideological warrant for maintaining law and order as it is now so that the privileged and powerful are the ones who defend civilisation against barbarism. In fact, that way of viewing revolution – as if it were an irrational breakdown of civilised life when the mob overwhelms rational decision-making – is a deeply 'psychological' way of looking at change.[2] It is an image of change that is fearful of what will happen if people take their lives into their own hands.

A revolution is an opportunity for discovering new ways of living, of bringing to the fore aspects of human creativity and hope that are usually suppressed. Artistic and scientific achievements and the material conditions in which it is possible to overcome the separation between 'work' and 'leisure' are transformed and extended by revolution, not done away with. At the same time as existing systems of knowledge are re-evaluated, revolution is an opportunity to take stock of what can be conserved from the old ways of understanding the world. It is at those moments that the disciplines like psychology which make a virtue of individual isolation are shaken to the core, and we can start to see something completely different emerge.[3]

---

[1] Curt (1994) tried to disrupt the way 'interdisciplinary' research operates to reify each separate disciplinary component in their appeal for 'transdisciplinary' research in social psychology; the book is a weird mixture of social constructionism and quantitative research written by a collective whose name 'Beryl Curt' was designed to parody and subvert British psychology's allegiance to the work of Cyril Burt.

[2] Le Bon's (1896) work on the crowd is the most influential text, and it was followed up by a number of psychological studies of the dangers of instincts of the 'herd' and the 'group mind' (see, e.g., Trotter, 1991; McDougall, 1927).

[3] Marxist attempts in psychology to address the nature of 'everyday life' have been concerned with the impact of routine and revolution on consciousness, and they usually find standard psychological theory to be of little use (see, e.g., Hayes, 1996; Hoggett, 1996); for good recent work on this topic which draws more extensively on social theory and political action as reference points, see Bratsis (2006) and Stephenson and Papadopoulos (2006).

A New Focus on Activity Appeared in the 1917 Russian Revolution

The October Revolution in 1917 was an event that was rather unexpected for many traditional Marxists (especially those who treated Marxism as an academic pursuit or a quasi-religious worldview), as well as for the ruling class. Those Marxists who held to the idea that feudal regimes would be replaced by capitalist ones before there was the possibility of socialist revolution saw these apparent 'stages' of history compressed and leapfrogged. Alternative conceptions of 'combined and uneven development' of the capitalist centres and the 'underdeveloped' periphery could now make better sense of what happened in Russia. These alternative conceptions rooted in the practice of changing Russian society showed that it would be impossible to develop the revolution on its own, as 'socialism in one country'.[4] The revolutionary changes included innovations in art, science and personal life, with laws relating to marriage, sexuality and childhood overturned and recognition given to the rights of those oppressed by the old regime. The revolutionary changes from 1917 through to the early 1920s were wide-ranging, but the isolation of the new regime and the crystallisation of the bureaucracy under Stalin saw repression of those who would not toe the party line. In the domain of personal life too, many progressive changes in the position of women, for example, were reversed, and Stalin reinforced his power by appealing once again to the old reactionary values of the 'nation' and the 'family'.[5]

Vygotsky's research in Russia led to new notions of development and language

The revolution was the context for new ideas about childhood that challenged fixed ideas about ages and 'stages'. The revolution confounded those who expected history to develop through an ordered sequence, and so developmental psychologists were also sensitised to the possibility of sudden qualitative changes as a child started to learn language. Language itself became viewed anew, not merely as a medium for communicating ideas from one individual's head to another, but as a collective social process through which people are

[4] For a history of the revolution by an insider that makes these points, see Trotsky (1977), and for an analysis of the rise of the bureaucracy, see Trotsky (1973).

[5] See, for example, Colletti's (1970) account of the revival of the old Tsarist ideology of nation and family under Stalin; see also Zaretsky (1976) for a discussion of implications for Marxist and feminist politics.

able to think about themselves and others. Our sense of individuality and separate 'psychology' is an effect of certain forms of language and ways of speaking it.[6]

We can see a contrast between the mainstream psychological theories of development that are still popular in US American and European textbooks based on the work of the Swiss psychologist Jean Piaget, and the work of the Russian psychologist Lev Vygotsky. Piaget saw internal 'cognitive' development leading the child to the point when they would learn language and move from individual 'egocentric' thinking into social relations with others. Vygotsky, on the other hand, showed how thought was separated off from language, and the 'individual' became separated off from collective activity, though still dependent on it.[7] A theory of language was fused with a theory of development to give rise to a quite new image of the human being as social through and through; it was a revolutionary psychology.[8]

The development of activity theory attempted to redefine what psychology was

Vygotsky's ideas were neither idiosyncratic nor context-free, any more than the thinking of an individual is separate from other people around them. His ideas were part of debates about the nature of language which treated it as a shared 'semiotic' system of meanings in which each element is defined by its relation with the other elements and by struggle between social classes and other social categories.[9] A wide-ranging redefinition of the relationship between language and 'development' was then elaborated by a set of approaches that are often grouped together under the label 'activity theory'.[10]

Instead of homing in on objects that appeared to be separated because they had been so thoroughly 'reified', turned into things,

[6] See Friedman (1990) on the 1920s Soviet Union as a backdrop for the development of Vygotsky's ideas.
[7] See Vygotsky (1962) for a rather truncated translation of one of his key works for a US American audience. Bickley (1977) discusses Vygotsky's work as a 'dialectical materialist' psychology. Walkerdine (1982) reviews and elaborates this distinction between Piaget and Vygotsky.
[8] For the argument that this was a 'revolutionary psychology', see Newman and Holzman (1993); see also Holzman (1996) on how Vygotsky's work should be 'completed' (by Newman). For a classic statement of this particular Marxist-Vygotskian alternative in psychology, see Hood and Newman (1983), and for a more current account of where Newman's work is going, see Holzman and Mendez (2003).
[9] Valentin Vološinov's (1973) revolutionary work on language is discussed by Greenslade (1996).
[10] See Holzman (2006) for a collection of papers that reviews the current status of Vygotskian and activity theory perspectives.

the complex dialectical relationships between things became the focus of study. This provides a way of thinking about alienation as the separation of thought from language and a consequence of treating such things as 'intelligence' and 'cognition' as measurable and then defining characteristics of one's individual identity. Vygotsky died in 1934, shortly before the Stalinist terror reached its height, and the activity theorists then had to adapt and adjust their work to escape too-close attention from the bureaucracy.[11]

Marxist work in France redefined personality in relation to work

The existence of the Soviet Union gave confidence to liberation movements fighting for independence from the Western imperialist powers, this at the very same time as the Stalinist bureaucracy tried to enforce its own rule over those it tactically supported. The existence of strong pro-Soviet communist parties in different parts of the world was also a mixed blessing for left-wing activists and scholars. The relationship between the imperialist powers and the old colonies was changed by the existence of the Soviet Union which, for all of the attempts of the bureaucracy to keep things under control, gave hope to those struggling against colonialism. The work of the radical psychiatrist Frantz Fanon is a case in point; originally from Martinique, he worked in Algeria alongside the liberation movement against French occupation and wrote about the effects of colonisation on what became the 'internal' world of the colonised and coloniser.[12]

In France, the communist party twisted and turned at the behest of the Soviet bureaucracy and conducted its own purges and witchhunts of dissidents; but at the same time it provided a space for relaying some of the innovations from revolutionary Russia and for elaborating these in relation to Marxist theory. The work of Lucien Sève redefining 'personality' is one key example.[13] Sève built on the Marxist insight that there is no 'essence' of the human being that could be captured and defined for all time by psychology, but that the human being was 'an ensemble of the social relations'.[14]

[11] For quite a good account of Vygotsky's ideas, see Kozulin (1989), and for a more extended (if at times quite reactionary) treatment of the wider context for Vygotsky's work, see Kozulin (1994).

[12] See Fanon (1967, 1970). Heartfield (2002) provides an interesting argument that the Algerian struggle was crucial to the development of existentialist and then 'post-structuralist' theory in France.

[13] Sève (1978); for an account of Sève's work, see Shames (1981); for a more critical account of the place of Sève's work in the context of the French communist party, see O'Donnell (1982).

[14] Marx (1845) uses this phrase in his 'Theses on Feuerbach'.

The work of the Russian activity theorists was thus taken forward to understand how 'personality' was linked to work, and how a worker's creative life was distorted by the time that was sold in capitalist society to an employer.[15]

German 'critical psychology' redefined activity, and then 'memory'

In West Germany the pro-Soviet communist party was in a much more difficult situation after the Second World War than its counterpart in France. However, while communists were often forced underground in the West – with ultra-leftists embarking on disastrous individual terrorist activities to try and shake things up – the proximity of East Germany did provide some intellectual comfort for some radicals. Again, we can see the paradoxical contradictory role of the Soviet bloc as condition of possibility of *and* obstacle to left-wing movements.

The student rebellions in the 1960s inspired a previously quite traditional psychologist, Klaus Holzkamp in West Berlin, to draw on and redefine activity theory.[16] More importantly, a large left-wing alternative psychology movement developed known as *Kritische Psychologie*, and this provided an audience for Holzkamp's work on a new Marxist 'science of the subject' with a focus on 'action potence'.[17] The work was taken forward by the Marxist-feminist Frigga Haug with a collective group methodology of 'memory work'. This notion of 'collective memory' is quite different from the studies of individual memory in psychology.[18]

A New Focus on Power Appeared After the 1968 Events in France

The May events in Paris, student and worker rebellions that were repeated around the world at the end of the 1960s, were as much a surprise to the left as they were to the French ruling class. Some

[15] See Leonard (1984) for an attempt to apply Sève's work in the context of British social work.

[16] Tolman (1994) provides an excellent introduction to Holzkamp's work and the political background to the development of German 'critical psychology'; for an account of this strand of critical psychology now in Germany, see Held (2006), and in Austria, see Sanin (2006).

[17] The collection by Tolman and Maiers (1991) is the most useful guide to the range of work in this tradition in English; for a brief account, see Maiers and Tolman (1996), and see Holzkamp (1992).

[18] See Haug (1987, 2000) for examples and theoretical discussion of 'memory work'.

of the first sparks for the student revolt – protests against segregation of the sexes in halls of residence – already indicated how important the link was between the policing of personal life and the big political issues of state power. As the student rebellion spread, links were made with strikes at car factories on the outskirts of Paris and in other parts of France. This revolutionary movement was in many ways to the left of the left, connecting with struggles around sex and sexual orientation, against racism and symbolic forms of power. The 'situationists', for example, aimed to disrupt the 'society of the spectacle' that bewitched and pacified individuals; and the slogans of the student movement reflected their romantic vision of something radical forcing its way up against state and personal repression.[19] As they ripped up the cobbles of Paris streets and threw them at the police it really did seem as if the slogan 'beneath the paving stones, the beach' could be true. After law and order was restored, however, the cynical response from the reactionary 'new philosophers' was that, human nature being what it was, the students should have recognised the harder truth that it was a case of 'below the beach, the paving stones'. Psychology, challenged by the events, was also back on track.

Foucault's work on madness traced the division between reason and irrationality

Some members of the French communist party and particularly its youth wing supported the revolts, but the leadership wanted to head off a revolution that was out of its control and prevent challenges to the party's authority. During the 1968 events Michel Foucault, who had trained as a clinical psychologist and carried out forensic work in prisons in the 1950s,[20] was teaching in Tunisia but was already caught up in events there, sheltering students protesting against the regime.[21] Foucault had left the communist party in 1953, partly because of anti-Semitism in the Stalinised communist parties immediately following the death of Stalin and partly because of Stalinist homophobia.[22] Already, the political and personal were intertwined in his own politics and then in his theoretical work.

[19] See Debord (1977) for analysis of the society of the spectacle, and Plant (1993) for a history and analysis of the impact of Debord and situationism.
[20] See Parker (1995b) for one brief account of Foucault's background in psychology.
[21] See Macey's (1994) intellectual biography for an account of Foucault's time in Tunis.
[22] For an account of this, see Macey (1994).

Foucault's work on the history of 'madness' and the way modern civilisation divides 'reason' from those aspects of human experience that are unbearable and disruptive, was still indebted to Marxism.[23] His work showed how 'madness' and the irrational stuff became reified, turned into an 'unconscious' to be deciphered by psycho-analysts, and in this way Foucault provided an alternative to versions of psychoanalysis that simply focused on what was repressed inside each individual.[24] Even though his work was cited by the 'anti-psychiatry' movement, he did not romanticise madness as if it were an essentially truthful experience bursting to be released from the chains of reason.[25]

Involvement with prison struggles led to new work on discipline and punishment

The real turning point came when Foucault was involved in rebellions by some of the movements that had emerged from the 1968 events. Prisoners, organised to protest against brutal dehumanising conditions, were given a voice by groups like the Group for Information on Prisons, which Foucault was part of. This practical involvement led him to write a ground-breaking book, *Discipline and Punish*, in which he showed how prison-like forms of surveillance had emerged in modern society from the beginning of the nineteenth century.[26]

The monitoring and recording of each individual was part of an apparatus of control in which people came to have a sense of them-selves as being observed even when they were not. A key discipline in this apparatus of individuation and control was the one that Foucault had been first trained in, psychology. Foucault's account of power as something that held people in relations of subjection to authority, as opposed to being a force that some individuals deliber-ately wielded over others, was actually still quite Marxist. Marx himself had not tried to explain why individual capitalists wickedly exploited poor workers; that kind of 'psychological' explanation was refused in favour of a political-economic explanation of how people came to be conscious of who they were inside particular historically

[23] Foucault (1991) reflects on the impact of Marx in his work in a series of interviews.
[24] Miller (1989) provides a (psychoanalytic) appraisal of Foucault's complex relationship to psychoanalysis; for a good Marxist critique of psychoanalysis, see Timpanaro (1976).
[25] Deleuze and Guattari (1977) come pretty close to such a romanticising of schizophrenia, mainly as a reaction to forms of psychoanalysis that seemed to demonise it.
[26] See Foucault (1977) for the analysis of surveillance in nineteenth-century capitalist society.

specific power relations. That is precisely why they need to interpret the world if they want to change it.

Studies of sexuality led to accounts of confession as linked with power

Foucault showed how a 'psychological' explanation was part of the problem, how it obscured what was really at stake. His historical analysis of 'sexuality' then turned to the stuff that seemed to be 'repressed' by power. People came to believe that there was something genuine and liberating under the surface – at times of revolution it was indeed as if 'under the paving stones, the beach'. This analysis throws new light on the allocation of biological males and females to their different historically constructed sexed bodies, and so on the entire concern with 'sex differences' in psychology. It also opens up questions of sexual orientation and moves beyond categories of 'heterosexuality' and 'homosexuality' as separate life-paths.

The lure of this appealing notion drew people into forms of therapy where they thought that if they spoke freely about it something would be released and they would be happier and healthier. Foucault showed how 'discipline' in psychology was accompanied by 'confession' as the smiling empathic face of the professional which invites someone to tell all and persuades them that they will feel better for it.

A new notion of subjectivity as historically constituted challenged psychology

The link between discipline and confession has provided a new way of thinking about the activity of psychologists – they are part of the system whether they like it or not, and all the more so when they try to be nice with it – and also about psychology itself. Foucault showed how it was possible to develop a completely different notion of the individual 'subject' and our reflexive understanding of our own subjectivity. His work is sometimes caricatured as entailing the 'death of the subject',[27] but what he produced was a 'history of the present' as a history that started from the way we are and showed how it had come to be like that.[28]

---

[27] For this argument, see Foucault's (1970) conclusion to *The Order of Things*; it is the 'figure' of man as a conceptual reference-point for explanations of how knowledge is produced that he throws into question, not individual human beings, and critics often seem to quite deliberately and obtusely overlook this distinction.

[28] Blackman (1994) gives a clear account for psychologists of Foucault's critical reworking of history as a 'history of the present' and of his development of 'genealogy' as a form of historical research and writing.

This work has been a liability to some Marxists, who see in it a threat to their own notions of leadership and power, but it has been an inspiration to critical Marxists and others for understanding aspects of the revolutionary process. His work is a particularly bitter blow against the Stalinist tradition in Marxist politics, and draws attention to residues of the impact of that tradition on the way that Maoist and some Trotskyist groups claiming allegiance to revolutionary Marxism form and maintain their organisations.[29] For all the problems in Foucault's work, it still provides a conceptual resource for re-energising genuine revolutionary politics, and shows how the fate of individual subjectivity is bound up with that social process.[30]

A New Focus on Nature Appeared from 1970s
Second Wave Feminism in the US

In US America the early communist activity of workers seeking an alternative to capitalism was more quickly and easily wiped out than in Europe. A combination of a tightly organised local communist party loyal to the Soviet Union and McCarthyite witch-hunts directed at those involved in 'un-American activities' after the Second World War made life very difficult for Marxists. Psychologists who did identify as Marxists had to be very careful, and it would have seemed outlandish to try and develop a 'Marxist psychology' there.[31] Expressions of discontent with capitalism took different forms, with a variety of movements building a critique of the status quo that focused on racial oppression or sexual exploitation. Anti-racist protests have found their way into academic work; they have been absorbed to an extent in psychology, and they now inspire 'postcolonial theory' which radicals in psychology might nonetheless still learn from. However, it has been socialist feminists

---

[29] Little surprise that it was from inside Stalinism that those disenchanted with what they saw as old authoritarian 'revolutionary' politics mistakenly turned to reformist social democratic 'Eurocommunism' as if it was an alternative. Given their experience of what 'Marxist' party politics was, it is understandable that they should conclude that the only way to go was into a form of 'post-Marxism' (see, e.g., Laclau and Mouffe, 2001). For an analysis of the impact of the lack of democracy inside the Stalinist tradition combined with the centrifugal logic of 'socialism in one country', see Mandel (1978).

[30] See Sawacki (1991) for a feminist critique of Foucault.

[31] See Harris (1990) for a survey of psychology in relation to the left in the US, and Harris (1996) for a discussion of the historical relationship between psychology and Marxism in the US.

from the 'second wave'[32] of the movement in the 1970s that have addressed connections between personal life and political struggle, and their work shook psychology. Analyses of the capitalist system as woven together and reinforced by 'patriarchy' as a system of oppression, in which men dominate women and older men dominate younger men, were very disturbing to the male psychologists. Now the critique has subsided and capitalism has found ways to incorporate women as managers and cover over what was most radical about feminism with the ideology of 'postfeminism'.[33]

Feminist studies of primatology raised questions about the construction of 'nature'

Detailed reading of 'primate research' showed that our ideas about 'nature' in psychology appear to be derived from studies of primate behaviour but those studies actually read into monkey behaviour our own culturally specific ideological presumptions.[34] Studies of attachment in baby monkeys, separated from their mothers and then forced to relate to wire-mesh substitutes, are an important part of Donna Haraway's work. Male control of reproduction is structured not only into the descriptions that the researcher Harry Harlow gives of 'primitive' behaviour, but in the very way in which the studies were set up. Isolated female monkeys were unable to conceive because of the peculiar conditions to which they had already been subjected, for example. They were artificially impregnated by use of what Harlow and colleagues refer to as a 'rape rack'.

Haraway showed how masculine fantasies of control of women's 'nature' were reproduced in the 'motherless monkey studies' to make it seem like Harlow had discovered this 'nature' when he was actually constructing it. This is 'second nature' which functions ideologically to oppress women, and which makes them seem more 'primitive', closer to nature than men.[35] This detailed study of

[32] 'First wave' struggles took place in the early years of the century, mainly around the right to vote; the 'second wave' was galvanised by the 1960s revolts, and the 'third wave' with the turn to the twenty-first century. See Rowbotham (1973) for histories of the first two waves, and Zavos et al. (2005) for material on the 'third wave' (particularly in relation to feminist activism around psychology).

[33] See Gamble (2001) for debates within feminism, and Eisenstein (1996) for an account of what it might mean in practice (focusing on femocrats in Australia).

[34] See Haraway (1990) for this detailed analysis of primatology and of the conclusions that psychologists draw from it.

[35] See Burman (1994) for an account of how this work functions ideologically in developmental psychology.

primatology thus showed the importance of differentiating between underlying biological, natural processes – a 'first nature' that cannot ever be captured and shown exactly as it is precisely because a description of it has to be in a particular language infused with cultural and ideological preconceptions – and 'second nature'. Psychological research too often pretends to be describing nature in the raw when it is actually recycling images of 'second nature', something that feels deep and permanent but which can be challenged and changed at times of revolution.

Feminism was 'situated knowledge', against 'objective' psychology

The Harlow studies, photographs from which still litter US American psychology textbooks, pretend to be neutral unbiased scientific investigation, but feminist research showed how they are forms of 'situated knowledge'. The response of feminist work, Haraway argued, should not be to pretend that it gives the real 'god's eye' view of reality, but to itself be reflexively aware of the way that it produces situated knowledge from a 'partial perspective'.

These notions of situated knowledge, partial perspective, and then 'standpoint' theories, which argue that those with less power in a society will see better how power works, have been crucial to re-orienting research.[36] This feminist research throws new light not only on what psychology looks like but also on how we come to know that we always look at it from a certain vantage-point. It then puts into question what psychology tells us we must be, and shows how who we are is intimately bound up with forms of knowledge about the mind that are constructed from a standpoint that is alien and hostile to human collective creative understanding and social change.

It led to proposals for socialist-feminist engagements with technology

Close examination of horrific technologies of control in primate studies did not lead to a rejection of technology. The lesson of primatology and images of raw nature that psychologists claimed to be discovering when they were actually reconstructing our 'second nature' was precisely that it would *not* be a solution to try and get 'outside' technology. Alienation is not a function of technology as

[36] For a feminist historical materialist argument for the importance of 'standpoint' in research and political action, see Hartsock (1987).

such, though it is tempting to blame our sense of ourselves as machines on the existence of technology. There is always technology of some kind or another, and the question is how we are positioned in relation to it and in relation to each other.[37]

Rather than turning to real nature as a romantic fantasy alternative to technology, socialist feminists needed to understand how particular kinds of technology create particular kinds of subjectivity. To combat the technophobia that many women experience in the face of technology – a fear that once again makes them seem more primitive and closer to nature – it became clear that new forms of distributed subjectivity might be a powerful resource for women.[38] This socialist-feminist 'second wave' feminism then became a resource for 'third wave' feminist arguments that take us beyond psychology to 'cyberpsychology', and then beyond that as well.[39]

The 'third wave' links with distributed subjectivities in cyberfeminist and queer politics

Haraway's 'cyborg manifesto' was an intervention in feminism and in the new realm of cyberspace.[40] While it may be true that cyberspace functions as 'a fantasy zone in which the masculinist desire to transcend the physical body reaches its zenith',[41] it is a contradictory technology that opens up spaces for movement as well as opportunities for new forms of surveillance and control. Proposals for a new cyberfeminism connect with emerging 'third wave' feminisms that are deliberately and explicitly plural, and that attend to divisions between women constructed around categories of race and sexuality. Just as Marxism has had to learn that anti-racism and feminism are not 'diversions' from the class struggle but crucial to the confidence and self-activity of the working class, so feminists have learnt that feminism itself must be a pluralistic politics. This pluralism is very different, however, from the liberal pluralism that tells us that the rights of every alienated 'individual' should be respected, and it draws on a different notion of 'rights' which is relational and which anticipates new forms of non-alienating relations of production and reproduction.

[37] Gordo López and Cleminson (2004) provide an account of the way different technological practices over the course of history have produced different forms of subjectivity and sexual relations.

[38] See Haraway (1991) for a discussion of these issues.

[39] See Gordo-López and Parker (1999) for a collection on these matters.

[40] Haraway's (1991) manifesto is also available online (of course).

[41] Marsden (1999), p. 73.

These feminisms encompass 'queer politics' that challenges the cultural division into 'normal' and 'abnormal' sexualities, and they are fluid in their political interventions as well as in their theories.[42] Diametrically opposed to psychological prediction and control, one of the watchwords of these new feminisms is 'precarity', an attempt to understand and reclaim the precarious nature of life and identity under capitalism.[43]

A New Focus on Consciousness Appeared in 1980s Latin America

The Soviet Union was far enough away from US America to function as a screen upon which to project all kinds of conspiracies and threats; for some it was an 'evil empire' that served to confirm the idea that a socialist alternative to capitalism must be a brutal dictatorship. For others, unfortunately, it seemed to be the place where paradise on earth had finally been realised. Revolutions in Latin America, in what the United States liked to think of as its own backyard, provided a more direct threat. What was worse for the ruling class about the revolutions that took place in Cuba in 1959, and then even more so in Nicaragua in 1979,[44] was that these revolutions were more genuinely democratic than the US-backed regimes they overturned. The Sandinistas in Nicaragua included Jesuit priests among their leadership, and 'liberation theology' was put on the agenda as a mobilising force that would change the way that people understood what 'spirituality' meant in practice. While Marx had treated religion as the 'opium of the people' or, more generously, as the 'heart of a heartless world', liberation theology showed that religious conceptions of the self and reality could lead to a commitment to changing the world.[45] Psychologists, who liked to explain away religious ideas as illusions at best in the case of neurotics and delusions in the worst case as a symptom of psychosis, were also in for a shock. The new generation of worker-priests had some lessons for psychological conceptions of 'mental health' that showed that

[42] For a more sceptical feminist psychological response to 'queer' theory, see Kitzinger and Wilkinson (1994).
[43] Precarias a la Deriva (2005) outline this feminist take on psychogeographical disruptive journeys through everyday locations.
[44] For a sympathetic discussion of mental health services in Nicaragua after ten years of revolution, see Harris and Shefer (1990); for a rather rosy account of the Cuban mental health system, see Michie (1979).
[45] There is a Marxist discussion of liberation theology and its implications for revolutionary politics in Löwy (1988).

revolution could be good for you. The effects of sanctions against Cuba, the fall of the Berlin Wall in 1989 and consequent loss of external economic support, together with the success of the US-backed 'Contras' against Nicaragua put increasing pressure on Castro. Just as 'socialism in one country' was impossible in the Soviet Union, so the stranglehold of imperialism on Cuba has led to a degree of bureaucratisation of the regime, even while the gains of the revolution still should be defended.[46] The heartless world is encroaching on Latin America more brutally than ever.

Martín-Baró linked interpretation of the world with change to combat lies

Ignacio Martín-Baró, to take one significant case, was a worker-priest originally from the Basque country but then based in El Salvador who was also trained as a psychologist, but 'psychology' was understood by him as something that was imposed through the process of colonisation. To treat 'behaviour' as something that could be 'conditioned' by rewarding it through 'positive reinforcement', as the US American behaviourists proposed, was to lose sight of the crucial capacity of human beings to be reflexive agents. What we know about the world affects what it is possible to do in it.

For Martín-Baró, a certain kind of mentality of the colonised needed to be tackled as part of the process of change. It was not possible to treat psychological problems with any 'objective' approach, but it was necessary to engage in subjective 'commitment' to 'de-ideologisation' in order to give people back the knowledge that had been stolen from them. This work became increasingly influential during the 1980s in Latin America from Mexico through Central America to the south of the continent.

Choice of certain questions and tactical use of psychological methods led to his murder

Once one adopts Martín-Baró's approach one starts to see that 'the role of experimental subjects is that of idiotic objects'.[47] However, it was necessary sometimes to use the attitude survey tools that have

---

[46] The question, of course, is whether one 'defends' a revolution by keeping quiet about abuses of power, in which case one ends up merely defending the leadership of the party apparatus, or whether one defends the revolutionary process itself by opposing imperialist intervention at the same time as supporting revolutionary democratic voices of dissent.

[47] Jiménez-Domínguez (2005), p. 66.

been developed by mainstream psychology tactically. Martín-Baró was insistent that political projects of the researcher working together with the oppressed must define what tools are used and how they are interpreted. We have seen how 'qualitative' methods in psychology are not necessarily more progressive than mainstream quantitative research, and there are many radical statisticians who are keen to use detailed scientific knowledge about the nature of social inequality to support movements for social change.[48]

Martín-Baró, for example, conducted opinion-poll surveys across the border in Nicaragua that showed, against the lies that were being spread by the US-backed 'Contra' terrorists, that the majority of people still supported the Sandinista regime. Similar survey work was being conducted by him in El Salvador in 1989 when a death squad from the military dictatorship broke into Universidad Centroamericana where Martín-Baró worked and gunned him down together with colleague priests and domestic workers.

Questioning of the taken-for-granted was linked with conscientisation

The task of 'education' is transformed in the liberation theology framework proposed by Martín-Baró. It is, as Marxists always argued, necessary to 'educate the educator' rather than assume that revolutionaries have an expertise that is above and beyond what is possible for ordinary people to comprehend. The 'conscientisation' process that Martín-Baró was engaged in led him to develop beyond 'liberation theology' to a perspective now known as 'liberation psychology'.[49]

Western psychologists assume that they already know what the world is like and what it is possible to be in it; meanwhile in Latin America Martín-Baró and other participant action researchers made it their job to work with people who were beginning to question what was possible. This tradition of work includes Paulo Freire in Brazil, Orlando Fals Borda in Colombia and Maritza Montero in Venezuela, and it changes where we look as psychologists for the real stuff of psychology. Critiques of this perspective within Latin America, that there is a risk that one simply immerses oneself in a community and loses any critical distance from everyday commonsense, have been developed in solidarity with the overall approach.[50]

---

[48] For collections by the Radical Statistics Group, see Irvine et al. (1979) and Dorling and Simpson (1999).

[49] See Martín-Baró (1994) for a collection of writings on liberation psychology.

[50] For a critique in sympathy with the overall project, see Jiménez-Domínguez (1996).

These critiques indicate that the field of consciousness-raising in liberation psychology is a field of diverse perspectives, conflictual, dialectical and rooted in practice.

From the 'centres' to the 'margins'

Liberation psychology is very different from the psychology that has been developed in the overdeveloped 'centres' of the world, and it shows us that the form of 'psychology' that has been developed in the centres will itself reflect that place of origin in the form it takes. There is an assumption in Western psychology that individual psychology must have a centre – a point of integrated mental functioning inside each person – and this assumption is a function of the old colonial assumption that economic and political systems can only function smoothly if there are 'centres' to guide them. This assumption then reinforces the individualism of Western psychology, and forms of psychologisation have operated by making each person feel that they have a little 'psychology' inside themselves.

New forms of globalisation and neoliberalism have transformed those assumptions about centres and margins, but we need to understand how new 'distributed' forms of control still perpetuate systems of economic production and consumption in which each individual worker and consumer is powerless to determine what happens to the fruits of their labour. Liberation psychology is indeed the 'sigh of an oppressed creature', and it forces psychologists in the West to look at what the nature of oppression is as something bound up with colonial control and neocolonial racism.

Resistance Is Necessary and Possible in Psychology and Against It

The Russian Revolution, the student rebellions in France, US American feminism and the Latin American liberation movements each shook and disturbed the assumptions psychologists made about the human being. The nature of psychology as a reductionist and individualising discipline was thrown into question, and different vantage-points were opened up on the nature of alienation. Most importantly, the ways of understanding what alienation was – and how economic exploitation intersected with sexual, gendered and cultural forms of oppression – were intimately linked with change. A dialectical relationship between interpretation and change was forged at these revolutionary moments.

It is necessary to understand the weight of the past and
what has been possible

It is as important to know how these possible new approaches to psychology have been closed down as how they emerged. Closure around a fixed, limited image of the individual makes the different kinds of work compatible once again with mainstream psychology.

The translation of Vygotsky's work into English, for example, has enabled some radical Western psychologists to know what revolutionary psychology might look like, but his work has also been absorbed back into mainstream developmental psychology, as if it was just another theory about how children turn into adults. The work of Sève, that of Holzkamp and that of Foucault still operate as reference-points for resistance to Western psychology, but they have also been depoliticised, and there is no reason why the discipline of psychology could not adopt and utilise them for its own purposes. Feminist perspectives are often still very disturbing to psychologists, for they put politics and subjectivity on the agenda, but there are already lucrative career paths in the 'psychology of women' and in 'lesbian and gay psychology' in the US that have turned radical work into academic specialities. Even the work of Martín-Baró, which shows how genuine understanding of the nature of oppression can only be developed through the process of revolution, can be formalised and incorporated into conservative 'community psychology'. There are no guarantees that ideas once revolutionary will always be radical, but there is potential, and that potential is dependent on us keeping the alternative histories alive that aim for emancipation.

We work in the fault-lines of the present power relations
to open up something new

The shockwaves from the revolutions changed how psychologists saw the world and the lessons are still rippling out from their places of origin: Haug's 'memory work' has been taken up and developed by feminist psychologists around the world, in critical studies of educational psychology in Australia, for example;[51] Foucault's work on power has been used in analyses of the new psychology of peace in South Africa;[52] precarious mobile struggles inspired in part by

[51] See, for example, Davies and Gannon (2006). There is a good discussion of conceptual issues in the development of 'memory work' by Stephenson (2003).
[52] Durrheim (1997) analyses the functions of the rhetoric about 'peace' during the transition period in which apartheid was dismantled. This piece is one of a series of

Haraway's work have been taken up by feminist 'psychologies' around the globe;[53] and participant action research has spread into the imperialist world, to educate the educators.[54]

The revolutions shook up psychology and put new concepts on the agenda; activity, power, 'second nature' and collective consciousness. But the question now is how we may link these concepts together. Instead of merely repeating the discoveries made during those revolutionary times, discoveries that were rooted in those particular contexts, we need to know how to learn from them so that we do something revolutionary in and against psychology today.

studies in 'discourse analysis' that shows that the political context in South Africa could produce something much more critical than British 'discursive psychology'; for other examples, see Levett et al. (1997), and on critical work in psychology in South Africa, see Hook (2004).

[53] Zavos et al. (2005) provide an overview and extension of feminist and activist work in and against psychology.

[54] See Collins (2003) for an example of 'action research' underpinned by revolutionary politics.

9
Commonsense: Psychological Culture on the Left

Radical political changes have always had profound repercussions for the psychology of those involved. The sense that things that were taken for granted can actually be changed and the experience of connecting theory with practice in the process of change are both disturbing and exhilarating. At these moments our everyday commonsensical psychology is thrown into question, and the ideological process of psychologisation unravelled. There have been a variety of responses to this; from the left, the left of the left, and the new revolutionary movements that put anti-racism, environmental issues and feminism on the agenda again. These movements are quite rightly suspicious of what capitalist society takes to be 'normal', but we need to go further than that; psychology is our flexible friend, quick to adapt and find new ways to adapt people to it. This chapter is about political challenges to reactionary commonsense, and about how psychology often smuggles this commonsense back into radical politics.

Ideological conditions are necessary for the individual
to be the focus of debate

At the very moment psychology was being formalised as a distinct discipline at the end of the nineteenth century, radical political movements were starting to tackle the role of the individual in history.[1] Marxists and anarchists debated the role of revolutionary 'leadership', for example, and the extent to which a strong individual could change the course of history. The question was already implicitly between politics and psychology. Should leadership be conceptualised as a democratic movement that would be in the

---

[1] The most well known text within Marxism on this question was produced by Plekhanov (1946), but this still adhered to a conceptual separation between the 'individual' who was formed by history and the 'society' they tried to change.

vanguard of struggle, building different forums and organisations for collectively debating what should be done? Or should it be reduced to secretive groups and charismatic individuals who would discover the real causes of oppression and guide those outside so that they could release themselves from it?[2]

On the one hand, it was conceivable that the working class would develop revolutionary consciousness as a direct result of miserable economic conditions combined with the experience of working together in the factories. On the other, it seemed that a theory of capitalist society and its weakest links may have to be developed by those already separated off from the working class to do intellectual work, with this theory then elaborated and tested in practice with workers themselves. Some anarchists looked to strong individuals, while some Marxists favoured a strong party as the best bet.[3]

The conditions for psychology to be experienced as real require false consciousness

The weight given to individual psychology in radical politics depends very much on the possibilities that there are for change, the material conditions for successful change. When the mass of the population is passive and pessimistic it does seem as if all the political innovations must be put down to the bright ideas of strong individuals. Then it is helpful to analyse the bureaucratic mindset of radical 'leaders' who are detached from everyday struggles and defending their own position in a trade union or in a 'workers' state'. A certain form of 'psychology' is called into being as part of the problem, and these 'leaders' sabotage movements for change while believing that they are getting the best deal in negotiations with employers and politicians.[4]

There is then 'false consciousness', but not as a kind of psychological weakness that deludes people, and often the rank and file can

[2] Marxist debates about 'democratic centralism' and the revolutionary 'Leninist' party were about how to develop forms of organisation that were necessary to take on the state without simply mirroring and repeating state forms of power; see, for example, Mandel (1977).

[3] Stirner (1995) provided one of the most individualistic of anarchist accounts, one that found its way into the Italian and then US American anarchist tradition as nihilism masquerading as progressive social change (see, e.g., Novatore, n.d.). Stalin's (C.P.S.U.(B), 1939) rewriting of the history of the party as the force leading the Russian Revolution and then guiding the transition to 'socialism in one country' is the most obvious template for authoritarian so-called 'Leninist' politics, one admired and adapted by Mao (see Rousset, 1987a, 1987b).

[4] See Mandel (1992) for an extended Marxist analysis of bureaucracy.

see very well what is going on when those that are supposed to be their representatives sell them out. This 'false consciousness' is a particular way of seeing the world that treats the individual and society as separated off from each other, one in which alienation seems inevitable. The material conditions that these leaders and their followers find themselves in lead them to really believe that there could be no other alternative to the way they do things now.[5]

Psychology Invokes a Certain Truth About the Individual, and Truths About Others

Some of the earliest Marxist introductions to the discipline for worker-activists tried to balance 'unbiased reasoning'[6] with political commitment 'concerned with psychology as part of the fighting culture of the proletariat'.[7] However, such analyses were written at a time when 'psychology' was a field of experimental inquiry closely tied to biology, and it seemed possible to fit the psychological bit of the puzzle into a larger theory of society and social change.[8] It was also before feminism put the question of personal politics on the agenda and posed a challenge for stereotypically masculine ways of seeing the world and trying to organise other people.

Psychology tells individuals to look deep into their selves to discover who they really are

Now psychology suffuses culture, and there is an increasingly powerful psychological culture that encourages people to look into themselves to understand why they feel anxious or depressed. The feminist challenge to male-dominated politics has also been absorbed and neutralised, turned into a stereotypically feminine concern with 'feelings'; even recuperated as hostility to politics as such. Hostility to politics is always actually profoundly political, and when women are mobilised against politics there are often

---

[5] For arguments about the problems with attempting to 'take power' without conceptualising what power relations are reproduced in the process, see Holloway (2002).

[6] Jameson (1947), p. 2.

[7] Jameson (1947), p. 156.

[8] Jameson's was one of the first Marxist introductions to psychology in the English language, written in 1921 and reprinted, revised and published by the 'Plebs League' in 1947; it restates Marx's interpretation of history and economics as a 'biological fact' that 'in the case both of individuals and of societies, *conduct, ideals, aspirations, and institutions depend on environmental influences and upon the inborn mechanisms by which men are forced to react to those influences in a particular way*' (Jameson, 1947, p. 5, emphasis in original).

reactionary agendas.[9] Psychological culture feeds upon this hostility and encourages people to look inward rather than outward for sources of change.

Disappointment is then the ground on which politics is reconfigured as a reflection on what the left invested in the working class; 'it is the working class who have had to hold the promise of revolution for the radical left – and the burden of failure when the revolution never came about'.[10] Different forms of feminist politics that do try to keep questions of women's oppression on the agenda, meanwhile, are also often sidelined and caricatured as being no more than amounting to a species of man-hating lesbianism.[11]

The truth of identity is treated as the underlying touchstone of personal truth

The resources that the left has drawn upon to understand the depth of defeat – failures to extend revolutions, rollback of the 'communist' bloc, neoconservative wars – often include attempts to address psychological dimensions. However, those very resources carry with them assumptions about the nature of psychology. One attempt to understand 'the mass psychology of Thatcherism' in the UK, a pamphlet by Chaplin and Haggart,[12] for example, drew upon the work of radical psychoanalysis to find grounds for optimism; the authors claimed that 'children are born with "natural" loving or rationally hating, creative, curious instincts. Through repression and punishment in the family the child learns to associate anxiety and fear with love and desire'.[13] The writers then went on to argue that 'Thatcherism appeals strongly to deep psychological constructs created by early experiences in the family'.[14]

The psychological alternative to this psychological diagnosis, 'useful for understanding and counteracting the appeal of Thatcherism',

[9] The mobilisation of women as mothers, for example, has often been used to defend the nation against 'outsiders' and so the opposition to big-party politics in the appeal to women turns out to be very political; for an example of this ideological ploy in Eastern Europe before and after the fall of the Berlin Wall, see Salecl (1994).
[10] Lucey and Reay (2000), p. 139; they go on to argue that 'the more defensive aspects of middle-class practices which so effectively protect the authority of bourgeois versions of rationality need to be exposed' (p. 154).
[11] This caricature of feminists blots out the intense debates inside feminism over power, gender, sexuality and oppression (see, e.g., Cartledge, 1983).
[12] Chaplin and Haggart (1983); the title of the pamphlet, published by the West London Socialist Society, alludes to Wilhelm Reich's (1975) book *The Mass Psychology of Fascism*.
[13] Chaplin and Haggart (1983), p. 5.
[14] Chaplin and Haggart (1983), p. 6.

was drawn from the ideas of Jung, not the best of friends of the left and of non-white 'races'.[15] Notwithstanding Jung's own reactionary politics, the authors of the pamphlet then go on to endorse the idea that there are 'masculine' and 'feminine' sides to the personality and 'shadow' sides to ourselves that we need to 'reconnect' with in order 'to develop as whole, mature individuals'.[16] The attempt to understand the depth of a defeat can be an opportunity to reflect on the importance of the emotions in politics.[17] But this is not helpful if we are thereby dragged so deep into psychological culture as for it to reinforce the idea that there are certain 'psychological' truths about the self that set limits to what we think can be changed in the world.

Psychology also requires acceptance of multiple truths about the self

The depth of defeat and demoralisation about the possibility for collective action and the construction of a genuinely democratic socialist alternative to capitalism has worked its way deeper and deeper into the left. Even before the fall of the Berlin Wall in 1989 and the disintegration of the bureaucratic fake-socialist regimes in the Soviet Union and Eastern Europe, there was an attempt to find a way out among the old communist parties. The development of 'Eurocommunism', seeking alliances with the liberal elements of the ruling class of different countries, included a critique of Stalinist conceptions of 'leadership'.[18]

The new politics drew upon feminist ideas but used these to shift attention from class struggle to class identity and people's feelings about how they identified themselves. Theoreticians of this shift to the right then treat class struggle as just one species of identity politics.[19] Working-class identity is seen as just one path to follow, a psychological path. This strand of left politics bought into psychological culture, and many of the leading activists later gave

---

[15] Dalal (1988) describes Jung's racism, and Samuels (1992) tackles his anti-Semitism.

[16] Chaplin and Haggart (1983), p. 12.

[17] Hochschild (2003) provides some interesting reflections on the then impending Bush 2004 election victory.

[18] 'Eurocommunism' is actually a misnomer; although there were often appeals to the writings of Gramsci (1971), the Italian communist party leader jailed by Mussolini, this centrifugal movement in which the Stalinised communist parties came to transfer allegiance from Moscow to social-democratic ideas in their own countries also existed outside Europe, with a large party of this kind existing in Japan; see the discussion in Mandel (1978).

[19] See Laclau and Mouffe (2001) for this argument as part of an attempt to escape old-fashioned socialist politics focused on political-economic struggle.

up politics altogether to go into therapy. This shift to 'identity' has found its way into analyses of class and gender;[20] it also has consequences for the way that anti-racist struggle becomes transformed into respect for different identities, and then to therapeutic respect for different identities defined by religious faith.[21]

Contemporary neoliberalism requires flexibility and adaptability

Capitalism was from the beginning a system that pulled the ground from under people's feet, throwing them into a world of constant change. Contemporary capitalism, neoliberalism, in which governments ruthlessly privatise services and appeal to each individual to make their own short-term contract with their employer, appears to have speeded up the process of dissolving traditional ways of relating to each other.[22] It seems as though people do have to be psychologically more flexible, and this requires that people should be more 'reflexive' and psychological about themselves as a precondition for that flexibility.[23]

New ideas from the new identities that will enable access to niche markets are welcomed, whether they be from minority cultures or from drawing on the 'pink pound', this even while racism and heterosexism are still used to mobilise people from other identity categories in order to divide and rule the workforce.[24] As capitalism rolls triumphant across Eastern Europe and into the old Soviet Union it is *individuals* who are enrolled as the new entrepreneurs, and psychologisation is one of the powerful ideological strategies used to divide people from one another and encourage competition in the so-called 'free' market.[25]

---

[20] See Skeggs (2003) for a sociological take on this, and Walkerdine (1990) for personal reflections linked with debates on subjectivity.

[21] Gordon (2001); for critiques of the tendency of Race Awareness Training to reduce racism to aspects of psychology, see Sivanandan (1985).

[22] For a good analysis of these changes by a sociologist who nonetheless ends up celebrating this transformation, see Giddens (1992).

[23] See Soldevilla (1999) for an analysis and critique of this related to new 'virtual' technologies; and see Sey (1999) for an account of the material historical preconditions for these transformations in early capitalism. For an extended analysis of the historical linking of technology and sexuality, see Gordo López and Cleminson (2004).

[24] Milligan (1979, p. 16) points out that 'workers' control of industry and the abolition of capitalism would create only the *possibility* of gay liberation. The abolition of gay oppression can only be brought about by breaking down sexism in the working class and by building up an understanding of the way male supremacy and the persecution of homosexuals represses everybody'.

[25] This also has an impact on the discipline of psychology itself, with pre-1989 Soviet psychology displaced by US American individualist psychology; see Dafermos et al. (2006).

Alternative Psychology Reproduces Ideas About
Transparency and Authenticity

It is understandable that capitalism should provoke a romantic hearkening back to 'the way things were' before people were separated and pitted against each other in brutal competition for work. Precapitalist society was never such a paradise, but the image of another more ideal world is some comfort in a real world organised around exploitation, oppression and alienation. Psychological explanations then get an even stronger grip when there is competition for goods and for status and 'identity'. Then, as psychological culture becomes more pervasive, that romantic hearkening back is treated as itself something to do with the individual. We then come to view childhood as a place where we were each freer and closer to nature, closer to each other and more authentically human.[26] This is the trap that forms of radical politics which have tried to move into the realm of human development and therapy have often fallen into, and this results in many problems in alternative psychology, an ostensibly new 'alt psy'.[27]

'Alt psy' rests upon a normative idea of childhood, transparency and optimism

One alternative practice came from 'co-counselling', an explicitly political therapeutic approach with roots in US American versions of Maoism (which in itself is not necessarily reason enough to avoid it).[28] Claims that different factions of organised 'co-counselling' are sects or 'cults' should be treated with care.[29] When an attempt is made to make sense of organisational problems by using the notion of 'cult' psychology, *political* problems are thereby obscured. Such accusations levelled against co-counselling are themselves using psychological explanations for why someone should be attracted to a certain political viewpoint, and so psychology as part of the problem that pretends to be part of the solution is also reinforced.

[26] See Ariès (1962) for the classic history of the construction of childhood.
[27] Totton (2000) gives a good overview of connections between the politics and psychotherapy.
[28] See Jackins (1978) for an indicative outline of co-counselling, and observations on a number of questions, including that 'We conclude that homosexuality (as distinct from the desire to touch or be close) is the result of distress patterns (often very early in origin and chronic) and will disappear by the free choice of the individual with sufficient discharge' (p. 411).
[29] See, for example, Tourish and Wohlforth (2000a) for a reductive psychologising attack on co-counselling.

The real problem with co-counselling is that this theory insists that rigid distress patterns from childhood must be discharged if we are to become healthy. One feminist assessment of the 'ecopolitics' of different psychological theories attempted to build co-counselling into 'embryonic green psychologies', for example. The author concludes that 'ecological activists need reflective knowledge of their own organizations, a way of noticing oppressive or exclusive assumptions and practices that have crept into [them], of loosening rigidities'.[30] There is then an explicit appeal to psychology, to 'healing' that is treated as an aspect of the kind of reflective knowledge that will enable radical politics.[31] This does not immediately reduce politics to psychology, and the attempt to put personal politics on the agenda for social change is a good one, but it does frame the activity of politics as a therapeutic one.[32]

'Alt psy' buys into the individualist lure of 'self-reliance' and personal strength

An alternative practice, also from within the US American Maoist tradition, built on the 'encounter groups' of the 1960s and questioned what 'psychology' is; this then took the form of 'social therapy' (which is a cover-all term for a range of different practices that evolved from within the group).[33] Again, we should be cautious about the label 'cult' that is thrown around too quickly by critics, and the Newman group is too-easy a target for smearing with such psychological diagnoses.[34] The problems need a political not a psychological assessment, and to psychologise Newman and his followers would then obscure what is progressive (as well as what is problematic) about their practice.[35] The 'social therapy' tradition builds upon sources as diverse as the Russian psychologist Lev Vygotsky and the Austrian philosopher Ludwig Wittgenstein to build a form of 'clinical psychology' that is critical of capitalist society.

---

[30] New (1996), p. 166.

[31] New (1996), p. 166.

[32] See Samuels (1993) for another attempt to see the radical 'citizen as therapist'.

[33] For a recent account of the theory and practice of social therapy, see Holzman and Mendez (2003).

[34] Tourish and Wohlforth (2000a) include a lurid and unhelpful 'analysis' of the Newman group in their book on cults; the chapter on Newman is available online (Tourish and Wohlforth, 2000b).

[35] See Parker (1995c) for a history and critical assessment of the development of social therapy, and Holzman (1995) for a response. For a serious critical engagement with Newman and Holzman's work, see Nissen et al. (1999).

Its leaders argue that it is Marxist insofar as it points to an alternative, but it cannot claim to be 'socialist', because we do not live in such a society and do not even know what it would be like.[36]

However, the shift of emphasis from the analysis of social conditions to an insistence that people can 'perform' better and better, as if they are developing in what Vygotsky termed a 'zone of proximal development', has led once again to therapeutic notions taking charge. Perhaps this is why the group behind 'social therapy' now concludes that 'the capitalists have won' and argues that the only hope is to intervene in the marketplace of ideas about possibilities for human growth.[37]

'Alt psy' flips quickly into its opposite, dependence and a victim mentality

The activities of the tightly organised left groups that have moved into the domain of psychology are instructive. The reactions to these interventions by others on the left reveal the power of psychological notions, and the way these notions can be used to pathologise certain kinds of political intervention. The testimonies of those who were once part of the groups concerned also reveal how important the 'psychological' aspect of the work was; dissidents often use precisely the same individualised claims, that they were 'brain-washed' for example, to account for why they made the mistake of going along with things they now disagree with.[38]

The lesson is that use of psychology as a political tool to try and confront capitalism is likely to rebound on those who use it. A 'feeling' or 'performance' of independence at one point is liable to turn into hopelessness and a sense of being a victim of evil forces at the next. The scrabble to claim status as a 'victim' and to then remain trapped in

[36] In an early paper, there is an excellent statement of their position then that is still worth reading now: 'our activity in developing a Marxist clinical psychology and, there-fore, its conceptualization, is reflective of the world (and, more particularly, of the society) in which we are living. To suppose it possible to have a socialist therapy in a nonsocialist world would clearly mean to deny reality' (Hood and Newman, 1983, p. 154).

[37] See Newman (1999), and for a restatement of their position and critical response, see Newman and Holzman (2003).

[38] This is precisely the problem of analyses of political 'cults' that draw on psycho-logical theory to explain how people made commitments to groups and then changed their minds; for discussion of the problems in treating political groups and new religious movements as 'cults', see Barker (1982); for a study of 'cults' in Britain that treats those who join them as just as daft as those who lead them, and which also shows how the anti-cult movements are tangled up in precisely the same problems they claim to expose, see Shaw (1995).

that new 'identity' is an increasingly popular one in contemporary psychological culture, and should not be endorsed by the left.[39]

'Alt psy' folds into grim psychoanalytic notions of unconscious aggression and 'lack'

Psychological culture also holds open a variety of explanations for those who were once on the left and have decided that they want to change direction. Their own 'disappointment' is recommended to everyone else as a psychologically healthy option,[40] and those who have turned to psychology end up wanting to tell the world what cannot be changed in human nature.[41]

Political projects that have been based on the premise that psychoanalysis is necessarily on the 'left', or is 'left of centre' enough to be amenable to persuasion by Marxists and feminists, all too often end up with the Marxists and feminists being persuaded to give up their politics. Then they put their energies into evangelising about what they think they have discovered about human psychology. Sometimes intense psychological reflection is designed to bring about change, and promises to provide the route to larger-scale economic change, and this has been the way of those looking to Jung for inspiration.[42] Sometimes the lesson concerns how an acceptance of 'lack' implies that we should give up trying to change the world, and this has been the way of those looking to Lacanian psychoanalysis.[43] Sometimes the lesson they draw is that they have discovered that 'unconscious aggression' puts paid to collective activity, and this has been the way of those drawn to the ideas of Melanie Klein.[44]

[39] For discussion of victimhood as a form of identity in contemporary culture, see Dineen (2001) and Furedi (2003).

[40] Craib's (1994) psychotherapeutic book is on the 'importance' (a sanctimonious word in therapeutic discourse) of disappointment.

[41] See Young (1996) for a Marxist argument about the role of evolutionary theory that turns into an advertisement for Kleinian psychoanalysis.

[42] See, for example, the collection edited by Totton (1996), and the journal founded in 2003, *Psychotherapy Politics International*, to link personal therapeutic change with political change.

[43] See, for example, Bar (2003) focusing on feminist politics; see also Miller (2001), Lacan's son-in-law and a former Maoist returning to political debate in his response to the 11 September 2001 attacks; also see *Journal for the Psychoanalysis of Culture and Society*, founded in 1996 with the claim that it is possible to find the 'psychological roots' of political problems.

[44] See, for example, Rustin (1982) on the socialist politics supposedly present in Klein's work, and Young (1996); see also the journal *Free Associations*, which was founded in 1984 to try and draw Kleinian psychoanalysts closer to the left.

Alternative Psychology Often Calls Upon a
Misreading of Psychoanalysis

Psychoanalysis has been a tremendous source of ideas about politics, most of them reactionary. When radical movements start to get interested in psychology, however, they conveniently overlook Freud's own suspicion of Marxism and feminism.[45] What psychoanalysis seems to offer is a way of accounting for the way that workers in capitalist society develop a 'fear of freedom' and fall in love with the very forms of oppression that grind them down.[46] They thus not only accept their servitude but revel in their own 'slavery' and despise those who want to rebel against law and order. These psychoanalytic perspectives aim to understand and unravel the deepest roots of alienation.[47]

Psychoanalysis is treated as if it were the radical
subversive opposite of psychology

One influential pamphlet on 'the irrational in politics' produced by 'Solidarity' – co-thinkers of the French *Socialisme ou Barbarie* group – argued that the focus should be on 'internalised patterns of repression and coercion, and with those intellectual prisons in which the "mass individual" is today entrapped'.[48] But, we need to ask, what kind of intellectual prison is psychoanalysis and is it really an alternative to psychology?

The 'Solidarity' pamphlet makes use of the work of the psychoanalyst Wilhelm Reich, who wrote *The Mass Psychology of Fascism*, an analysis of the way the family produced a certain kind of personality structure admiring of leadership and ripe for Nazism. Reich's political interventions in 1930s Germany included connecting political struggle with 'the sexual struggle of youth', and 'Sex-Pol'

---

[45] For a fascinating overview of these questions through an analysis of the popularity and then suppression of psychoanalysis in Russia, see Miller (1998).

[46] In Latin America, the ideas of Erich Fromm (1960, 1962) combining psychoanalytic with existentialist perspectives have been important as a humanist alternative to the sexual and 'orgone' energy theories of Wilhelm Reich and theories of 'lack' purveyed by Lacanians. In the UK there have been some attempts to connect left politics with the work of Karen Horney (see, e.g., Southgate and Randall, 1989).

[47] See Ollman (1979) for an attempt to tackle alienation by combining Marxist and psychoanalytic theory.

[48] Brinton (1975), p. 5. The 'Solidarity' pamphlet writer 'Maurice Brinton' was, it transpired later upon his death in 2005, a pseudonym for Christopher Pallis, a respected neurologist working in London. 'Solidarity' also published pamphlets by 'Paul Cardan', a pseudonym for the psychoanalyst Cornelius Castoriadis.

demands for free contraception and abortion on demand anticipated the feminist and socialist movements of the 1960s.[49] Other far-left groups also drew on Reich's ideas, but there was always a temptation to idealise psychoanalysis, and especially to idealise Reich as being on the left of the left.[50]

*Notions of liberation of the self that lies within
the unconscious are invoked*

The version of psychoanalysis that flowed from Reich's work treated it as a political theory and clinical practice that would be able to access the unconscious desires that were 'repressed' by capitalism. This led to a simplistic idea of 'liberation' as meaning that if oppression is combated and repression is overcome, then freedom will well up. It is as if the 'unconscious' is always already revolutionary and will necessarily bring people together. The idea that violence during a revolutionary struggle is 'cathartic' is of a piece with this romantic view of the unconscious, and work within the black liberation movement that drew on the writings of the psychiatrist Frantz Fanon also bought into this way of looking at things.[51]

The problem that psychology poses as a material practice through which people are divided from each other on the basis of their 'normality' or 'abnormality', also needs a better response than that of romanticising the unconscious. The 'anti-psychiatry' movement was a necessary response to the brutal coercion meted out to patients through confinement, electroshock and psychosurgery, and it still is.[52] However, when anti-psychiatry became linked to the left it tended to romanticise 'madness' as the 'other' of, as alternative to, rationality under capitalism. It then served to relay romantic ideas about essential underlying psychological truths into the left.[53] Even now the appeals to 'anti-Oedipus' and 'schizoanalysis' often serve to

[49] For a collection that provides a better translation than some of the earlier English-language pamphlets, see Reich (1972).

[50] See, for example, the pamphlet by Knight (1976) produced by the Chartist Tendency (a British Trotskyist grouping); a pamphlet a few years later on revolutionary consciousness did not refer to Reich (Knight, 1980).

[51] See Fanon (1967, 1970).

[52] For attempts to connect radical approaches to mental health with politics, see Banton et al. (1985); see Sedgwick (1982) for an excellent Marxist analysis of the 'anti-psychiatry' movement. Totton (2000) provides a good overview of intersections between politics and psychotherapy.

[53] Sedgwick (1982) makes this point in his review of the politics of psychiatry and anti-psychiatry. See also Parker et al. (1995).

reproduce rather than challenge the power of psychological categories among leftist academics.[54]

Contemporary expressions are to be found in notions
of 'empire' and 'multitude'

Psychoanalysis is an example of a practice of control that constitutes the very stuff which it represses; at the very moment that it shuts 'irrationality' out, it creates that irrationality as something that may then erupt at times of crisis, as if it were always already there. In this sense, psychoanalysis is rather like capitalism, for capitalism *creates* the very collective force that will be able to overthrow it. This is not surprising, since psychoanalysis came into being as a psychological practice to address the particular forms of alienation that capitalism produced; psychoanalysis and capitalism are twins, even if one can be used to highlight contradictions in the other.[55] The 'proletariat' did not exist before capitalism, and as the working class becomes conscious of itself in the process of struggle it will bring about the proletarian revolution thereby abolishing the division between classes.

This view of the conditions of possibility for things to be constructed to inhibit change or to operate as a potential force for change informs recent anti-capitalist theories of 'empire'.[56] However, there are aspects of the uptake of the theory that are problematic in a heavily psychologised culture. The danger is that one comes to believe that underneath this 'empire' which represses human creativity there is supposed to be an elemental mobile force, 'multitude'.[57] Resistance does not bubble around and up against 'empire' any more than the 'unconscious' really exists as a thing that needs to be released. What this 'anti-capitalist' analysis does is to lay the way for an appeal to something essential under the surface, and so there is a risk that psychological elaboration of these theories for the new

[54] Deleuze and Guattari (1977) attacked mainstream psychoanalysis (including Lacanian approaches) in France, accusing it of 'oedipalising' family relationships and thus dividing 'normal' from 'abnormal' family structures, but they also used psychoanalytic theory to carry out this attack (and Guattari was a Lacanian psychoanalyst). It is often forgotten that some of the most well known figures in the so-called 'anti-psychiatry' movement, like R. D. Laing and Thomas Szasz, were trained as psychoanalysts.
[55] See the argument in Parker (1997) that psychoanalytic culture is intimately tied to capitalism as a political-economic system.
[56] Hardt and Negri (2000).
[57] Hardt and Negri (2004). For critical reflections on the notion of 'multitude', see Laclau (2001).

anti-capitalist movements could prepare the ground for appeals to real hidden psychology under the surface.

Alternative Psychology Ends Up Treating the Political as Only Personal

The appeal to 'alternative psychology' always takes the risk of presenting it as something hidden under the surface that needs to be released. The way this also tends to be interpreted by those who get drawn into psychology, as if it were an alternative, is to treat psychology as something personal that needs to be released from politics.

Feminist arguments are remade and betrayed, with appeals to 'the feminine'

Feminist politics has been an invaluable part of the struggle against mainstream psychology. Socialist-feminist critiques of the nonsense spouted about innate aggression in popular texts about human nature, for example, have put those reactionary ideas in their place, in history.[58] However, the appeal to 'femininity' as something essential that women need to connect with in order to become their real authentic selves then risks undoing this good work. In psychological culture this appeal is sometimes mistakenly seen as a progressive response to the devaluation of women.

What the celebrations of femininity tackle is the problem that women have always been simultaneously admired and despised in modern patriarchal society. However, they then attempt to switch the emphasis from negative to positive images of women, and increasingly the emphasis is particularly upon women as mothers. The split between the two aspects of woman is something that reflects the material separation of their positions as child-bearer and as sexual object; feminism that has become a personal project, become psychologised, then loses sight of the way that material separation is a function of the position of women in the workforce and of the difference between the position of bourgeois and working-class women. The preoccupation with essential underlying 'masculinity' that draws on Jungian psychology then drums home the old reactionary message that men are men and women are women, and ever more will be so.

---

[58] See, for example, Reed (1971).

Different forms of organisation give rise to different forms of subjectivity

The 'personal' is necessarily part of political struggle; this is the crucial lesson that 'second wave' feminism put back on the agenda of socialist politics, but now we need to be especially critical of the role of psychology in society and on the left. If we are not, the lesson will be transformed and twisted into the lesson that *only* the 'personal' is politics worth bothering with, and that other forms of politics are bad for women. And, at the same time, if that personal aspect of the struggle is not taken seriously it will still influence the way that leftist political organisations are formed and conceptions of 'leadership' that activists take on for themselves.

Organisations that are run by men and concerned with keeping women in their place will indeed produce certain kinds of subjectivity for those who inhabit them. Controlling individuals who try to defend their place in the pecking order will then have little time for the 'feelings' that are treated as the concern only of women. This recognition that forms of subjectivity are bound up with forms of organisation, however, is not at all the same as an understanding of the 'psychology' of those involved. To give a 'psychological' account is to pretend that it is possible to wipe away the conditions in which feelings take a particular shape and have a particular force.[59]

There is always organisation, sometimes obscured by the tyranny of structurelessness

The attempt to bring about complete transparency in organisations can also have the consequence that real power relations remain hidden. Work on the 'tyranny of structurelessness' draws attention to the role of the illusion that everyone is equal in a radical organisation; such an organisation is then not so much challenging as maintaining power.[60]

There is a further problem, which is that intense personal reflection then becomes seen as the only way to guarantee radical political activity against the emergence of power structures, and the idea starts to gain hold that therapeutic activity can replace political activity. Therapeutic activities which demand that individuals speak

---

[59] Chaplin and Haggart (1983) do say that their work 'complements' political analysis.

[60] See Freeman (1996) for the feminist argument, mainly directed at the anarchist movement, which attempts to pretend that there is no structure in a genuinely radical political organisation, arguing that this pretence can serve to render invisible the way that women, for example, are positioned. See also Holloway (2002).

about their innermost feelings and share their perceptions of each other are, in psychologised capitalist society, precisely the way that power is exercised. A consequence of turning to therapeutic practices as an attempt to escape power relations – an attempt that is itself futile – is that a range of reactionary group practices are ratified. A consequence of reducing everything to a personal level, focusing only on the 'psychology' of those involved, is that the real psychological structure of leftist organisations is not attended to.[61]

There needs to be liberation in psychology and from psychology

This is where the attempt to build a 'liberation psychology' modelled on the liberation theology movements in Latin America is problematic, for in the origins of 'liberation psychology' there already lie deeply ideological practices of leadership and confession. Liberation theology was a progressive movement that challenged the Catholic Church and reconfigured the opposition between heaven and hell as a real material contradiction that was already here on earth in the struggle of the poor.[62] However, at the same time it sought to 'empower' the poor by drawing them into activities in which they would take responsibility, it linked politics with the long-standing Christian practice of searching within the core of the self for one's sins so that one could better find redemption. The liberation theologians also served as charismatic leaders who would guide their flocks in this new political movement.

There are thus already structural and ideological preconditions for Western psychology, and the psychologisation of each individual involved in this radical politics, to take hold. Charismatic authority and personal self-reflection provide the breeding ground for all manner of reductionist and individualising strategies for pathologising politics; in the opportunity that liberation theology and 'liberation psychology' provided lies the threat of neoliberal subjectivity and successful implantation of the discipline of European and US American psychology in Latin America. This is a question for the left anti-capitalist movement, so that it can maintain what has been progressive about liberation theology and ensure that the 'liberation psychology' is not psychology, but something better.

---

[61] For a discussion of the personal politics of left organisations, see Slater (2003).
[62] See Löwy (1988) for an excellent account of and argument for the progressive role of liberation theology in Latin America.

There Is No Fully Formed Alternative Psychology, nor Should There Be

The bad news for left, feminist and anti-racist politics is that psychologists have nothing to offer. This is also bad news for academic and professional psychologists who are sympathetic to movements for change or even involved themselves in revolutionary politics. It is difficult for those who have status because of the expertise they are supposed to have to say clearly that they do not have the answers. We should not buy into psychological answers, nor try to find the 'real thing' hidden under the surface, for that will not be 'anti-capitalist' or necessarily progressive in any way.

We cannot simply refuse psychology as part of the texture of life under capitalism

Capitalism draws us into a chase after the things that will, we hope, really make us happy. Psychology should be treated as one of those ideals; an understanding of individual identity and personal fulfilment always seems almost within our grasp, but the attempt to plug the psychological bit into a progressive politics should be avoided. The psychologisation of culture and the uptake of psychological ideas in opposition movements make these arguments all the more important.

Psychology is a powerful ideological force, and those who really believe it suffer from false consciousness, but as suffering that they actually enjoy. It is then a mystery to them how others cannot want to be similarly enlightened. For those who are drawn into psychology it is as if the revolution has already taken place; this is one reason why the discipline is such a dangerous and pernicious part of psychological culture on the left.

We should not get lured into psychology by the nice psychologists who are trying to improve it

Some of the attempts of the left to intervene in psychology have made it seem as if there is a possibility of changing the discipline from within. While there are undoubtedly nice people who trained to be psychologists, and some of them even stay true to their principles when they work as psychologists, we should be very careful. Psychology is bad for the left, and when psychology has been used by the left it has had the effect of transforming the left into something else, all too often transforming those who want to change the world into those who say that nothing can be done to change it.

When we turn to attempts to forge new progressive practices inside psychology in alliance with those outside, we will need to attend to the role of psychologisation. We will see how psychology as a force of social control has never been monolithic. On the contrary, there is a history of disagreement and division inside the discipline and the remainders of revolutionary upheavals that gave rise to new ideas. There are also contradictions within the very alienated consciousness we have of the world and of who we are, fault-lines and openings to emancipation in and against psychology.

10
Elements of Opposition: Psychological Struggles Now

It is not surprising that so many people feel bad and seek help in a world driven by the search for profit, and a world organised to make it seem normal and natural that workers should be exploited and divided from each other on the basis of race and sex. Psychology as a discipline bears some responsibility for the anguish and distress that people feel as the glimmering distorted consciousness of their alienation. The discipline worries away at race and sex differences, examining culture and sexuality with the aim of making things seem all the more 'normal' and 'natural' and unchangeable. Because it is so deeply embedded in oppressive practices and in the ideological justification for exploitation, most of the time psychology makes distress worse. Even so, there are struggles for alternative ways of doing psychology, and sometimes they come up against capitalism and the state. This chapter describes how elements of the opposition brush against the grain of the discipline.

There are many existing practices that resist psychology

The struggles to build another world that would put people before profit have left their mark on psychology. Most-times the debates that have been forced on the discipline by revolutionary shocks and upheavals in the real world have been neutralised and absorbed. Sometimes the debates are treated as historical curiosities, but there are still many different practices that prefigure something better than psychology that have been kept going.

There are a number of vital elements to prefigurative work to rethink and rework the stuff of human experience and action so that the contradictory, collective and transformative aspects of our historically constructed 'second nature' provide the ground for progressive self-reflection and social change. First, it is necessary to take on the disciplinary aspects of psychology, the way it observes and regulates individuality. Second, we need to tackle psychologisation, the way that political-economic questions are reduced to how we think and feel in psychological culture. Third, we need to link with progressive political struggles, and put these questions on the agenda in such a way as to challenge psychological culture on the left.

There are practices that have implications for what other professions should do

The best, most progressive psychologists are those who do something else with their time than practice, teach and research psychology. Sometimes they do radical networking to help people understand and mobilise against exploitation; at these points there is networking between the psychologists, other professionals and those involved in political practice. These psychological struggles are often built upon a simple premise, that people have basic rights to collectively and democratically determine their own lives. Far from being a luxury for the chattering classes, psychological struggle is also class struggle; it is part of the fight against the sexist and racist society that intensifies alienation and separation of us from each other.

This struggle is also a struggle to make alliances across the range of professions that are dependent on and subordinate to psychology, and with those radicals in professions that psychologists compete with. The elements of opposition are at the edges of psychological practice, and they disturb the boundaries between psychology and other professions, as well as the boundaries between psychological and political activity. The oppositional practices vary – from disability activism, to deinstitutionalisation, to networks for alternative forms of normality and for reconfiguring individual problems as social problems – and they are imperfect and contradictory, but they serve to open up different ways of interpreting, changing and emancipating the domain of individual 'psychology'.

Psychological Reductionism Is Challenged in the Fields of Ability and Disability

Education pretends to give us the tools to become more civilised and grown-up, but the school is a battlefield where people are psychologically scarred for life as they learn what their place in the world is. Whether they are driven to compete and succeed or persuaded to accept their inability and failure, people learn something deep down about the nature of capitalism when they go through school. This is why struggles for inclusion in the field of 'disability' have such deep consequences for psychology. These are consequences not only for the children segregated into 'special' schools or units, but also for the relationship between educational psychologists, called upon to give advice, and educational welfare officers, for example, who are usually forced to bow to the wisdom of the psychologist. The class relations between children are, in this way, reflected in the class relations between different professionals, with huge disparities in their salaries and in their power. Political action around disability refuses the usual psychological move, which is to reduce a political problem to being one of individual inability.[1]

Embodied oppression is the lived interrelation of bodies that psychology occludes

Educational psychologists step in to describe things that are hidden to everyone else, and this is where the experience of being separated out and excluded becomes confused with the underlying disorder that the psychologist pretends to discover. The class-based assumptions of the psychologists have often been apparent in their expectation that sensitive middle-class children, who are expected to suffer more from emotional problems, will benefit from talking about it, while working-class children will respond better to drug treatments.[2]

This class structure in assessment is now gathering pace in schools where services have been privatised and middle-class parents are able to find and often pay a psychologist to give a diagnosis of 'dyslexia' or some other hidden psychological impairment that will explain why their children are not succeeding as well as expected. The question posed by 'dyslexia' as a label used to identify children who need more help with reading is how to provide opportunities for all children to read, not a select few who will end up paying for having a diagnosis.[3] In processes of assessment and diagnosis class differences are embodied in children, in the different places in which they must learn, and in whom they will learn alongside.

[1] For a path-breaking radical sociological analysis of the way the education system operates to reproduce class structure, see Bourdieu and Passeron (1990), and for an ethnographic perspective on this process, see Willis (1980). For the broader question of masculinity and schooling, see Frosh et al. (2002). For critical studies of 'special' education as a form of exclusion, see Clough and Barton (1998). For key analyses of disability from a Marxist perspective, see Oliver (1990, 1996) and Shakespeare (1998), and for work that brings these analyses into psychology, see Goodley and Lawthom (2004).

[2] See Newnes and Radcliffe (2005) and Timimi (2002), and on the use of Ritalin to drug children, see Scruggs and Breggin (2001).

[3] See Elliott (2005a) for an argument against applying the label 'dyslexia', and Elliott (2005b) for further discussion and responses to critics.

School league tables based on educational achievement then increase the segregation of clever from stupid children, even when this is camouflaged by the political rhetoric of each school 'playing to its strengths'.[4]

Description of behavioural processes is not in itself psychology

The first ideological trick that the activists who are mobilised around the 'social model' of disability expose is the claim that a redescription of behaviour is necessarily something 'psychological'. When a psychologist writes a report saying that a child is having difficulty in class, and concludes that this is because they have a 'disability' of some kind, they focus on something to do with the individual. This description is not in itself a discovery of a 'psychological' problem, however, even though the poor child may really experience themselves as having a problem because of the reaction of others.[5]

The disability action movement shifted focus back to the environments of the schools, to what was 'disabling' the child, and this showed that psychology can be reframed when the focus is on what is disabling in the environment.[6] This is why those in the movement refuse to say that someone has a disability; the question is, what is it that is happening to the child that is disabling them and how should that be tackled? The argument goes well beyond physical disability. The pervasive racism in a society, for example, will impact on the way children from different cultures will be able to learn. The exclusion of a disproportionate number of black children from school is not just an error but a structuring force which disables them and enables racists.[7] The experience of girls who are given less attention by teachers in mixed-sex classes and who then perform less well in tests is another example of how a disabling environment insidiously blames the victims.[8]

[4] On the management of children in school as a political and ethical question, see Dahlberg and Moss (2005).

[5] See Billington (2000) for an account by a radical educational psychologist trying to bend and break the rules; see also Billington and Pomerantz (2004).

[6] See Goodley and Lawthom (2004) for a collection on disability approaches in psychology and schools.

[7] On studies of racism in education, see the edited collection by Connolly and Troyna (1998) and analysis of 'multiculturalism' by Kincheloe and Steinberg (1997); and for a radical activist account, see Coard (1971).

[8] For a wide range of perspectives on gender and schooling, see Arnot and Weiner (1987); on the way that the education system regulates sexuality, see Epstein and Johnson (1998); for general perspectives on disability and the emergence of the 'social model', see Marks (1999); and on feminism and disability activism, see Morris (1996). For a disability activist perspective on new technologies, see Cromby and Standen (1999).

The social model gave rise to a practice
that opposes psychology

The 'social model' of disability linked its own interpretation of the world with change so that schools, for example, would be less disabling of certain categories of people – whether those are categories that are already visible to us or categories invented by psychologists and the drug companies. In schools that are pressurised to come up with good results for government targets, and for anxious parents who themselves know what the consequences might be of a school record for their child's career, anything that disturbs the school and its own success is a problem.[9] Attempts to 'protect' children, and to keep them out of school on the grounds that their little brains are not yet ready for educational activity, reinforces a quite artificial separation between 'work' as adult activity and 'play' as defining the life of the child; and such psychologising responses to the problems children face at school also provide perfect ammunition for a neoliberal agenda which aims to cut the provision of free education.

Children in contemporary society are doubly cursed: at one moment they are assumed to be liars, fabricating stories of sexual abuse; at the next moment they are idealised, romanticised as inno-cent flowers who need to be protected for as long as possible from the adult world. When they do behave badly they are now patholo-gised by the psychologists, and may even be put on medication to shut them up. Bad behaviour that is labelled 'ADHD', failure to read that is labelled 'dyslexia', or clumsiness that is labelled 'dyspraxia', each need to be treated as instances in which the child is failing to conform to the demands of the school. A school that disables the children really is an institution that is failing, and the political forces that disable the school need to be tackled. There is a psychological problem here, but it is a problem that the psychologist is part of.[10]

Psychological Essentialism Is Challenged in the Process of Deinstitutionalisation

Demands that things must be done differently cause conflict, and the lesson of struggles against institutions that imprison and punish people for being unable to cope with life under capitalism is that social divisions need to be tackled and fought through. Once again, there is a correlation between class and professional status on the

[9] See Goodley and Lawthom (2004) for accounts by academics and activists.
[10] For an example of the way 'inclusive education' is tackled in teacher training, see Evans (2002).

one hand, and the fate of people treated for different disorders on the other. A 'talking therapy' rather than physical treatment is more likely to be offered to a middle-class patient, with the unspoken assumption that the working class consists of dumb brutes who will only respond to drugs and electroshock. A cursory examination of the class background of medical doctors and psychiatrists reveals that they are much more likely to come from the ruling class and middle class than nurses and auxiliary support workers in hospitals and clinics. Psychologists are usually located somewhere between the two groups, and in some ways this makes them more dangerous; they are more anxious about their status and willing to crawl to the doctors to gain acceptance and step on those whom they are keen to see as lesser than themselves. The focus on deinstitutionalisation provides a way of tackling the role of psychology in its home bases and in the wider 'community'.[11]

Analyses of institutionalisation show how it fixes individuals in place

The political movement for deinstitutionalisation entails an alternative to psychological attempts to treat disorder as some essential quality of the people who are diagnosed. The movement to close the mental hospitals in Trieste in the north of Italy in the late 1970s showed that psychiatry and psychology not only divide the expert 'doctors' from the stupid 'patients', but it divides the different workers in the hospital against each other. The Italian 'democratic psychiatry' movement has had an impact around the world, and is still alive in struggles against institutionalisation.[12]

Franco Basaglia, the psychiatrist who initiated the closure of San Giovanni mental hospital in Trieste as part of the mass movement 'Psichiatria Democratica', argued that 'deinstitutionalisation' needs to focus not only on what happens in the hospital itself, but on what happens outside. As Basaglia pointed out, 'when the mentally ill are no longer segregated – conceptually as well as spatially – we are forced to recognise their peculiarities and at the same time to discover our own'; this then enables us to see that ' "normality" can be just as much of a distortion as madness'.[13] The 'institution' of the

[11] Basaglia (1987) brings together descriptions of the Italian 'democratic psychiatry' movement and theoretical analyses.
[12] Ramon and Giannichedda (1989) provide a good outline of key issues in the Italian debates and a useful contrast with the process of closing the mental hospitals and turning to 'community care' in the UK.
[13] Basaglia (2004), p. 192.

hospital is present also in the community when people are still treated as 'patients' who are made to take their medication.[14]

The struggle includes changing images of
what psychological 'disturbance' is

The demand to close the old mental hospitals was not only a humanitarian demand, but one designed to ensure that there would be no guarantee of medical authority lying in the background. The existence of the mental hospital as a 'last resort' meant that psychiatrists would always have the final say in 'extreme' cases that could not be handled by the psychologists, or by those even further down the pecking order. In addition, the mental hospital put different grades of mental health workers in their place, institutionalising them almost as much as the patients. This led to some difficulties that had to be tackled when the hospital was closed. Many of the nurses were organised by fascist 'trades unions', for example, and intense political struggle took place between them and those organised with the radical psychiatrists and psychologists in 'Psichiatria Democratica', in which there were activists from the Italian communist party and 'autonomist' far-left groups.

Some of the psychologists in San Giovanni in Trieste carried on working in the 'clinical psychology' department in the grounds of the hospital, a chilling steel and linoleum medical ward run by people in white coats. However, those psychologists who threw themselves behind the reforms did not seek new positions of power in the community mental health centres; instead they spent their time working in the new public cafeteria and in the gardens. This transformation of professional identity has been followed by some psychologists outside Italy who have been inspired to spend more of their time as activists rather than as 'clinical' practitioners. In this way the transformation of images of madness that was so important in Trieste has been taken forward in other places, and there has been an emergence of 'mad pride' as the self-organisation of those who have been labelled by psychiatric institutions in different countries around the world.[15]

Democratic psychiatry and psychology require a political context

The formation of a network of community mental health centres and work cooperatives meant that a wide range of political divisions

[14] See Basaglia (1987) for discussion of deinstitutionalisation.
[15] See Curtis et al. (2000) for examples of 'mad pride' activities.

had to be tackled. There is a question here of the role of 'work' for example, and new cooperatives were set up which then enabled those who had been hospitalised to creatively produce alongside others and democratically decide how products should be sold. There are limits, of course, to what is possible, and the reconfiguration of working-class consciousness in the Trieste cooperatives was determined by the need to compete in the capitalist market.[16] The lessons of the struggle for deinstitutionalisation cannot be learnt if the limitations are not also taken seriously. Similarly, mental health problems always impact on women in a different way than on men, and women in families usually bear the brunt of responsibility for care when 'patients' are released from the hospital into the 'community'. They may be thrown back into the care of their families, but those families may then become the relay for power just as surely as the hospital was.

In addition, in Trieste there were cultural minorities that posed particular demands; the Slovenes, for example, had a community mental health centre on the outskirts of Trieste and were more likely to demand psychotherapy. This demand was treated as a reflection of their greater concern with identity by the psychiatrists leading the reforms, but the Italian experiment still had a deep impact over the border in Slovenia, an impact that is still evident today in the capital, Ljubljana. Cultural, 'ethnic' and 'racial' differences always serve a function in the production of images of 'madness' and these images need to be addressed if there is to be a genuinely progressive alternative to the institutionalisation of those who suffer their alienation to the breaking point called 'madness'.[17]

Psychological Pathologisation Is Challenged in the Production of New Normalities

Cultural norms about what is normal are deeply embedded in psychology, and these questions of culture very quickly turn into questions of institutionalised racism when diagnoses are made of

---

[16] There were graffiti on the walls in Trieste in the 1980s that accused Basaglia of releasing the mad from the hospital only to put them in the chains of work; the story was that supporters of Guattari, the French anti-psychiatrist, had been responsible for these graffiti. Deleuze and Guattari (1977) were not as convinced as traditional Marxism that creative work could overcome alienation.

[17] For a discussion of political lessons of 'democratic psychiatry' and future perspectives, see T. McLaughlin (2003). For examples of the way the context for political struggle in South Africa led to more radical ways of thinking about what 'mental health' might be, see Eagle et al. (1989).

those who are 'abnormal'. One of the most active radical movements currently in the field of mental health mobilised around 'hearing voices', began when a Dutch psychiatrist, Marius Romme, was questioned by one of his patients about his religious beliefs. Patsy Hage (the patient) heard 'voices', which in the diagnostic system of the DSM is a 'first rank' symptom of schizophrenia. As Patsy Hage pointed out, it was a bit strange that she should be diagnosed by a psychiatrist who was also a good Catholic who must have heard the voices of God. Romme was provoked by this encounter, and put out a call to people who heard voices in Holland, and then brought them together; many had no contact with the psychiatric system, though some participants in this meeting had worries about telling a psychiatrist about their experiences. This led to the formation of a network of people who 'hear voices', the Hearing Voices Network, drawing attention to new ways of being human, new ways of being normal.[18]

Explanations define what it is normal for those who are disturbed to hear

The study of 'hearing voices' has been conducted by psychiatrists, psychologists and now by researchers in a range of other professions. While psychiatrists still tend to see the phenomenon as a symptom of an underlying schizophrenic illness, psychologists have responded by focusing on it as a discrete symptom that may be treated with 'cognitive' focusing techniques.[19] Some of those who hear voices use these techniques if they are unhappy with their experiences, and find it useful, for example, to find ways of being able to talk back at particular times of the day to the voices. Some people in the groups decide to take the medication prescribed by their psychiatrist, and discuss the effects and 'side effects' in the self-help groups.

However, the movement has gone further than this, to show that there is no one correct way to define a problem, and that for some people it is not a problem at all. Some meetings show that the

[18] There is an early account of the work by Romme and Escher (1989) for *Schizophrenia Bulletin* (a mainstream psychiatric journal), and Romme et al. (1992) for *British Journal of Psychiatry*, and then Romme and Escher (1993) published a more accessible version for MIND (an alliance of fairly progressive mental health groups in the UK). For histories and analyses of the development of the Hearing Voices Network, see Blackman (2001) and James (2001). For insider accounts by key activists in the movement, see Coleman (1999) and T. McLaughlin (1996).
[19] Haddock and Slade (1995) argue that CBT can be used to treat 'psychotic disorders'.

process of diagnosis can be interpreted as an occasion where the doctor hears the 'voices' of science. Studies of child development in the Vygotskian tradition – where there is an analysis of the way the individual thinking alone emerges out of a collective linguistic interaction – show that it is likely that everyone hears 'voices' as a condition of being able to think in the first place.[20]

The formation of a new network changes who is heard and what can be heard

People who hear voices are often put in positions where their experiences are treated as pathological. People who come from 'other' cultures – other to the Western psychiatric tradition – may have experiences of 'hearing voices' as a necessary part of being in a local religious system.[21] When they turn up in front of a psychologist with a problem, the experience of hearing voices may be detected and diagnosed as a disorder connected with the problem, and they may then end up being 'sectioned', compulsorily detained in hospital under the Mental Health Act.[22]

At a time when Muslim communities are being targeted for housing 'fundamentalists' who, we are told, hear the voice of God and think that they will be rewarded in heaven for carrying out suicide attacks, the 'pathology' of hearing voices urgently needs to be put in question. The question is not what the community is like that has fundamentalist and abnormal psychological states, but what the dominant culture is like that is so intent on pathologising experiences that are deemed to be scarily different.[23]

The struggle over voices connects with the politics of mental difference

Just as the movement in Trieste had to challenge popular views of 'madness', so the Hearing Voices Network has been concerned with media images of people who are often depicted as violent because they 'hear voices'. One result of the challenge to psychiatric bound-aries between people who hear voices and 'normal' people who do not (or claim that they do not) is that there has been a proliferation

---

[20] See Vygotsky (1962), and Vološinov (1973) for a more explicitly Marxist, non-psychological analysis of the relationship between thought and language.
[21] Littlewood and Lipsedge (1993) provide a good review of the issues, and for one attempt within psychiatry to tackle this, see Rack (1982).
[22] On this problem in the UK, see Black Health Workers and Patients Group (1983).
[23] See Mamdani's (2004) account of the construction of identity in the context of colonialism in Africa.

of practices to create different ways of being visible. The Hearing Voices Network gave rise to a variety of other networks. One network brought together women who cut themselves.[24]

Another response was the formation of the 'Paranoia Network' in 2003 by people who have been labelled for being 'paranoid'.[25] Two disciplines, psychology and psychiatry, tried to keep a tight grip on knowledge over the last century and, together with their various hangers-on, these disciplines ruled the roost at the centre of the psy-complex as a dense web of theories and practices. The paradox is that while those in the psy-complex observed and regulated thinking and behaviour – they are part of the very enterprise that makes it so people do feel they are being watched – at the same time the professionals always felt fearful and suspicious about what people who are 'abnormally' paranoid might do next. The Paranoid Network has brought those who have been labelled psychotically 'paranoiac' together with practitioners to find new ways of living in a political economic system which requires a degree of paranoia for individuals to survive.[26]

Psychological Explanation Is Reframed by Embedding It in Narrative and History

Some radical alternatives have come out of the ideological heart of capitalist society. The nuclear family is the place where boys and girls learn to become normal men and women, and family therapy has historically been one of those forms of psychological intervention that served to glue men and women who are unhappy, and unhappy with each other, back together again.[27] The compulsory heterosexuality that is maintained by a 'healthy' family system ensures that power is distributed in line with patriarchal values, and ensures that property is passed on from father to son in clear unbroken succession. While this inheritance of property is most important for the bourgeois families that own the means of production, the moral

[24] Spandler (1996) draws on accounts given by young women who self-harm, and Cresswell (2005) provides a history of this strand in the 'survivor' movement in England.

[25] For a typical psychological review of approaches to paranoia which draws attention to some of the problems in the mainstream psychiatric categories but then ends up trying to conceptualise the problem in psychological terms, see Bell et al. (2003).

[26] For an overview and critique of the way 'paranoia' figures in psychiatric and psychological discourse, see Harper (1994).

[27] For a discussion of the role of family therapy traditions that normalise family relations, see Poster (1978). For an example of this work, see Minuchin (1974).

lesson in family values that has percolated through the rest of society is just as important for the working class.[28] In some ways, that lesson is more important for the working class because it is more likely to be observed and pathologised when individual workers do not fit in, when they are not productive.[29] In this respect fundamentalism really is a problem, but it is actually fundamentalist Christianity as a force that enforces the nuclear family that we should be most beware of; Christian moral crusades against other cultures then link sexual subordination of women with the racist images of 'others'. It is in this context that alternative therapeutic approaches have emerged that locate the 'problem' neither in the individual nor in the family but in the fabric of culture, society and political activity.[30]

Diagnostic categories and definitions of the 'problem' are reframed in narrative

The most powerful approaches in family therapy were those that treated the family as a 'system', a system which may itself be pathological when it tries to pin the blame on a particular individual – the 'identified patient' or 'index patient' – for its problems. These approaches that were at the time so conservative, actually undid themselves, for they provoked ways of thinking about family systems that widened the scope of the 'problem'; therapists and social workers using the approach started looking at the cultural systems in which the particular family was embedded.[31] The turn to narrative that emerged from within the systemic tradition provided an alternative way of conceptualising practice for psychiatrists and it gave an

[28] Engels (1972) outlines the classical Marxist account of the necessary entwinement of the family, private property and the state. Foucault (1981) argued that the practice of 'confessing' our innermost desires in a therapeutic mode to a professional was something that started in the middle class and then was advertised as a good thing to the whole population.

[29] See Hill (1983) for an account of psychiatric oppression that locates it in the context of class society; Pilgrim and Rogers (1983) provide a sociological overview of the relationships between mental distress and class, sex and race; Pilgrim (1997) focuses on the role of psychotherapy and its relationship to different axes of oppression.

[30] The classic early statements of the most radical narrative position in therapy were by White and Epston (1989, 1990); these accounts were published by the Dulwich Centre in Adelaide, Australia (Michael White is based in Australia and David Epston in New Zealand). There are restatements and extensions of this work in Monk et al. (1997), Madigan and Law (1998), and Parker (1999b).

[31] See Selvini et al. (1978) for work within the systemic therapy tradition that was already starting to address wider questions of language and society; Selvini-Palazzoli et al. (1980) is the widely cited paper on clinical practice within this framework.

opening for social workers to engage in therapy in such a way as to challenge mainstream psychiatry. It then also served as an opportunity for clinical psychologists to take what their clients said seriously. Until then there had been a behaviourist-oriented focus on 'social skills' in clinical psychology, sometimes supplemented with 'cognitive' models of the way someone with a mental 'disorder' functioned in the world.[32]

The way was opened for language and self-reflection to be taken seriously, and so also for the contrasting definitions of the problem, definitions beyond psychiatric categories, to be explored. Someone who came to one of the new systemic therapists – now fashioning themselves as 'narrative therapists' or 'discursive therapists' – would be asked where they first heard the diagnoses they gave themselves and how those diagnoses functioned for them. These questions will vary according to cultural context, and there are specific variants of the narrative approach to attend to gender and sexuality.[33]

The re-articulation of the narrative changed
the relationship to the 'problem'

Speaking and reflecting on the ways in which one has been labelled has the effect of changing the relationship to the problem. Rather than the person being the problem, the problem itself is treated as the problem. This, however, is merely a step to redefining how the problem operates and finding ways to tackle it. This has enabled connections between 'narrative' perspectives in therapy and broader collective projects that redefine 'empowerment' in ways that are more suited to socialist and feminist politics.[34]

In this way a space is opened for externalising the problem and addressing it as cultural. The 'problem' is moved out of the realm of the particular individual, hitherto treated as someone who carried it around with them as part of their particular pathological personality structure, into the realm of narrative. The problem is thus 'externalised'. Rather than being problem-focused, however, these

---

[32] On the 'social skills' model, see Trower et al. (1978), and for a humanist critique, see Yardley (1979).

[33] For a discussion of the relationship between narrative therapy and feminism, see Swan (1999); for an elaboration of the approach to tackle questions of gender and culture (in the context of work in Ireland), see O'Reilly Byrne and Colgan McCarthy (1999); and for narrative work with men and male violence, see Law (1999).

[34] For examples, see the volume edited by Paré and Larner (2004).

alternative approaches are 'solution-focused',[35] and the techniques that these therapists use can be employed by psychologists, social workers or other professionals who do not want to pathologise people who are suffering.

There is a collective practice for addressing problems as questions of power

The 'narrative' therapies have provided a way of 'deconstructing' the problems that have been constructed by powerful pathological processes, those that psychologists are too often happy to participate in. This has opened the way for linking people who have externalised the same kind of problem and mobilising them to address those problems together. The 'Anti-Anorexia League', for example, brings together young women who have been labelled and who have shaken off the label in order to be able to move on to challenge the images of women that make some body shapes seem normal and others abnormal.[36]

The power relations between psychiatrists, psychologists, psychotherapists and their patients are also challenged. While the motifs of 'respect' and 'cultural respect' in these practices can sometimes seem to avoid the material structures of class, race and sex oppression when people come into the psychiatric system, they do open a different way of working with categories of distress. The practice of 'reflecting teams' (an innovation from Norway in which therapists discuss how they have made sense of a 'problem' while the clients observe them), for example, throws the expertise of the professional into question, and it can make them more accountable for the decisions they make about diagnosis and treatment. It also means that the discussions that happen in self-help groups about

[35] Steve de Shazer (1985) is best known for 'solution-focused' therapy, and linked it to philosophy more explicitly when it became popular as an approach in family therapy (de Shazer, 1991); the problematic role of 'post-structuralism' in this work is discussed by Fish (1999). For a discussion of the relationship between Michael White and de Shazer's work, see Chang and Phillips (1993), and for a scathing comparison of Michael White and Michel Foucault (upon whom Michael White claims to draw for his narrative therapy), see Leupnitz (1992).

[36] White (1986) offers a narrative approach to 'anorexia'; and for an account of the work of the narratively oriented 'Anti-Anorexia League' in Vancouver, see Grieves (1997, 1998). Madigan and Epston (1995) link the questioning of psychiatry to collective action; see also Madigan (1999).

therapeutic options and 'side effects' are less likely to be based on paranoid speculation about what is being done to us when we are patients.[37]

Oppositional Practices Change Relations of Ruling, and in Relation to Psychology

There are clearly serious political limitations to oppositional practices inside the discipline of psychology (and oppositional practices in adjacent disciplines) when they are led by professionals. Many of the most radical 'anti-psychiatry' initiatives, for example, have been led by psychiatrists, and this is the case in the classical anti-psychiatry movement – with R. D. Laing and Thomas Szasz as the most well known examples – and in the attempts to deinstitutionalise psychiatry and set up hearing voices networks (with Franco Basaglia and Marius Romme as initiators of those movements).[38] Similarly, the development of the radical disability movement has tended to be based in education institutions, and narrative therapies have emerged from within social work; while these are lower-status professions than psychology, they can hardly be seen as 'grass-roots' movements. Nevertheless, they lay the ground for us to reconfigure what psychology is, and to find better alternative practices for reflecting upon and changing alienated life conditions.

Oppositional practices succeed when those with power are unable to rule any longer

New practices disturb the certainties of the professionals in psychology so they can define what ability really is. The lesson of the struggles against reductionism and essentialism in psychology is that even psychologists can be broken from their understanding of what is normal and what is abnormal. When they are shown that there are alternatives to psychology that work better than the old tried and tested procedures, then some psychologists will join those labelled by the discipline and find new ways of working with them.

Some clinical psychologists have recently broke down the boundaries between expert and patient by revealing that they too were

[37] Monk et al. (1997) include discussions of this from within psychiatry, psychotherapy and counselling. For a specific discussion of the role of the 'reflecting team' in relation to psychiatry, see Madigan and Epston (1995).
[38] See Coppock and Hopton (2000) for an account of the rise and fall of the 'anti-psychiatry' movement, and Spandler (2006) for a history of the Mental Patients Union as the more radical wing. See also Foucault's (2006) reflections on anti-psychiatry.

once incarcerated, that they had to keep this history secret to be able to be accepted into clinical training.[39] This opens the space for new practices that redefine what the problem is and where the problem lies. It is then possible to move from alienation to emancipation.

Oppositional practices succeed when those without power are unwilling to be ruled any longer

The movements for emancipation have always had to link the domain of 'personal' change with 'political' change; this is a lesson that the new social movements – left, ecological, feminist, anti-racist and anti-capitalist movements – have already learnt from their own history. The problem is that these movements for change are also now operating in a political-economic environment that is not only hostile to change; it has developed strategies for persuading the oppressed that their problems are really only deep psychological problems. This means that 'radicals' in psychology have to be careful not to play into this deeply ideological psychological culture and not to reinforce the psychologisation of politics and resistance.

The lesson of struggle against pathologisation and for the acceptance of a variety of ways of being 'normal' is that those who seemed to be without power are actually the ones who turn out to be able to redefine the terms of the debate. The power of psychology is dissolved in the process, and psychology is thrown into question. The conditions are bit by bit put in place for psychology as a separate discipline to disappear.

---

[39] See May (2000) for one inspiring account in British clinical psychology.

11
Transitional Demands: Taking on Psychology

The discipline of psychology is part of a sprawling network of theories and techniques concerned with the way we think and behave, and it all too often operates as an apparatus of social control. That sprawling network has come to have immense power in capitalist society; so much so that it seems impossible now to escape it. At the very same time that new versions of this psychological fake-science pretend to avoid 'psychobabble', then, the enthusiasts insist that we need to work with the 'human givens'.[1] Whether it is laboratory research recognised by mainstream psychological associations or new-age pop-psychology peddled as an alternative to save us from stress or help us discover our inner potential, there is the same reactionary assumption at work: fix the individual and you will solve social ills.

There are real alternatives to psychology, however; and this chapter describes different political perspectives in and against psychology developed in alliance with those who make use of psychological services. It sets out a series of demands that will put social change on the agenda of psychological practice. The task we are engaging in here is two-fold, and we need to interlink the two aspects dialectically so that they each draw strength from, and question, the other. The tactical and strategic nature of the 'transitional' demands we make should be designed to take us up to the limits of psychology and enable us to imagine what life might be like without it.[2]

---

[1] One example here is 'Mindfields College' in the UK which claims to teach 'the practical application of sound psychological knowledge' (and it has the front-of-brochure tagline: 'WORKING WITH THE HUMAN GIVENS – No psychobabble!'. Linked to the 'Human Givens Institute', this 'college' offers a range of courses conducted by no doubt well-meaning folk keen to make a profit out of psychology, and it merely makes explicit what is being generated in established mainstream university psychology departments.

[2] A series of 'transitional demands' was built into the founding programme of the Fourth International by Leon Trotsky (1938) to take forward the analysis elaborated by Karl Marx and Frederick Engels (1965) in the Communist Manifesto. Transitional demands

There are first and second 'human nature'
which bind and separate us

The first aspect of a progressive engagement with psychology is to take human nature seriously, but to do this in such a way as to cut the ground from under the feet of those who try to define and limit our experience of ourselves and others.[3] There has always been resistance to psychological explanations of who we are and what we can do, and this resistant reflexive questioning aspect of human nature has been very troublesome to the psychologists. As we learn to speak we thereby reflect on who we are for the significant others we speak to and who speak to us. Our different languages provide the symbolic resources to transform our underlying human nature, our 'first nature' endowed by the peculiar biological material of the human species.

The social 'second nature' we have no choice but to construct as we 'develop'. We construct our second nature alongside and in contrast to those around us in a common language, and this enables us to refuse already existing definitions of what we are, definitions that usually lock us in our place (whether those definitions are given by bureaucrats, clerics or psychologists). In capitalist society that second nature is the stuff of alienation. This historically constructed second nature – the particular psychological content that we feel so

---

are reasonable requests, for a sliding scale of wages or opening the books of companies, for example, but they function in two ways: they cannot be met under capitalism, so they take us up to and beyond the limits of what is possible in this society; and they prefigure a more democratic society which is based on human needs (and the creative possibilities opened up by new, as yet unimagined kinds of subjective experience) rather than profit (and the brutal inequality and secrecy required to extract profit more efficiently).

[3] Although some Marxists have tried to pretend that there is no such thing as human nature, this argument is actually a travesty of Marxism, which does rest on assumptions about human needs and potentials (see Geras, 1983). We should, however, take care not to slide into the so-called 'critical realist' attempts to specify exactly what the 'first nature' is that defines human psychology. Although critical realism has been useful as a counterweight to relativist approaches (which make it seem as if we can know nothing about underlying social and economic mechanisms that structure power inequalities), it is a big mistake to try and outdo the psychologists at their own game by telling us what psychology really is like (see, e.g., Archer, 2003). Thus 'psychology' sometimes figures in critical realist accounts as just one more piece of the jigsaw (see, e.g., Collier, 1994), and is then used to warrant alternative 'co-counselling' approaches outside mainstream psychology (see, e.g., New, 1996). Some ostensibly 'critical' approaches in psychology concerned with 'embodiment' (as a counter to the focus on language at the expense of everything else) fall into the same trap when they try to defend quasi-psychoanalytic brain research (see, e.g., Cromby, 2005). Recent 'critical realist' work has, in a bizarre turn to God, argued for a level playing field in debates between secular and religious theorists (see Archer et al., 2004).

deep at the core of our being – distances us from our first underlying nature, that forever lost and mythical stuff many psychologists desperately try to discover and then represent to us in anthropological fairy tales or glowing brain-scan images.

Political analysis is necessary for interpretation that is also transformation

The second aspect of our task is made possible and necessary by the creative possibilities opened up by our second nature – a sense that there is more to life than blind obedience to mute biology.[4] The task includes creative collective activity that works at the limits and fault-lines of ideology and power. The ideological mystification that psychology perpetuates in its peculiar images of human mental processes, and the power that psychologists reproduce when they label and limit behaviour, lie in the realm of politics. This politics is broader and deeper than the machinations of professional politicians though, and progressive political analysis is necessary to grasp the role of psychology as a discipline if we want to change it.

We need to know how psychology functions in the service of capitalism, how it reinforces the alienated and individualised sense that people have of themselves which makes them happy enough to sell their labour to others, and despair of any other way of living. But we also need to know how this particular kind of exploitation that was the setting for psychology to emerge as a separate discipline is interwoven with other axes of oppression – around gender and culture, for example – and how psychology is used to set the subjects of one kind of oppression against the others.[5] The political alliances

---

[4] Note here the way metaphors of sight and speech themselves also privilege certain kinds of life, certain kinds of psychology built upon these senses, in the image of limits and liberation that they evoke here. This problem, that we are still trapped in certain metaphors that are so useful to convey what is wrong with existing society, is addressed in critical disability research (see, e.g., French and Swain, 2000; and Goodley and Lawthom, 2004). It could be argued that making language central to the development of our historically constituted 'second nature' sidelines those who do not speak; however, this 'language' could be any shared symbolic system; deaf people, for example, will have a certain form of sign language that performs the same functions (see Sacks, 1991), and blind children will still have a certain kind of mirror-like relationship with their care-givers even if the 'mirror' operates through the medium of sound and touch (see Urwin, 1998).

[5] Here the radical updating of Marxist politics offered by 'transitional demands' is already informed by the socialist-feminist tradition in which there is an emphasis on the way that power is relayed in the most intimate of relationships, even in the realm of what we think of as being 'psychology', and that our forms of struggle must connect the means we employ with the ends we want to achieve. So, this is feminist 'prefigurative' politics built upon the argument that the personal is political (see, e.g., Rowbotham et al., 1980), reinforcing the 'transitional' aspect of more traditional Marxist politics (see Parker, 1996).

we can then make will include different kinds of people who suffer at the sharp end of psychology, the professional psychologists who realise that something is wrong, and even some academic researchers who are worrying away at what psychology has turned people into. The demands push open the door that leads from psychology to social change.

Using and Abusing, and Turning the Tables

The discipline is organised around a sharp divide between those who discover and deliver psychological expertise (in which there is another weird separation between 'pure' and 'applied' work) and those who are subjected to it. There has been some attention given to professional abuse by psychologists, but this has often tended to let the academics off the hook.[6] Simply portraying those who consume psychology as helpless dupes fails to take account of the way that psychological explanations have come to saturate contemporary society. Psychological culture seeps into the everyday life of the professional and academic so that they come to believe the false explanations and solutions offered by the discipline as much as those they dish it out to. We all 'use' and are used by psychology at different points in our lives, so then the question is how we can find the resources to do something with it that take us beyond what psychology offers. A first set of transitional demands is needed that will position those who use psychological services not as victims but as autonomous agents who have the strength to resist psychology, and also get something useful from it in the meantime.

1.   The right to refuse physical treatments for 'psychological' problems

Physical treatments – including lobotomy, leucotomy, electroshock and psychopharmacology – operate on assumptions about human distress that would not even be made by most psychologists. These treatments are used when the psychologist has failed to provide their own treatment but hands over responsibility to medics who know even less about what goes on in the mind. The treatments do

---

[6] Studies of the high incidence of clinical psychologists who have sex with their clients, for example, do draw attention to the abuse of power. However, there is also an endemic problem of male lecturers preying on younger women students which does not receive so much attention, and when these issues are discussed there is often an appeal to the spurious notion of 'boundaries', as if we would all be OK if we kept strictly to our given identities and roles. The problem of power is once again neatly displaced into something that seems to have a psychological origin and solution.

not reach the 'causes' of psychological problems, but they do often cause damage that then really impairs mental processes. There are sometimes reasons why drugs are useful to stabilise and give breathing space for reflecting on what is happening, but none of these treatments are 'psychological' at all, and psychologists can be mobilised alongside users of psychological services to refuse them.[7]

2.   Transparency over the rationale for psychological treatments

Treatment programmes that are implemented without the knowledge and agreement of those subjected to them inevitably take on a coercive form. This then erases the reflexive capacities of those involved, turning them into mechanisms, and the scene is set for people to be turned from subjects into objects. Every psychological treatment must necessarily, for good or ill, include space for that reflexive capacity to choose to participate and to puzzle about what the consequences are. The 'process notes' made by practitioners help them make sense of what is going on in counselling or psychotherapy, though there may be agreement at the outset that these will be shared. The key issue here is the right to know what that process might involve at the outset, and to know of any diagnostic labels that will be shared with other practitioners.[8]

3.   No agreed 'correct' terminology for psychological phenomena

The descriptions psychologists give of different aspects of behaviour, thinking and feeling are specific to the models they use, and their models draw on and feed into how we make sense of ourselves in everyday life. This diversity is potentially a source of strength and it needs to be defended and opened up further so that there can be challenge to the use of different labels. This is a question of control and ownership of our right to describe ourselves, whether that is as 'mad' or 'queer' or 'neurologically diverse'. Star signs are as valid descriptions for who we are as 'personality traits', and the reclaiming and reworking of psychological terms is part of the struggle to put

---

[7] The 'democratic psychiatrists' in Trieste knew that they could reduce the amount of medication when they were no longer using it to 'cure' patients, but they still had to make diagnoses so they could get European Union grants for their community mental health centres; the key issue was how to enable people to get off the drugs when they had done their work (see Ramon and Giannichedda, 1989).

[8] For a discussion of narrative therapeutic work with 'case notes', see Simblett (1997); for a discussion of the way behavioural packages to treat such things as phobias can be democratically agreed upon, see Goldiamond (1974).

our individual psychology in social context so that we can reflect on it and change it ourselves.[9]

4.   The right to reply to representations of ourselves in research

Observations about the behaviour of others and reflections on those things can be made by anyone, whether they are a psychologist or not. However, when a psychologist asks permission for inclusion of 'personal' responses – through a questionnaire, interview or focus group – they often hope that they will scoop up 'data' which they can then interpret so that they can publish their speculations about what their participants really think. Taking transparency in research all the way robs the psychologist of their power, and this includes insisting on the right to see any interview transcripts, to delete or amend portions of transcripts, to have responses to any interpretations made of personal material included, and to withdraw from the study at any point.[10]

Professionals In and Against the Discipline

Practising psychologists are often put in the position of acting as gate-keepers, and the routine assessment and testing that take up much of their time mean that they do open or close access to other services. However, the psychologist is also under threat from rival professions, and the history of any sub-discipline – whether it is clinical, educational or occupational psychology – is marked by turf wars in which the psychologist has to claim a particular kind of knowledge and right to practice.[11] The upshot of the precarious

---

[9] Medieval popular psychology in England was much weirder than horoscopes in newspapers today (see Bates, 1983); if we can refuse psychology now, we would then be in a stronger position to refuse other mystical 'explanations' for human behaviour that pretend to be universal.

[10] Sometimes descriptions of patterns of behaviour can be illuminating without intruding into the 'psychology' of those involved, and it would be ridiculous to insist that everyone who was observed should give their consent (see, e.g., Fox, 2004); on the other hand, those who take part in research should not be forced to be anonymous, and they should demand the right to be named if they want this (see Parker, 2005a).

[11] Clinical psychology in Britain nearly disappeared during the 1980s, for example, because psychologists could not find a way of persuading service providers (hospitals and local authorities) that they had something distinct to offer (see Pilgrim and Treacher, 1992). Eventually they triumphed over the occupational health and social workers and, in an uneasy truce with the psychiatrists, the psychologists have become the designated experts on Cognitive Behaviour Therapy (CBT) as a supplement to medical treatments for made-up diseases like 'schizophrenia' (see, e.g., Bentall, 1990). In this way psychologists did not challenge the notion of 'psychopathology', but merely fought to have the right to define and tackle it in their own way (see Parker et al., 1995).

position of many psychologists is that they actually have most to lose from radical alternatives. The particular demands that psychologists make have to be embedded in other political programmes so that they might find a place to do some of the good things that they imagined would be possible when they first trained. There are those who make a mint as lifestyle gurus; for them any radical demand will radically curtail their lifestyle, but there are also many more psychologists now in 'independent' practice; and because they are working privately they are tied into the continued success of their discipline. Our task here is to open up more space for change, to expand and go beyond their limited room for manoeuvre.

5. Diagnostic categories are only tactical or strategic devices

The labels used in different diagnostic systems – the most notorious being the International Classification of Diseases (ICD) and the *Diagnostic and Statistical Manual of Mental Disorders* (DSM) – fix people in categories that then often follow them throughout their lives. The question is always how a category has come to be applied (how, for example, did someone come to believe this description of themselves, and what are the consequences?), and then how the label operates as a shorthand term to access certain resources (in which case they should also know how this is being used only for these purposes). Psychological categories should be open to question and transformation, never used to classify and compare one group with another.[12]

6. No secret diplomatic deals with the other professionals

The worst abuses occur when there is collusion between different groups of professionals, and psychology is in a particularly dangerous position because it is below psychiatry in the pecking order and it then enjoys power over other 'lesser' professions. This structural position – 'kiss up, kick down' – makes the slide between psychological diagnosis and psychiatric diagnosis very prevalent. The risk is then that a 'difficult' case is already marked for treatment, and the precise reasons for distress come to be obscured, especially when other professionals are recruited to agree with what a psychologist says.

---

[12] The general campaign against 'labels' in education and clinical psychology also needs to include recognition that a diagnosis can sometimes be useful as a tactic to gain access to services (see, e.g., Hare-Mustin and Marecek, 1997); the issue here is how the tactic is to be used, and whether the person who is labelled knows it is a tactic or comes to believe it as a life sentence.

When someone is a problem we always need to ask for whom they are a problem, and every cover-up designed to keep things quiet needs to be exposed.[13]

7.   Refuse 'tried and tested' psychological expertise

Psychologists have a privileged position in relation to other disciplines when they are allowed to relay their 'knowledge' in academic and professional training courses. This knowledge should be refused by other professionals, and treated as inappropriate to the work they do. When a psychologist presents certain forms of knowledge as 'findings' they should be challenged. These 'findings' in 'experiments' and observational studies should be carefully teased apart to show the ideological assumptions that are at work. There is no such thing as tried and tested psychology that can be exported into the domain of other professions, and nothing can be taken for granted in psychological knowledge.[14]

8.   Against 'boundaries' that protect professional roles

The preoccupation with gate-keeping and safeguarding of expertise is one of the reasons why psychologists have become so obsessed with 'boundaries'. This motif of boundaries then becomes one of the touchstones of therapeutic practice, and in the process it seals off the realm of political activity from psychological change. Psychologists who will only relate to others from within a professional role may do so because they are operating in a certain theoretical model, but then they have no right to pretend that they have expertise to adjudicate about the decisions a person may make about their life. Obedience to a certain etiquette which rules out discussion of politics in the consulting room only serves to guarantee the position of the psychologist, which needs to be questioned.[15]

Academics Who Know How Not to Know, and Why

Academic psychologists are torn in two. On the one hand, they have the luxury to carry out research and then imagine that they have

[13] Support for the 'whistle-blowers' is only possible when there is a network of activists, and here the role of collective activity as standing over individual isolated moral choices is clear (see, e.g., Virden, 2006).

[14] This is where the 'social constructionist' and 'discursive' approaches in psychology have provided useful ammunition for those struggling to make sense of and dismantle psychological knowledge (see, e.g., Hansen et al., 2003).

[15] Debates about different forms of knowledge that are led by those who use psychological services and that call professionals to account are invaluable in this process (see, e.g., Bates, 2006).

really 'discovered' things about mental processes. Driven by a passion to find out more about other people, they quickly forget that they are themselves part of the problem; the history of the discipline is littered with cases where they have remembered this and left in a crisis of conscience. And those who remain have resources and nagging doubts about the value of their work that we must now do our best to intensify and exploit. On the other hand, academic researchers are expected to produce something for their employers; the search for funding for projects, the pressure to carry out investigations within a strict timescale, and the push to publish or perish, each place limits on creative work. The bizarre idea that in this context they can really be 'objective' in their research, that they could have no interest in what they study or find, merely makes things worse. Meanwhile, there is an expectation that they should teach new generations of psychologists, and we have to find ways of turning their pearls of wisdom back into bits of grit around which we can build something better.

9.   Include the psychologist in what they research

The opposition between 'objectivity' and 'subjectivity' is used in psychology to exclude the interests of the researcher from the equation in research. We need to put that subjective component back into the equation again and encourage the psychologists to reflect on what they are getting out of the research they carry out. There is no such thing as neutral disinterested research that simply uncovers the 'facts' about human psychology, and there is no such thing as knowledge about psychology without political effects. To include the psychologist in the research is to examine how they operate as voyeur on things they are curious about and to make them own up to what they might expect to find in any piece of research, and why.[16]

10.   Turn the spotlight on the psychologists

The study of psychology has traditionally been the study of other people outside the discipline, those who are positioned as the 'non-psychologists'. Against this we need to redefine the academic discipline of psychology as the study of psychologists – where they come from, how they are trained, what they do – so we can understand better what alternatives to this fake-science are possible.

---

[16] Researchers in the qualitative research tradition have questioned the stark distinction between 'objectivity' and 'subjectivity' (see, e.g., Reason and Rowan, 1981), and the argument that what we think of as 'objective' in psychology is a peculiar form of subjectivity has been insisted on in feminist research (see, e.g., Hollway, 1989).

The starting assumption of this new psychological study would be that there is actually no such thing as 'psychology'; rather there is a process of 'psychologisation' in which observations from biology or sociology, for example, are taken up and transformed into something that looks as if it is occurring inside an individual mind.[17]

11.   Unravel psychological culture

The study of psychological culture is a necessary complement to the study of psychologists. This enables us to take our distance from claims about 'development' and 'personality', for example, for we are concerned here with what is being done in the explanations that are offered by the experts and by the pop-psychologists. This study of psychological culture also means that we should take care not to participate in it, not to relay 'findings' about psychology to the media as if they were the good or bad news about human thinking and behaving. The question to be posed to a journalist asking for information about psychology should also be concerned with why it is that they think it would be worthwhile to know this. Psychologists should admit that they do not know.[18]

12.   Refuse to turn politics into psychology

Psychology should never be used to provide an explanation as to why certain things occur at the political level. Images of normality and abnormality are used to perpetuate ideological assumptions about what is possible and what should be placed outside the limits of change. Such questions about changing social relations are ethical questions in a domain of political argument about the nature of the society we want to live in. To reduce such questions to the level of psychology is to introduce a normative and moralising element into the debate. Psychologists should be encouraged to participate in political life, but as political agents, not as operating with the identity of a psychologist. The identity of 'psychologist' in politics should be treated with suspicion and derision.[19]

[17] For a good example of non-psychological historical research on how our 'psychology' is bound up with different forms of technology, see Gordo López and Cleminson (2004).

[18] For an example of the study of psychoanalytic culture, see Parker (1997), and for an attempt to extend this framework to analyse cognitive and humanistic kinds of psychology in culture, see Parker (1998b).

[19] In Latin America there are many psychologists who have entered government, and other psychologists paid by the military (and CIA) to keep tabs on radicals; in this context, 'liberation psychology' developed not as a new form of political identity but as a set of arguments and techniques that could be used by the liberation movements (see, e.g., Martín-Baró, 1994).

Politics Without Putting All the Pieces Together

Conservative politicians have started to realise that an explicit appeal to things psychological might win more support than boring people with arguments about the economy.[20] Calls for a shift of emphasis from GDP (Gross Domestic Product) to GWB – 'General Well Being' – are not meant as covert propaganda for more military intervention.[21] Rather, this General Well Being is aimed specifically at middle-class women voters who are encouraged to 'balance' their work and their life. In a cruel parody of the socialist-feminist argument that the personal is political, the role of psychology in political argument is now designed to put the personal bit of the jigsaw in a privileged place, as if it is the feminine bit of us that is most authentic and deserving of our devoted care. This is in some ways an old reactionary ruse, and support for women as mothers and mainstay of the family as the pillar of society has been popular in many authoritarian societies.[22] However, 'psychology' as such is handier nowadays as a tried and tested bit of this nonsense, so what demands can we make to take this seriously and so to take psychology out of the equation again?

13.   Against psychology as a component of a bigger picture

Distinctions between 'reason' and 'madness', between rationality and irrationality, are historically constructed in such a way as to reinforce reactionary notions of 'civilisation' and the development of supposedly lesser cultures. These distinctions map the way we come to understand the domain of society and political action so that it seems as if we must have a special 'psychological' account of

[20] For a socialist-feminist analysis of why people do not read the financial pages of the newspaper because it is 'boring', see Haug (1987). What is notable about Haug's analysis, which is developed from within the German 'Kritische Psychologie' tradition (see Tolman and Maiers, 1991; Hook, 2004), is that it traces the way things are structured as interesting or boring in the media without dredging around for a 'psychological' explanation for why people are bored. There is a rich tradition of analysis of 'boredom' in philosophy that neatly sidesteps all of the daft things that psychology has to say about it (see Osborne, 2006).

[21] The British Conservative Party leader David Cameron made this call for an emphasis on 'well-being' in 2006 after remodelling himself as an ecologically sensitive politician concerned with 'work-life balance' (the limits of which were neatly illustrated by him cycling to Parliament to save the ozone layer while having a car ferry his documents to work).

[22] For analyses of fascist propaganda around the place of women, and for analysis of the position of women in east European Stalinist societies, see Salecl (1994). The organisation 'Women Against Fundamentalism' developed analyses of the way religious leaders reinforce the subordinate status of women by romanticising them as mothers and child-bearers (see http://waf.gn.apc.org).

what happens at the level of the individual. Such a map is profoundly ideological, and it opens the way to writing off collective activity, as irrational mob behaviour, for example, or political protest as driven by resentment. Psychological explanation is always poisonous, and no less so when it is incorporated into a bigger picture to complete it.[23]

14.   Against any state definition of what psychology should be

Attempts to register psychologists or regulate psychotherapeutic practice always have the effect of defining how psychology should be understood. The variety of different models gives breathing space for those who are subjected to psychology, room for manoeuvre that would be closed down if there was state regulation of the discipline. Physical or sexual abuse is already a matter for the criminal courts regardless of the kind of professional practice within which such abuse takes place. Possible alternative approaches within and against traditional psychology that might emerge in the future are also thereby made more difficult, if not prohibited by well-meaning 'protective' regulation. This kind of regulation does no one any favours.[24]

15.   Against psychological definitions of 'identities' or 'communities'

Professionals of different kinds, not only psychologists, try to define what 'communities' are so that community 'representatives' can then speak for everyone and tell the authorities what 'identities' should be respected and what might be dismissed. Attempts to develop 'transcultural' psychiatry reveal the dangers for those who fail to match up to the images of 'health' and 'normality' specified for each particular category of identity. The notion of 'identity' itself puts the individual in their place, and the attempts to disrupt identity within 'queer politics' are a valuable corrective to psychological notions. Community development and identity development are twin dangers to be refused in any radical politics.[25]

[23] For a detailed analysis of suspicion of the 'masses' linked to contempt for feminisation, shop-girls, grocers, clerks, newspapers and tinned food among the English middle classes and their favourite writers, see Carey (1992); here we see laid bare the political-economic conditions in which individual psychology is assumed to be a part of the picture to guarantee civilised life.

[24] See Bates and House (2003) for a range of arguments against the 'professionalisation' of psychotherapy and counselling.

[25] The experience of members of minority ethnic communities who are doubly pathologised when they fail to show culturally appropriate mental distress – damned because they are mad, and damned because they are not mad in the way the psychiatrist expects them to be – is discussed by Mercer (1986).

16.   For psychology that is always different somewhere else

Psychology emerged in Western Europe and then took root in the United States, and it now relays certain models of the individual to different parts of the world. Different 'psychologies' in different cultures throw colonialist definitions of what a civilised, reasonable subject should look like into question. There is then a temptation to turn these more exotic psychologies into a romantic vision of what life used to be like or into something more authentic. We need to encourage the development of new spaces for new modes of thinking and relating, and show how every new technological development gives rise to something new in psychology. Every kind of 'psychology' that departs from US American and European models effectively disrupts and unravels the truth claims of the discipline.[26]

Success and Failure and Two Steps More

There have been many alliances of users of psychological services working alongside professional psychologists who are willing to break ranks and challenge the discipline, and with academic researchers who help us question the limits psychology places on progressive change. But those alliances are transitory and organised around particular kinds of activity. It is not a sign of failure that such alliances shift focus from one moment to the next and that the organisations that tried to hold them together disintegrated. Rather, the failure is when psychological explanations are wheeled in to explain why we got it wrong.[27]

Accountability is partial, particular and contradictory

The overriding question that needs to run through these demands is to do with accountability; how is this particular position from which the demand is made to be made accountable? This very basic and limited question does not have to be filled out now with content of some kind or other. How it will be answered is a matter

---

[26] See Dafermos et al. (2006) for a wide range of arguments about the limitations of mainstream psychology in different parts of the world.

[27] One example draws on psychoanalytic theory to examine 'disappointment', and so drum home the message that the hopes of the left were always too unrealistic and need a dose of reality-testing and therapeutic knowledge to help us come to terms with failure (Craib, 1994). When ex-radicals indulge in this kind of agonised heart-searching the psychologists must be rubbing their hands with glee. The reactionary effect is then enhanced when 'feminist' arguments are stirred in, to claim that the old leftist politics was always too 'macho' and doomed to failure because activists did not take psychology into account (see, e.g., Rustin, 2000).

that will be decided by the context in which psychology operates and what forces and relations govern what it is possible to demand. At the very least the emphasis on accountability puts on the agenda the idea that activity is embedded in collective projects, and that idea is already a significant break from mainstream psychology.

A further twist, which helps us break further from psychological logic, is to highlight contradictory partial alliances; what is most important is what we can do, not how we can justify it in a consistent argument that a psychologist will understand.[28] Against 'objective', 'neutral' or 'scientific' criteria, and against the isolated individual decision-making of someone faced with the psychologist, or someone employed as a psychologist, or someone trying to find out what psychology really is, we have an ethical question about how a particular course of action will be carried through and how this will be justified to others who are positioned to question and challenge us.[29]

Autonomy, self-organisation and political debate

The different clusters of demands in this chapter are not designed to be taken forward by each separate group on their own, as if there were certain objectives for those who use psychology or those who practice it or those who teach it to others. In most cases it would not actually be possible for a particular group to be able to operate independently, even if we would ideally love to see autonomous organisations of those who are usually subjected to psychology refusing it and then developing much better alternatives from scratch. Different social movements that insist that another world is possible know that they need to make alliances, and the demands they make also need to take on questions of psychology; the tensions and contradictions between those involved are what makes social change possible.

[28] Feminist practices which emphasise the 'precariousness' of multiple practices of resistance which are not organised by a political party or movement headed by leaders are useful antidotes to the psychological assumption that each individual should be consistent (see, e.g., Zavos et al., 2005).

[29] While 'ethics' is understood in psychology as being concerned with the 'consent' of participants in research (that is, with the way an individual understands the consequences of what someone else is going to do to them when 'data' is being collected), outside psychology there has been more sustained examination of the way that ethics entails a 'fidelity' to events in which one is implicated, remaining true to the commitment that one has made in one's action (see, e.g., Badiou, 2001). This is very different to a psychological logic which encourages us to falter, to fail, and then to be paralysed by the thought that attempts to change the world were always doomed. We need to remain steadfast, faithful to a political ethics that enables us to escape the grip of psychologisation and keep open possibilities of social change.

Each set of demands entails demands posed to the others involved, and a fierce debate is necessary. If psychology is not put on the agenda by the left it will reappear through the back door to pathologise collective action and pathologise those who are driven crazy by a crazy world. This 'psychology' needs to be understood and tackled as a political question. Appeals to the pure and free 'experience' of those who use psychological services, for example, are not much more useful than drawing only on the experience of those who practise psychology for their living or those who are expected to produce psychological knowledge. The turn to the viewpoint of each group, or to the ideas of the most enlightened members as their representatives, is merely to reintroduce a psychological logic into what is really a political problem.

The arguments between those who are challenging psychology from different positions should not be taken as signs of weakness; they are signs of strength, for as long as these arguments keep going psychology as a system of social control is prevented from closing how we think down around its own peculiar and reactionary models of human behaviour. We are taking on psychology together here so that we can shake it off, and this process can then take us from alienation toward emancipation.

12
What Next? Reading and Resources

The discipline of psychology is contradictory, and its internal debates reveal much discontent about the way it operates ideologically to enforce law and order at the level of individual behaviour and experience. This last chapter suggests some reading – from within and outside psychology – to explore some of the arguments in this book in more detail. I also give details of some internet resources that include more texts and some organisations campaigning around psychological questions. The sub-categories of research and sub-disciplinary areas of psychology reflect the ideological assumptions psychologists make about the world. So, while I have followed some of these ways of cutting up subjectivity, I have also tried to problematise those dividing lines here.

General Psychology: History and Philosophy

The best historical overview of the development of psychology is the Richards (1996) book *Putting Psychology in its Place: An Introduction from a Critical Historical Perspective*. It provides acute discussion of emerging trends of research and locates these well in political-economic traditions. Newman and Holzman (1996) flesh out the philosophical background in *Unscientific Psychology: A Cultural-Performatory Approach to Understanding Human Life*. They have a particular line on what should take the place of psychology, and those suggestions are also interesting, but the main value of this book is the argument about the conceptual mistakes psychology carried through from philosophy at the end of the nineteenth century, and the political consequences. There are a number of texts now on 'critical psychology', and by far the best one is the edited volume produced from South Africa by Hook (2004). This *Critical Psychology* text brings the political consciousness forged through the struggle against apartheid to bear on the discipline, with a variety of perspectives on history, theory and research.

Selves: Personality and Individual Differences

The category of 'personality' and 'individual difference' is one that psychology stole from everyday life, and Sloan (1996), in *Damaged Life: The Crisis of the Modern Psyche*, explores how personality and personal experience might be reclaimed in this thoughtful book. A psychoanalytic perspective, by a writer who eventually gave up practising as an analyst to focus on political issues, is provided by Kovel's (1981) *The Age of Desire: Case Histories of a Radical Psychoanalyst*. These are composite case studies, and used to lay bare some of the contradictions in personal experience under capitalism. Anthropology can be a handy resource to show the limitations of models of the self in psychology, and the Heelas and Lock (1981) edited collection, *Indigenous Psychologies: The Anthropology of the Self*, includes some very nice chapters which show the variety of ways human beings understand themselves, often ways that are not 'psychological' at all.

Developmental and Educational Psychology

It is tempting to start with an idealised image of the child in developmental research, and then to show how 'socialisation' enables the innocent child to become civilised or to show how society destroys that original innocence. The Newnes and Radcliffe (2005) edited collection *Making and Breaking Children's Lives* brings together perspectives on the way children are faced with a world hostile to development as such. Billington and Pomerantz (2004) provide an overview of issues facing children in education in *Children at the Margins: Supporting Children, Supporting Schools*. This is a practical as well as conceptual guide produced by educational psychologists who know that something is deeply wrong with the way psychology deals with children. There is a detailed critical companion to mainstream developmental psychology in Burman's (1994) *Deconstructing Developmental Psychology*. This book, which is about to be published in an extended revised edition, also tackles images of children and the theories in the discipline that feed upon and contribute to those images.

Social Psychology

The area of 'social psychology' is one of the areas of the discipline that should really be redundant if psychology took social and political issues seriously in the first place. This sub-discipline actually churns out some of the most stupid research; there are valuable reflections on the history and current state of this research context in Cherry's (1995) *The Stubborn Particulars of Social Psychology: Essays on the Research Process*. For an example of good social psychological research that is intervening in political debate and exploring assumptions made about such things as 'prejudice' and 'authoritarianism' in the discipline, see Billig's (1978) *Fascists: A Social Psychological View of the National Front*. Haug's (1987) *Female Sexualisation* shows how 'memory' can be reconfigured and researched as a political phenomenon, and it provides a completely different way of tackling issues that social psychology took on, but failed to understand.

Culture, Colonialism, Racism and Identity

Traditional psychology likes to reduce what it calls 'race' either to individual differences and sense of identity or to anthropological accounts of what everyone in an 'ethnic' group must think and feel. The most useful alternative perspectives come from outside the discipline, and need to be taken seriously by radical psychologists. Mamdani's (2005) *Good Muslim, Bad Muslim: America, the Cold War, and the Roots of Terror* tackles the way that 'identity' is enforced by the imperialist powers, and the way cultural groups are homogenised and managed. The counterpart is Achcar's (2006) analysis, in *The Clash of Barbarisms: The Making of the New World Disorder*, of the way that different forms of 'civilisation' incite certain forms of 'barbarism'; then we can see how racism infuses the image that the West has of its own civilised status. Ahmed's (2004b) *The Cultural Politics of Emotion* is a complex detailed exploration of the way that racism operates at the level of 'affect', and it provides a quite different way of addressing experience than that assumed by psychology.

Psychopathology and Abnormal Psychology

Psychologists love to discover what is wrong with people, and they like to think that if they can slap on the right label then they can help the poor individual get back to normality. A quite different approach is provided by Johnstone (2000) in a book, *Users and Abusers of Psychiatry: A Critical Look at Psychiatric Practice*, that is designed for those who come up against psychologists and psychiatrists in the mental health system. Alternative approaches are also explored by Monk et al. (1997) in the edited volume *Narrative Therapy in Practice: The Archaeology of*

Hope. There are frameworks for thinking about what distress is without pathologising it and practical examples of how a problem can be taken seriously and tackled. Critiques of mainstream psychiatry are covered in Sedgwick's (1982) classic study *Psycho Politics*.

Cognition, Reason and Technology

The sub-area concerned with 'cognition' has in some cases already broken away from the rest of psychology to declare that it is a 'cognitive science', rather like business schools of universities who make a bid for independent status because they want to keep the profit to themselves. Gordo López and Cleminson (2004) show, in *Techno-Sexual Landscapes: Changing Relations Between Technology and Sexuality*, that what we think of as 'cognition' is a complex historical process bound up with forms of technology. Walkerdine (1988), in *The Mastery of Reason*, shows how 'cognition' is bound up with a particular kind of political economic system and how studies of the 'development' of cognition in studies of children reflect and reinforce a peculiarly masculine way of seeing the world. The edited volume by Costall and Still (1991), *Against Cognitivism: Alternative Foundations for Cognitive Psychology*, includes critiques and alternative ways of thinking about what thinking is.

Biological Bases of Behaviour

Against mainstream 'bio-psycho-social' psychology, which in practice boils down to 'bio-bio-bio' psychology, there are alternative ways of exploring how a human being lives in a body and deals with neurological changes. One example is by the humanist psychiatrist Sacks (1973) who shows, in *Awakenings*, how an illness and the drugs used to treat it have quite different psychological effects on different people. Timimi (2005) focuses, in *Naughty Boys: Anti-Social Behaviour, ADHD and the Role of Culture*, on the practical consequences of diagnosing different ways of being in the world as if they were organic diseases, and shows the way to addressing such 'disorders' in a different way. A good attempt to think through how socialist-feminist politics might engage with biology and ecology is provided by New (1996) in *Agency, Health and Social Survival: The Ecopolitics of Rival Psychologies*. This book outlines different models of science and therapy, and is a useful intervention in psychology and politics around these questions.

Counselling and Psychotherapy

We need to start with the fiercest attack on the whole project of therapy by the former psychoanalyst Masson (1990) in *Against Therapy*.

This scythes its way through psychodynamic and humanist approaches, and shows how well-meaning counsellors and therapists get caught in impossible tangles as they try to put their theories into practice. The edited volume by Bates (2006), *Shouldn't I Be Feeling Better By Now? Client Views of Therapy*, brings together accounts by 'clients' and then juxtaposes these accounts with responses by some practitioners. These critiques of therapy are useful, and in many ways correct, but a different way of thinking about psychoanalysis is provided by Bettelheim (1986) in *Freud and Man's Soul*. He argues that the translation of Freud's work into the English-speaking world has distorted what was originally a humanist approach.

Women, Gender, Sexuality and Psychology

The discipline is sometimes a little nervy now about talking about 'sex differences' and prefers to study 'gender', and then feminist arguments are neatly co-opted in courses on 'the psychology of women'. Against this, there are a number of texts from feminists in psychology that turn the study of women around to argue that mainstream psychology is really often the psychology of men. Sayers (1986) provides a neat review of theories and debates around 'sex' and 'gender' in *Sexual Contradictions: Psychology, Psychoanalysis and Feminism*. The role of psychologists in enforcing gender norms and heterosexual behaviour is explored in Raymond's (1980) study, *The Transsexual Empire*. A detailed analysis of the way research into sex in primatology constructs 'nature' is given by Haraway (1989) in the massive path-breaking book *Primate Visions: Gender, Race, and Nature in the World of Modern Science*.

Work, Class and Industrial Psychology

The history of industrial psychology starts with the obsessive study of time and motion, and this is beautifully uncovered in Kakar's (1974) book, *Frederick Taylor: A Study in Personality and Innovation*. While psychology sometimes likes to treat class as a kind of identity, and thus reduces class relations to thoughts and feelings inside individuals, a different tack is taken by Sennett and Cobb (1972) in the classic study, *The Hidden Injuries of Class*. A thorough analysis of capitalism, work and alienation is provided by Mandel (1992) in *Power and Money: A Marxist Theory of Bureaucracy*. These texts are not mentioned in books on work and 'organisational' psychology because they do not show managers how to be more efficient. Rather, they show the need for interpreting and changing the way the economy produces 'psychology' and then worries away at improving it through specialist disciplines.

Language, Conversation and Discourse

The study of language in 'conversation analysis' and 'discursive psychology' promised to provide a completely new way of doing research, and much 'critical psychology' in the English-speaking world now just redescribes how people talk about things. One exception to this is Hansen et al.'s (2003) *Beyond Help: A Consumer's Guide to Psychology*, which provides a sharp account of the way problems are psychologised and opens the way to alternative ways of addressing what are usually seen as 'psychological' problems. Cameron (1995) shows how the concern with language is a cultural phenomenon in her series of essays in *Verbal Hygiene*. A complex theoretical argument which draws on 'post-structuralist' and psychoanalytic theories of language is outlined in Henriques et al.'s (1998) *Changing the Subject: Psychology, Social Regulation and Subjectivity*.

Research Methodology

The best outlines of research methodology – how psychology goes about collecting and interpreting its 'data' – come from outside the colonial centres. One good example is Terre Blanche and Durrheim's (1999) edited volume *Research in Practice: Applied Methods for the Social Sciences* from South Africa. This book includes outlines of and critical reflections on psychological research methods, and the examples are rooted in processes of resistance and change. Parker's (2005a) *Qualitative Psychology: Introducing Radical Research* focuses on recent qualitative methodologies and explores the way they can be used to dismantle rather than shore up ideology and social control. The assumption that the people who are researched by psychologists and other social scientists are avidly keen to contribute to the development of academic knowledge is explored by Cooke and Kothari (2001) in the edited volume *Participation: The New Tyranny?*

Psychological Fictions

It would be possible to say that all psychology is fiction, and it would be just as possible to argue that in psychological culture all fiction concerns 'psychology'. The novel is, after all, a form of writing that usually traces the life path and experiences of a single individual, and so it is already intensely psychological. Three great books to while away the time when you get sick of academic and professional psychology and to help you to reflect on these questions are the following: Piercy's (2000) *Woman on the Edge of Time* explores intersections between gender, culture, violence and mental distress; Høeg's (1996) *Borderliners* focuses on childhood and institutions; and Oe's (1996) *Nip the Buds, Shoot the Kids* provides a quite different account of childhood 'nature' to that circulating in Western ideological representations of development.

Cyberpsychology

Floating around among all the junk-psychology sites in cyberspace are a number of sites with details of more critical text resources and organisations. The ones listed here provide some reliable starting points with links that will be useful. The Discourse Unit site (www.discourseunit.com) includes papers on the development of critical psychology in many different countries, a selection of papers from the organisation 'Psychology Politics Resistance' (PPR), downloads of out-of-print books, texts and links to online journals and details of activist organisations. The magazine for 'democratic psychiatry', *Asylum*, which now includes the newsletter of PPR, has a site (www.asylumonline.net). The Critical Psychology International site is a very useful open-access place for links to radical work (www.criticalpsychology.com). There are online journals, such as *Radical Psychology Journal* (www.yorku.ca/danaa), *Social Practice / Psychological Theorizing* (www.sppt-gulerce.boun.edu.tr/default. htm), *Annual Review of Critical Psychology* (www.discourseunit.com/ arcp.htm), and other critical journals with information sites, such as *International Journal of Critical Psychology* (www.l-w-bks.co.uk/journals/ criticalpsychology/contents.html) and *Journal of Critical Psychology, Counselling and Psychotherapy* (www.pccs-books.co.uk/section.php? xSec=76).

References

Achcar, G. (2006) *The Clash of Barbarisms: The Making of the New World Disorder*. London: Saqi.

Adorno, T. W. (1967) 'Sociology and psychology I', *New Left Review*, 46, pp. 67–80.

Adorno, T. W., Frenkel-Brunswik, E., Levinson, D. and Sanford, R. (1950) *The Authoritarian Personality*. New York: Harper and Row.

Ahmed, S. (2004a) 'Declarations of Whiteness: The non-performativity of anti- racism', *borderlands e-journal*, 3 (2), available at www.borderlandse-journal. adelaide.edu.au/vol3no2_2004/ahmed_declarations.htm (accessed 15 August 2006).

Ahmed, S. (2004b) *The Cultural Politics of Emotion*. Edinburgh: Edinburgh University Press.

Albee, G. W. (1990) 'The futility of psychotherapy', *The Journal of Mind and Behavior*, 11 (3/4), pp. 369–84.

American Psychiatric Association (2000) *Diagnostic and Statistical Manual of Mental Disorders*, Fourth Edition, Text Revision (DSM-IV-TR®). Arlington, VA: American Psychiatric Publishing.

Anderson, P. (1976–77) 'The antinomies of Antonio Gramsci', *New Left Review*, 100, pp. 5–78.

Anderssen, N. (2001) 'A critical look at psychological research on the children of lesbian and gay parents', *International Journal of Critical Psychology*, 1 (3), pp. 173–81.

Antaki, C. (ed.) (1981) *The Psychology of Ordinary Explanations of Social Behaviour*. New York: Academic Press.

Antaki, C. (ed.) (1988) *Analysing Everyday Explanation: A Casebook of Methods*. London and Thousand Oaks, CA: Sage.

Archer, M. S. (2003) *Structure, Agency and the Internal Conversation*. Cambridge: Cambridge University Press.

Archer, M. S., Collier, A. and Porpora, D. V. (2004) *Transcendence: Critical Realism and God*. London and New York: Routledge.

Ariès, P. (1962) *Centuries of Childhood: A Social History of Family Life*. New York: Knopf.

Arnot, M. and Weiner, G. (eds) (1987) *Gender and the Politics of Schooling*. London: Hutchinson.

Aronson, E., Wilson, T. and Akert, R. (2004) *Social Psychology*, Fifth Edition. Englewood Cliffs, NJ: Prentice-Hall.

Ashmore, M. (1989) *The Reflexive Thesis: Wrighting Sociology of Scientific Knowledge*. Chicago: Chicago University Press.

Atkinson, J. M. (1984) *Our Masters' Voices: The Language and Body Language of Politics*. London: Methuen.

Augoustinos, M. (1999) 'Ideology, false consciousness and psychology', *Theory & Psychology*, 9 (3), pp. 295–312.

Austin, J. L. (1962) *How to Do Things with Words*. Oxford: Clarendon Press.

Bacciagaluppi, M. (1989) 'The role of aggressiveness in the work of John Bowlby', *Free Associations*, 16, pp. 123–34.

Badiou, A. (2001) *Ethics: An Essay on the Understanding of Evil*. London: Verso.

Banton, R., Clifford, P., Frosh, S., Lousada, J. and Rosenthall, J. (1985) *The Politics of Mental Health*. London: Macmillan.

Bar, V. (2003) 'Can the good of one be for the good of all?', *European Journal of Psychotherapy, Counselling and Health*, 6 (1), pp. 7–19.

Barker, E. (1982) *New Religious Movements*. Lampeter: Edwin Mellen.

Barker, M., Hagger-Johnson, G. E., Hegarty, P., Hutchison, C. and Riggs, D. (in press) 'Responses from the Lesbian and Gay Psychology Section to Crossley's "Making sense of 'barebacking' " ', *British Journal of Social Psychology*.

Barker, P. and Davidson, B. (1998) *Psychiatric Nursing: Ethical Strife*. London: Edward Arnold.

Barrett, M. and McIntosh, M. (1982) *The Anti-Social Family*. London: Verso.

Basaglia, F. (1987) *Psychiatry Inside Out: Selected writings of Franco Basaglia*. New York: Columbia University Press.

Basaglia, F. (2004) 'Breaking the circuit of control', in D. Ingleby (ed.) *Critical Psychiatry: The Politics of Mental Health*. London: Free Association Books.

Bates, B. (1983) *The Way of Wyrd*. London: Century Publishing.

Bates, Y. (ed.) (2006) *Shouldn't I Be Feeling Better By Now? Client Views of Therapy*. London: Palgrave Macmillan.

Bates, Y. and House, R. (eds) (2003) *Ethically Challenged Professions: Enabling Innovation and Diversity in Psychotherapy and Counselling*. Ross-on-Wye: PCCS Books.

Batur, S. and Aslıtürk, E. (2006) 'On critical psychology in Turkey', *Annual Review of Critical Psychology*, 5, available at www.discourseunit.com/arcp/5.htm (accessed 13 September 2006).

Baumeister, R., Smart, L. and Boden, J. (1996) 'Relation of threatened egotism to violence and aggression: The dark side of self-esteem', *Psychological Review*, 103, pp. 5–33.

Beck, A. T. (1976) *Cognitive Therapy and the Emotional Disorders*. New York: International Universities Press.

Beechey, V. (1979) 'On patriarchy', *Feminist Review*, 3, pp. 66–82.

Bell, D. (1965) *The End of Ideology: On the Exhaustion of Political Ideas in the Fifties*. New York: Free Press.

Bell, V., Halligan, P. W. and Ellis, H. (2003) 'Belief about delusions', *The Psychologist*, 16 (8), pp. 418–23.

Bem, S. (1976) 'Probing the promise of androgeny', in A. G. Kaplan and J. P. Bean (eds) *Beyond Sex Roles: Readings Towards a Psychology of Androgeny*. Boston: Little, Brown.

Bem, S. (1983) 'Gender schema theory and its implications for child development: Raising gender-aschematic children in a gender-schematic society', *Signs*, 8, pp. 598–616.

Bensaïd, D. (2002) *Marx for Our Times: Adventures and Misadventures of a Critique*. London: Verso.

Bentall, R. P. (ed.) (1990) *Reconstructing Schizophrenia*. London and New York: Routledge.

Bentall, R. P. (2004) *Madness Explained: Psychosis and Human Nature*. Harmondsworth: Penguin.

Berger, J. (1990) *Ways of Seeing*. Harmondsworth: Penguin.

Berger, P. L. and Luckmann, T. (1971) *The Social Construction of Reality: A Treatise in the Sociology of Knowledge* (originally published 1966). Harmondsworth: Penguin.

Berman, M. (1983) *All That is Solid Melts into Air: The Experience of Modernity*. London: Verso.

Bettelheim, B. (1986) *Freud and Man's Soul*. Harmondsworth: Pelican.

Bhavnani, K.-K. (1990) 'What's power got to do with it? Empowerment and social research', in I. Parker and J. Shotter (eds) *Deconstructing Social Psychology*. London and New York: Routledge.

Bhavnani, K.-K. and Phoenix, A. (eds) (1994) *Shifting Identities, Shifting Racisms: A Feminism and Psychology Reader*. London and Thousand Oaks, CA: Sage.

Bickley, R. (1977) 'Vygotsky's contributions to a dialectical materialist psychology', *Science & Society*, 41, pp. 191–207.

Billig, M. (1976) *Social Psychology and Intergroup Relations*. London: Academic Press.

Billig, M. (1977) 'The new social psychology and "fascism" ', *European Journal of Social Psychology*, 7, pp. 393–432.

Billig, M. (1978) *Fascists: A Social Psychological View of the National Front*. London: Academic Press.

Billig, M. (1979) *Psychology, Racism and Fascism*. Birmingham: Searchlight, available at www.ferris.edu/isar/archives/billig/homepage.htm (accessed 9 February 2004).

Billig, M. (1982) *Ideology and Social Psychology: Extremism, Moderation and Contradiction*. Oxford: Basil Blackwell.

Billig, M. (1987) *Arguing and Thinking: A Rhetorical Approach to Social Psychology*. Cambridge: Cambridge University Press.

Billig, M. (1988) 'Methodology and scholarship in understanding ideological explanation', in C. Antaki (ed.) *Analysing Everyday Explanation: A Casebook of Methods*. London and Thousand Oaks, CA: Sage.

Billig, M. (1994) 'Repopulating the depopulated pages of social psychology', *Theory & Psychology*, 4 (3), pp. 307–35.

Billig, M. (1995) *Banal Nationalism*. London and Thousand Oaks, CA: Sage.

Billington, T. (2000) *Separating, Losing and Excluding Children: Narratives of Difference*. London: RoutledgeFalmer.

Billington, T. and Pomerantz, M. (eds) (2004) *Children at the Margins: Supporting Children, Supporting Schools*. Stoke-on-Trent: Trentham Books.

Black Health Workers and Patients Group (1983) 'Psychiatry and the corporate state', *Race & Class*, 25 (2), pp. 49–64.

Blackman, L. (1994) 'What is doing history? The use of history to understand the constitution of contemporary psychological objects', *Theory & Psychology*, 4 (4), pp. 485–504.

Blackman, L. (2001) *Hearing Voices: Contesting the Voice of Reason*. London: Free Association Books.

Blackman, L. (ed.) (2003) 'Spirituality Special Issue', *International Journal of Critical Psychology*, 8.

Blackman, L. and Walkerdine, V. (2001) *Mass Hysteria: Critical Psychology and Media Studies*. London: Palgrave.

Blass, T. (2004) *The Man Who Shocked the World: The Life and Legacy of Stanley Milgram*. Jackson, TN: Perseus Books.

Block, N. and Dworkin, G. (eds) (1977) *The IQ Controversy: Critical Readings*. London: Quartet.

Blum, J. M. (1978) *Pseudoscience and Mental Ability: The Origins and Fallacies of the IQ Controversy*. New York: Monthly Review Press.

Bond, C. F. and Titus, L. J. (1983) 'Social facilitation: A meta-analysis of 241 studies', *Psychological Bulletin*, 94, pp. 265–92.

Bookchin, M. (2004) *Post-Scarcity Anarchism*, New Edition. Oakland, CA: AK Press.

Boring, E. G. (1929) *A History of Experimental Psychology*. London: The Century Co.

Boston Women's Health Book Collective (2005) *Our Bodies, Ourselves: A New Edition for a New Era*, Eighth Edition. New York: Simon and Schuster.

Boswell, J. (1994) *The Marriage of Likeness: Same-Sex Unions in Pre-Modern Europe*. London: HarperCollins.

Bottomore, T. (ed.) (1991) *A Dictionary of Marxist Thought*, Second Edition. Oxford: Blackwell.

Bourdieu, P. and Passeron, J.-C. (1990) *Reproduction in Education, Society and Culture*, Second Edition. London and Thousand Oaks, CA: Sage.

Bowers, J. (1990) 'All hail the great abstraction: *Star Wars* and the politics of cognitive psychology', in I. Parker and J. Shotter (eds) *Deconstructing Social Psychology*. London and New York: Routledge.

Bowlby, J. (1944) 'Forty-four juvenile thieves: Their characters and home lives', *International Journal of Psycho-Analysis*, 25, pp. 19–53, 107–28.

Bowlby, J. (1951) *Maternal Care and Mental Health*. Geneva: World Health Organization.

Boyle, M. (2002) *Schizophrenia: A Scientific Delusion?*, Second Edition. London and New York: Routledge.

Bracken, P. (1995) 'Beyond liberation: Michel Foucault and the notion of critical psychiatry', *Philosophy, Psychiatry and Psychology*, 2 (1), pp. 1–13.

Bracken, P. (2002) *Trauma: Culture, Meaning and Philosophy*. Beckenham: Whurr.

Bracken, P. and Thomas, P. (2001) 'Postpsychiatry: A new direction for mental health', *British Medical Journal*, 322, pp. 724–7.

Brady, J. V. (1958) 'Ulcers in "Executive" monkeys', *Science*, 199, pp. 95–100.

Braithwaite, J. (1989) *Crime, Shame and Reintegration*. Cambridge: Cambridge University Press.

Bramel, D., and Friend, R. (1981) 'Hawthorne, the myth of the docile worker, and class bias in psychology', *American Psychologist*, 36, pp. 867–78.

Bratsis, P. (2006) *Everyday Life and the State*. Boulder, CO: Paradigm.

Braverman, H. (1976) *Labor and Monopoly Capital: The Degradation of Work in the Twentieth Century*. New York: Monthly Review Press.

Breggin, P. (1993) *Toxic Psychiatry: Why Therapy, Empathy and Love Must Replace the Drugs, Electroshock and Biochemical Theories of the New Psychiatry*. London: Flamingo.

Breggin, P. (1995) *Talking Back to Prozac*. New York: St Martin's.

Breggin, P. and Cohen, D. (2000) *Your Drug May Be Your Problem: How and Why to Stop Taking Psychiatric Medications*. Cambridge, MA: De Capo.

Brinton, M. (1975) *The Irrational in Politics* (originally published 1970). London: Solidarity.

Brohm, J. M. (1989) *Sport: A Prison of Measured Time*. London: Pluto.

Broughton, J. (1988) 'The masculine authority of the cognitive', in B. Inhelder (ed.) *Piaget Today*. Hillsdale, NJ: Lawrence Erlbaum.

Broughton, J. M. (ed.) (1987) *Critical Theories of Psychological Development*. New York: Plenum.

Brown, P. (ed.) (1973) *Radical Psychology*. New York: Harper & Row.

Brown, S. D. and Lunt, P. (2002) 'A genealogy of the social identity tradition: Deleuze and Guattari and social psychology', *British Journal of Social Psychology*, 41, pp. 1–23.

Bryman, A. (2004) *Disneyization of Society*. London and Thousand Oaks, CA: Sage.

Bulhan, H. A. (1981) 'Psychological research in Africa', *Race & Class*, 23 (1), pp. 25–81.

Bulhan, H. A. (1985) *Frantz Fanon and the Psychology of Oppression*. New York: Plenum.

Bulhan, H. A. (1993) 'Imperialism in studies of the psyche: A critique of African psychological research', in L. J. Nicholas (ed.) *Psychology and Oppression: Critiques and Proposals*. Johannesburg: Skotaville.

Burks, B. S., Jensen, D. W. and Terman, L. (1930) *Genetic Studies of Genius: Volume III, The Promise of Youth: Follow-up Studies of A Thousand Gifted Children*. Stanford, CA: Stanford University Press.

Burman, E. (ed.) (1990) *Feminists and Psychological Practice*. London and Thousand Oaks, CA: Sage.

Burman, E. (1994; revised and expanded edition in press) *Deconstructing Developmental Psychology*. London and New York: Routledge.

Burman, E. (1995) 'The abnormal distribution of development: Policies for southern women and children', *Gender, Place and Culture*, 2 (1), pp. 21–36.

Burman, E. (1997) 'Telling stories: Psychologists, children and the production of "false memories" ', *Theory & Psychology*, 7 (3), pp. 291–309.

Burman, E. (2004) 'Taking women's voices: The psychological politics of feminisation', *Psychology of Women Section Review*, 6 (1), pp. 3–21.

Burman, E. (2005) 'Engendering culture in psychology', *Theory & Psychology*, 15 (4), pp. 527–48.

Burman, E. (2006) 'Emotions and reflexivity in feminised action research', *Educational Action Research*, 14 (3), pp. 315–32.

Burman, E. (in press) 'Between orientalism and normalization: Lessons from Japan for developmental psychology', *History of Psychology*.

Burman, E. and Chantler, K. (2002) 'Service responses to South Asian women who attempt suicide or self harm: Challenges for service commissioning and delivery', *Critical Social Policy*, 22 (4), pp. 641–68.

Burman, E., Aitken, G., Alldred, P. Allwood, R., Billington, T., Goldberg, B., Gordo-López, Á. J., Heenan, C., Marks, D. and Warner, S. (1996) *Psychology Discourse Practice: From Regulation to Resistance*. London: Taylor & Francis.

Burr, V. (2003) *Social Constructionism*, Second Edition. London and New York: Routledge.

Burton, M. and Kagan, C. (1994) 'The verbal community and the societal construction of consciousness', *Behavior and Social Issues*, 4 (1/2), pp. 87–96.

Butler, J. (1990) *Gender Trouble: Feminism and the Subversion of Identity*. London and New York: Routledge.

Butler, J. (1993) *Bodies That Matter: On the Discursive Limits of 'Sex'*. London and New York: Routledge.

C.P.S.U.(B) (1939) *History of the Communist Party of the Soviet Union (Bolsheviks): Short Course*. Moscow: Foreign Languages Publishing House.

Callinicos, A. (1989) *Against Postmodernism: A Marxist Critique*. Cambridge: Polity.

Cameron, D. (1995) *Verbal Hygiene*. London: Routledge.

Cameron, D. (2000) *Good to Talk? Living and Working in a Communication Culture*. London and Thousand Oaks, CA: Sage.

Cammack, P. (2003) 'The governance of global capitalism: A new materialist perspective', *Historical Materialism*, 11 (2), pp. 37–59.

Campbell, R. and Foddis, W. (2005) 'Is high self-esteem bad for you?', available at www.objectivistcenter.org/showcontent.aspx?ct670&printerTrue (accessed 13 December 2005).

Campbell, R. L. (1999) 'Ayn Rand and the cognitive revolution in psychology', *Journal of Ayn Rand Studies*, 1, pp. 107–34.

Carey, J. (1992) *The Intellectuals and the Masses: Pride and Prejudice among the Literary Intelligentsia, 1880–1939*. London: Faber & Faber.

Cartledge, S. (1983) *Sex and Love: New Thoughts on Old Contradictions*. London: The Women's Press.

Chang, J. and Phillips, M. (1993) 'Michael White and Steve de Shazer: New directions in family therapy', in S. Gilligan and R. Price (eds) *Therapeutic Conversations*. New York: W. W. Norton.

Chantler, K. (2004) 'Double edged sword: Power and person-centred counselling', in R. Moodley, C. Lago and A. Talhite (eds) *Carl Rogers Counsels a Black Client*. Ross-on Wye: PCCS.

Chantler K. (2005) 'From disconnection to connection: "Race", gender and the politics of therapy', *British Journal of Guidance and Counselling*, 33 (2), pp. 239–56.

Chantler, K. (2006) 'Re-thinking person-centred therapy', in G. Proctor, M. Cooper, P. Sanders and B. Malcolm (eds) *Politicizing the Person-Centred Approach: An Agenda for Social Change*. Ross-on Wye: PCCS.

Chaplin, J. and Haggart, C. (1983) *The Mass Psychology of Thatcherism*. London: West London Socialist Society.

Chappell, V. C. (ed.) (1981) *Ordinary Language: Essays in Philosophical Method*. New York: Dover.

Cherry, F. (1995) *The Stubborn Particulars of Social Psychology: Essays on the Research Process*. London and New York: Routledge.

Chesler, P. (1973) *Women and Madness*. London: Allen Lane.

Chomsky, N. (1959) 'Review of B. F. Skinner's *Verbal Behavior*', *Language*, 35, pp. 26–58.

Chomsky, N. (1972) 'Psychology and ideology', *Cognition*, 1, pp. 11–16.

Chomsky, N. (1979) *Language and Responsibility*. Hassocks: Harvester.

Clifford, J. and Marcus, G. (eds) (1986) *Writing Culture: The Poetics and Politics of Ethnography*. Berkeley, CA: University of California Press.

Cloud, D. (1998) *Control and Consolidation In American Culture And Politics: Rhetoric Of Therapy*. London and Thousand Oaks, CA: Sage.

Clough, P. and Barton, L. (1998) (eds) *Articulating with Difficulty: Research Voices in Special Education*. London: Paul Chapman.

Coard, B. (1971) *How the West Indian Child is Made Educationally Sub-Normal in the British School System*. London: New Beacon Books.

Cocks, G. (1985) *Psychotherapy in the Third Reich: The Göring Institute*. Oxford: Oxford University Press.

Cohen, C. I. (1986) 'Marxism and psychotherapy', *Science and Society*, 1 (1), pp. 4–24.

Cohen, D. (1988) *Forgotten Millions*. London: Paladin.

Cohen, D. (1989) *Soviet Psychiatry: Politics and Mental Health in the USSR Today*. London: Paladin.

Cohen, D. and Jacobs, D. (1998) 'A model consent form for psychiatric drug treatment', *International Journal of Risk & Safety in Medicine*, 11, pp. 161–4.

Cohen, S. (2006) *Standing on the Shoulders of Fascism: From Immigration Control to the Strong State*. Stoke-on-Trent: Trentham Books.

Coleman, R. (1999) 'Hearing voices and the politics of oppression', in C. Newnes, G. Holmes and C. Dunn (eds) *This Is Madness: A Critical Look at Psychiatry and the Future of Mental Health Services*. Ross-on-Wye: PCCS.

Colletti, L. (1970) 'The question of Stalin', *New Left Review*, 61, pp. 61–81.

Collier, A. (1994) *Critical Realism: An Introduction to Roy Bhaskar's Philosophy*. London: Verso.

Collins, C. (2003) ' "Critical psychology" and contemporary struggles against neo-liberalism', *Annual Review of Critical Psychology*, 3, pp. 26–48.

Coltart, N. (2000) *Slouching towards Bethlehem*. New York: The Other Press.

Coltart, N. E. C. (1988) 'The assessment of psychological-mindedness in the diagnostic interview', *British Journal of Psychiatry*, 153, pp. 819–20.

Condor, S. (1997) 'And so say all of us?: Some thoughts on "experiential democratization" as an aim for critical social psychologists', in T. Ibáñez and L. Íñiguez (eds) *Critical Social Psychology*. London and Thousand Oaks, CA: Sage.

Connolly, P. and Troyna, B. (eds) (1998) *Researching Racism in Education: Politics, Theory and Practice*. Buckingham: Open University Press.

Cooke, B. and Kothari, U. (eds) (2001) *Participation: The New Tyranny?* London: Zed.

Cooperrrider, D. L. and Whitney, D. (2005) *Appreciative Inquiry: A Positive Revolution in Change*. San Francisco: Berrett-Koehler.

Coppock, V. and Hopton, J. (2000) *Critical Perspectives on Mental Health*. London and New York: Routledge.

Costall, A. and Still, A. (eds) (1991) *Against Cognitivism: Alternative Foundations for Cognitive Psychology*. Englewood Cliffs, NJ: Prentice-Hall.

Craib, I. (1994) *The Importance of Disappointment*. London and New York: Routledge.

Crawford, M. (1995) *Talking Difference: On Gender and Language*. London and Thousand Oaks, CA: Sage.

Cresswell, M. (2005) 'Self-harm "survivors" and psychiatry in England, 1988–1996', *Social Theory and Health*, 3 (4), pp. 259–85.

Cromby, J. (2005) 'The morphogenesis of subjectivity: Between constructionism and neuroscience', in A. Gülerce, A. Hofmeister, J. Kaye, G. Saunders and I. Steauble (eds) *Theoretical Psychology*. Toronto: Captus.

Cromby, J. and Standen, P. (1999) 'Cyborgs and stigma: technology, disability, subjectivity', in Á. J. Gordo López and I. Parker (eds) *Cyberpsychology*. London: Palgrave.

Crossley, M. (2000) *Introducing Narrative Psychology: Self, Trauma and the Construction of Meaning*. Buckingham: Open University Press.

Crossley, M. (2003) 'Formulating narrative psychology: The limitations of contemporary social constructionism', *Narrative Inquiry*, 13 (2), pp. 287–300.

Crossley, M. (2004) 'Making sense of "barebacking": Gay men's narratives, unsafe sex and the "resistance habitus" ', *British Journal of Social Psychology*, 43 (2), pp. 225–44.

Cullen, C. (1991) 'Experimentation and planning in community care', *Disability, Handicap & Society*, 6 (2), pp. 115–28.

Cullen, C., Hattersley, J. and Tennant, L. (1981) 'Establishing behaviour; the constructional approach', in G. Davey (ed.) *Applications of Conditioning Theory*. London: Methuen.

Curt, B. C. (1994) *Textuality and Tectonics: Troubling Social and Psychological Science*. Buckingham: Open University Press.

Curtis, T., Dellar, R., Leslie, E. and Watson, B. (eds) (2000) *Mad Pride: A Celebration of Mad Culture*. London: Spare Change Books.

Cushman, P. (1991) 'Ideology obscured: Political uses of the self in Daniel Stern's infant', *American Psychologist*, 46 (3), pp. 206–19.

Dafermos, M., Marvakis, A. and Triliva, S. (eds) (2006) 'Critical psychology in a changing world: Contributions from different geo-political regions, Special Issue', *Annual Review of Critical Psychology*, 5, available at www.discourseunit.com/arcp/5.htm (accessed 13 September 2006).

Dahlberg, G. and Moss, P. (2005) *Ethics and Politics in Early Education*. London and New York: RoutledgeFalmer.

Dalal, F. (1988) 'The racism of Jung', *Race & Class*, 29 (1), pp. 1–22.

Danziger, K. (1979) 'The positivist repudiation of Wundt', *Journal of the History of the Behavioural Sciences*, 15, pp. 205–30.

Danziger, K. (1985) 'The methodological imperative in psychology', *Philosophy of Social Science*, 15, pp. 1–13.

Danziger, K. (1990) *Constructing the Subject: Historical Origins of Psychological Research*. Cambridge: Cambridge University Press.

Danziger, K. (1997) *Naming the Mind: How Psychology Found its Language*. London and Thousand Oaks, CA: Sage.

Davies, B. and Gannon, S. (2006) *Doing Collective Biography*. Buckingham: Open University Press.

De Beauvoir, S. (1968) *The Second Sex* (originally published 1949). London: Jonathan Cape.

De Shazer, S. (1985) *Keys to Solution in Brief Therapy*. New York: W. W. Norton.

De Shazer, S. (1991) *Putting Difference to Work*. New York: W. W. Norton.

Debord, G. (1977) *Society of the Spectacle*. Detroit: Black and Red.

Deleuze, G. and Guattari, F. (1977) *Anti-Oedipus: Capitalism and Schizophrenia*. New York: Viking.

Dineen, T. (2001) *Manufacturing Victims: What the Psychology Industry is Doing to People*. Montreal: Robert Davies.

Donzelot, J. (1979) *The Policing of Families*. London: Hutchinson.

Dorling, D. and Simpson, S. (eds) (1999) *Statistics in Society: The Arithmetic of Politics*. London: Edward Arnold.

Double, D. B. (ed.) (2006) *Critical Psychiatry: The Limits of Madness*. London: Palgrave Macmillan.

Drever, J. (1964) *A Dictionary of Psychology (revised by H. Wallerstein)*. Harmondsworth: Penguin.

Drury, J. (2002) ' "When the mobs are looking for witches to burn, nobody's safe": Talking about the reactionary crowd', *Discourse & Society*, 13 (1), pp. 41–73.

Drury, J. (2003) 'What critical psychology can('t) do for the "anti-capitalist movement" ', *Annual Review of Critical Psychology*, 3, pp. 90–113.

Duckett, P. S. (2005) 'Globalised violence, community psychology and the bombing and occupation of Afghanistan and Iraq', *Journal of Community and Applied Social Psychology*, 15 (5), pp. 414–23.

Durrheim, K. (1997) 'Peace talk and violence: An analysis of the power of "peace" ', in A. Levett, A. Kottler, E. Burman and I. Parker (eds) *Culture, Power and Difference: Discourse Analysis in South Africa*. London: Zed.

Eagle, G., Hayes, G. and Bhana, A. (eds) (1989) *Mental Health: Struggle and Transformation (OASSSA Third National Conference Proceedings)*. Durban: Organisation for Appropriate Social Services in South Africa.

Eagly, A. H. (1995) 'The science and politics of comparing women and men', *American Psychologist*, 50, pp. 145–58.

Easthope, A. (1988) *British Post-structuralism, since 1968*. London: Routledge.

Easthope, A. (1990) ' "I gotta use words when I talk to you": Deconstructing the theory of communication', in I. Parker and J. Shotter (eds) *Deconstructing Social Psychology*. London: Routledge.

Easthope, A. (1999) *Englishness and National Culture*. London: Routledge.

Edwards, D. (1992) *Discourse and Cognition*. London and Thousand Oaks, CA: Sage.

Edwards, D. and Potter, J. (1992) *Discursive Psychology*. London and Thousand Oaks, CA: Sage.

Edwards, D., Ashmore, M. and Potter, J. (1995) 'Death and furniture: The rhetoric, politics, and theology of bottom-line arguments against relativism', *History of the Human Sciences*, 8 (2), pp. 25–49.

Eisenstein, H. (1996) *Inside Agitators: Australian Femocrats and the State*. Philadelphia, PA: Temple University Press.

Eiser, J. R. (1986) *Social Psychology: Attitudes, Cognition and Social Behaviour*. Cambridge: Cambridge University Press.

Elliott, J. G. (2005a) 'Dyslexia: Diagnoses, debates and diatribes', *Special Children*, 169, pp. 19–23.

Elliott, J. G. (2005b) 'The dyslexia debate continues', *The Psychologist*, 18 (2), pp. 728–9.

Emler, N. (2001) *Self-Esteem: The Costs and Causes of Low Self-Worth*. York: Joseph Rowntree Foundation.

Engels, F. (1892) *Socialism: Utopian and Scientific*. London: George Allen & Unwin.

Engels, F. (1972) *The Origin of the Family, Private Property and the State* (originally published 1884). New York: Pathfinder.

Epstein, D. and Johnson, R. (1998) *Schooling Sexualities*. Buckingham: Open University Press.

Epstein, R., Lanza, R. P. and Skinner, B. F. (1981) 'Self-awareness in the pigeon', *Science*, 212, pp. 695–6.

Erikson, E. H. (1965) *Childhood and Society*, Revised Edition (originally published 1950). Harmondsworth: Penguin.

Ernst, S. and Goodison, L. (1981) *In Our Own Hands: A Book of Self-Help Therapy*. London: The Women's Press.

Evans, R. (2002) 'Ethnography of teacher training: Mantras for those constructed as "other" ', *Disability & Society*, 17 (1), pp. 35–43.

Eysenck, H. J. (1952) 'The effects of psychotherapy: An evaluation', *Journal of Consulting Psychology*, 16, pp. 319–24.

Eysenck, H. J. (1975) *The Inequality of Man*. London: Pan.

Eysenck, H. J. (1977) *Crime and Personality* (originally published 1964). London: Paladin.

Eysenck, H. J. (1982) 'The sociology of psychological knowledge, the genetic interpretation of IQ, and Marxist-Leninist ideology', *Bulletin of the British Psychological Society*, 35, pp. 449–51.

Eysenck, H. J. (1985) *Decline and Fall of the Freudian Empire*. London: Viking.

Eysenck, H. J. and Wilson, G. C. (1973) *The Experimental Study of Freudian Theories*. London: Methuen.

Fanon, F. (1967) *The Wretched of the Earth*. Harmondsworth: Penguin.

Fanon, F. (1970) *Black Skin White Masks: The Experiences of a Black Man in a White World*. London: Paladin.

Farr, R. M. and Moscovici, S. (eds) (1984) *Social Representations*. Cambridge: Cambridge University Press.

Feyerabend, P. (1975) *Against Method: Analytical index and concluding chapter*, available at www.marxists.org/reference/subject/philosophy/works/ge/feyerabe.htm (accessed 15 March 2004).

Fine, M. (ed.) (2004) *Off White: Readings in Power, Privilege, and Resistance*. London and New York: Routledge.

Finison, L. J. (1976) 'Unemployment, politics, and the history of organized psychology', *American Psychologist*, 31, pp. 747–55.

Finison, L. J. (1977) 'Psychologists and Spain: A historical note', *American Psychologist*, 32, pp. 1080–4.

Finlay, L. and Gough, B. (eds) (2003) *Reflexivity: A Practical Guide for Researchers in Health and Social Sciences*. Oxford: Blackwell.

Fish, V. (1999) 'Clementis's hat: Foucault and the politics of psychotherapy', in I. Parker (ed.) *Deconstructing Psychotherapy*. London and Thousand Oaks, CA: Sage.

Fonagy, P. and Target, M. (2004) 'What can developmental psychopathology tell psychoanalysts about the mind?', in A. Casement (ed.) *Who Owns Psychoanalysis?* London: Karnac.

Fonagy, P., Gergely, G., Jurist, E. L. and Target, M. (2004) *Affect Regulation, Mentalization, and the Development of Self*. London: Karnac.

Forrester, J. (1980) *Language and the Origins of Psychoanalysis*. London: Macmillan.

Foster, D. (1993) 'On racism: Virulent mythologies and fragile threads', in L. J. Nicholas (ed.) *Psychology and Oppression: Critiques and Proposals*. Johannesburg: Skotaville.

Foster, J. B. and Braverman, H. (1998) *Labor and Monopoly Capitalism: The Degradation of Work in the Twentieth Century*. New York: Monthly Review Press.

Foucault, M. (1977) *Discipline and Punish: The Birth of the Prison.* Harmondsworth: Penguin.

Foucault, M. (1981) *The History of Sexuality, Vol. I: An Introduction* (originally published 1976). Harmondsworth: Pelican.

Foucault, M. (1991) *Remarks on Marx: Conversations with Duccio Trombadori.* New York: Semiotext(e).

Foucault, M. (2006) *Psychiatric Power: Lectures at the Collège de France, 1973–1974.* London: Palgrave Macmillan.

Fox, D. and Prilleltensky, I. (eds) (1997) *Critical Psychology: An Introduction.* London and Thousand Oaks, CA: Sage.

Fox, K. (2004) *Watching the English: The Hidden Rules of English Behaviour.* London: Hodder.

Freeman, J. (1996) 'The tyranny of structurelessness', available at www.hartford-hwp.com/archives/45/112.html (accessed 16 February 2004).

French, C. (2001) 'The placebo effect', in R. Roberts and D. Groome (eds) *Parapsychology: The Science of Unusual Experiences.* London: Edward Arnold.

French, S. and Swain, J. (2000) ' "Good intentions": Reflecting on researching in disability research the lives and experiences of visually disabled people', *Annual Review of Critical Psychology*, 2, pp. 35–54.

Frenkel-Brunswik, E., Levinson, D. J. and Sanford, R. N. (originally published 1947) 'The antidemocratic personality', in E. E. Maccoby, T. M. Newcomb and E. L. Hartley (eds) (1958) *Readings in Social Psychology*, Third Edition. New York: Henry Holt.

Freund, K. (1960) 'Some problems in the treatment of homosexuality', in H. J. Eysenck (ed.) *Behavior Therapy and Neurosis.* London: Pergamon.

Friedman, D. (1990) 'The Soviet Union in the 1920s: An historical laboratory', *Practice*, 7 (3), pp. 5–8.

Fromm, E. (1960) *The Fear of Freedom* (originally published 1942). London: Routledge & Kegan Paul.

Fromm, E. (1962) *Beyond the Chains of Illusion: My Encounter with Marx and Freud.* London: Abacus.

Fromm, E. (1974) *The Anatomy of Human Destructiveness.* London: Jonathan Cape.

Frosh, S. (2005) *Hate and the 'Jewish Science': Anti-Semitism, Nazism, and Psychoanalysis.* London: Palgrave Macmillan.

Frosh, S., Phoenix, A. and Pattman, R. (2001) *Young Masculinities.* Basingstoke and New York: Palgrave.

Fukuyama, F. (1992) *The End of History and the Last Man.* Harmondsworth: Penguin.

Furedi, F. (2003) *Therapy Culture: Cultivating Vulnerability in an Uncertain Age.* London and New York: Routledge.

Gamble, S. (2001) *The Routledge Critical Dictionary of Feminism and Postfeminism.* London and New York: Routledge.

Gambles, R., Lewis, S. and Rapoport, R. (2006) *The Myth of Work-Life Balance: The Challenge of Our Time for Men, Women and Societies.* Chichester: Wiley.

Geras, N. (1983) *Marx and Human Nature.* London: Verso.

Gergen, K. J. (1991) *The Saturated Self: Dilemmas of Identity in Contemporary Life.* New York: Basic Books.

Gibson, J. J. (1966) *The Senses Considered as Perceptual Systems*. Boston, MA: Houghton Mifflin.

Giddens, A. (1979) *Central Problems in Social Theory: Action, Structure and Contradiction in Social Analysis*. London: Macmillan.

Giddens, A. (1992) *The Transformation of Intimacy: Sexuality, Love and Eroticism in Modern Society*. Cambridge: Polity.

Giddens, A. (1998) *The Third Way: The Renewal of Social Democracy*. Cambridge: Polity.

Gill, R. (1995) 'Relativism, reflexivity and politics: Interrogating discourse analysis from a feminist perspective', in S. Wilkinson and C. Kitzinger (eds) *Feminism and Discourse*. London and Thousand Oaks, CA: Sage.

Goldiamond, I. (1974) 'Toward a constructional approach to social problems', *Behaviourism*, 2, pp. 1–84.

Goleman, D. (1996) *Emotional Intelligence: Why It Can Matter More than IQ*. London: Bloomsbury.

Goodley, D. and Lawthom, R. (eds) (2004) *Psychology and Disability: Critical Introductions and Reflections*. London: Palgrave Macmillan.

Goodley, D. and Parker, I. (2000) 'Critical psychology and action research', *Annual Review of Critical Psychology*, 2, pp. 3–16.

Gordo López, Á. J. (2000) 'On the psychologization of critical psychology', *Annual Review of Critical Psychology*, 2, pp. 55–71.

Gordo López, Á. J. (coord.) (2006) *Jóvenes y Cultura Messenger: Tecnología de la Información y la Comunicación en la Sociedad Interactiva*. Madrid: FAD/INJUVE.

Gordo López, Á. J. and Cleminson, R. (2004) *Techno-Sexual Landscapes: Changing Relations Between Technology and Sexuality*. London: Free Association Books.

Gordo López, Á. J. and Parker, I. (eds) (1999) *Cyberpsychology*. London: Palgrave.

Gordo López, Á. J. y Linaza, J. L. (comps) (1996) *Psicologías, Discursos y Poder (PDP)*. Madrid: Visor.

Gordon, P. (2001) 'Psychoanalysis and racism: The politics of defeat', *Race & Class*, 42 (4), pp. 17–34.

Gough, B. and McFadden, M. (2001) *Critical Social Psychology: An Introduction*. London: Palgrave.

Gould, S. J. (1996) *The Mismeasure of Man*. New York: W. W. Norton.

Gramsci, A. (1971) *Selections from the Prison Notebooks* (ed. by Quinton Hoare and Geoffrey Nowell Smith). London: Lawrence & Wishart.

Gray, J. A. (1979) *Pavlov*. London: Fontana.

Green, V. (ed.) (2003) *Emotional Development in Psychoanalysis, Attachment Theory and Neuroscience: Creating Connections*. Hove and New York: Brunner-Routledge.

Greenslade, L. (1996) 'V. N. Volosinov and social psychology', in I. Parker and R. Spears (eds) *Psychology and Marxism: Coexistence and Contradiction*. London: Pluto.

Grieves, L. (1997) 'From beginning to start: The Vancouver Anti-Anorexia League', *Gecko*, 2, pp. 78–88.

Grieves, L. (1998) 'From beginning to start: The Vancouver Anti-Anorexia League', in S. Madigan and I. Law (eds) *Praxis: Situating Discourse, Feminism and Discourse in Narrative Therapies*. Vancouver: Yaletown Family Therapy.

Grogan, S. (1998) *Body Image: Understanding Body Dissatisfaction in Men, Women and Children*. London and New York: Routledge.

Guerin, D. (1973) *Fascism and Big Business*. New York: Monad.

Guilfoyle, M. (2005) 'From therapeutic power to resistance?: Therapy and cultural hegemony', *Theory & Psychology*, 15 (1), pp. 101–24.

Guthrie, R. V. (1976) *Even the Rat Was White: A Historical View of Psychology*. New York: Harper & Row.

Haaken, J. (1998) *Pillar of Salt: Gender, Memory, and the Perils of Looking Back*. New Brunswick, NJ: Rutgers University Press.

Haddock, G. and Slade, P. (1995) *Cognitive-Behavioural Interventions with Psychotic Disorders*. London and New York: Routledge.

Haney, C., Banks, W. C. and Zimbardo, P. G. (1973) 'Interpersonal dynamics in a simulated prison', *International Journal of Criminology and Penology*, 1, pp. 69–97.

Hannon, J. W., Ritchie, M. and Rye, D. R. (2001) 'Class: The missing discourse in counselling and counsellor education in the United States of America', *The Journal of Critical Psychology, Counselling and Psychotherapy*, 1 (3), pp. 137–54.

Hansen, S., McHoul, A. and Rapley, M. (2003) *Beyond Help: A Consumer's Guide to Psychology*. Ross-on-Wye: PCCS.

Haraway, D. J. (1989) *Primate Visions: Gender, Race, and Nature in the World of Modern Science*. London and New York: Routledge.

Haraway, D. J. (1991) *Simians, Cyborgs, and Women: The Reinvention of Nature*. London and New York: Routledge. 'A cyborg manifesto: Science, technology, and socialist-feminism in the late twentieth century', included in this book, is available at www.kitchenmedialab.org/download/cyborgmanifesto1.rtf (accessed 24 August 2006).

Hardt, M. and Negri, A. (2000) *Empire*. Cambridge, MA: Harvard University Press.

Hardt, M. and Negri, A. (2004) *Multitude: War and Democracy in the Age of Empire*. New York: Penguin.

Hare-Mustin, R. T. and Marecek, J. (1997) 'Abnormal and clinical psychology: The politics of madness', in D. Fox and I. Prilleltensky (eds) *Critical Psychology: An Introduction*. London and Thousand Oaks, CA: Sage.

Harper, D. (1994) 'The professional construction of "paranoia" and the discursive uses of diagnostic criteria', *British Journal of Medical Psychology*, 67, pp. 131–43.

Harré, R. (ed.) (1986) *The Social Construction of Emotion*. Oxford: Blackwell.

Harré, R. (2004) 'Staking our claim for qualitative psychology as science', *Qualitative Research in Psychology*, 1, pp. 3–14.

Harré, R. and Secord, P. F. (1972) *The Explanation of Social Behaviour*. Oxford: Blackwell.

Harris, A. and Shefer, T. (1990) 'Mental health services in Nicaragua: Ten years of revolution', *Psychiatric Bulletin*, 14, pp. 346–50.

Harris, B. (1990) 'Psychology', in M. J. Buhle, P. Buhle and D. Georgakas (eds) *Encyclopedia of the American Left*. New York: Garland.

Harris, B. (1995) 'Psychology and Marxist politics in America', in I. Parker and R. Spears (eds) *Psychology and Marxism: Coexistence and Contradiction*. London: Pluto.

Hartmann, H. (1958) *Ego Psychology and the Problem of Adaptation* (originally published 1939). New York: International Universities Press.

Hartsock, N. (1987) 'The feminist standpoint: Developing the ground for a specifically feminist historical materialism', in S. Harding (ed.) *Feminism and Methodology: Social Science Issues*. Bloomington, IN: Indiana University Press.

Haslam, A. and Reicher, S. (2006) 'Debating the psychology of tyranny: Fundamental issues of theory, perspective and science', *British Journal of Social Psychology*, 45, pp. 55–63.

Haug, F. (1987) *Female Sexualisation*. London: Verso.

Haug, F. (2000) 'Memory work: The key to women's anxiety', in S. Radstone (ed.) *Memory and Methodology*. Oxford: Berg.

Hayes, G. (1996) 'The psychology of everyday life', in I. Parker and R. Spears (eds) *Psychology and Society: Radical Theory and Practice*. London: Pluto.

Hayes, G. (1998) 'We suffer our memories: Thinking about the past, healing and reconciliation', *American Imago*, 55, pp. 29–50.

Healy, D. (1997) *The Anti-Depressant Era*. Cambridge, MA: Harvard University Press.

Healy, D. (2002) *Psychopharmacology*. Cambridge, MA: Harvard University Press.

Healy, D. (2002) *The Creation of Psychopharmacology*. Cambridge, MA: Harvard University Press.

Healy, D. (2004) *Let Them Eat Prozac: The Unhealthy Relationship Between the Pharmaceutical Industry and Depression*. New York: New York University Press.

Healy, D. and Cattell, D. (2003) 'The interface between authorship, industry and science in the domain of therapeutics', *British Journal of Psychiatry*, 183, pp. 22–7.

Hearnshaw, L. (1976) *Cyril Burt, Psychologist*. Ithaca, NY: Cornell University Press.

Heartfield, J. (2002) *The 'Death of the Subject' Explained*. Sheffield: Perpetuity.

Heather, N. (1976) *Radical Perspectives in Psychology*. London: Methuen.

Hedges, L. V. (1987) 'How hard is hard science, how soft is soft science?', *American Psychologist*, 42, pp. 443–55.

Heelas, P. and Lock, A. (eds) (1981) *Indigenous Psychologies: The Anthropology of the Self*. London: Academic Press.

Hegarty, P. (2003) 'Pointing to a crisis: What finger-length ratios tell us about the construction of sexuality', *Radical Statistics*, 83, pp. 16–30.

Hegarty, P. (in press) 'Gendered intelligence and inverted genius: Lewis Terman and the power of the norm', *History of Psychology*.

Held, J. (2006) 'Beyond the mainstream: Approaches to critical psychology in the German-speaking community and their international significance', *Annual Review of Critical Psychology*, 5, available at www.discourseunit.com/arcp/5.htm (accessed 13 September 2006).

Henriques, J., Hollway, W., Urwin, C., Venn, C. and Walkerdine, V. (1998) *Changing the Subject: Psychology, Social Regulation and Subjectivity* (originally published 1984). London: Routledge.

Hepburn, A. (1999) 'Derrida and psychology: Deconstruction and its ab/uses in critical and discursive psychologies', *Theory & Psychology*, 9, pp. 641–67.

Hepburn, A. (2000) 'On the alleged incompatibility between relativism and feminist psychology', *Feminism & Psychology*, 10 (1), pp. 91–106.

Hepburn, A. (2003) *An Introduction to Critical Social Psychology*. London and Thousand Oaks, CA: Sage.

Hepworth, J. (1999) *The Social Construction of Anorexia Nervosa*. London and Thousand Oaks, CA: Sage.

Herrnstein, R. J. and Murray, C. (1994) *The Bell Curve: Intelligence and Class Structure in American Life*. New York: Free Press.

Hewstone, M. and Stroebe, W. (2001) *Introduction to Social Psychology: A European Perspective*, Third Edition. Oxford: Blackwell.

Hill, D. (1983) *The Politics of Schizophrenia: Psychiatric Oppression in the United States*. London: University Press of America.

Hinshelwood, R. D. (1996) 'Convergences with psychoanalysis', in I. Parker and R. Spears (eds) *Psychology and Society: Radical Theory and Practice*. London: Pluto.

Hochschild, A. R. (1983) *The Managed Heart: Commercialisation of Human Feeling*. Berkeley, CA: University of California Press.

Hochschild, A. R. (2000) 'Global care chains and emotional surplus value', in W. Hutton and A. Giddens (eds) *On the Edge: Living with Global Capitalism*. London: Jonathan Cape.

Hochschild, A. R. (2003) 'Let them eat war', *European Journal of Psychotherapy, Counselling and Health*, 6 (3), pp. 175–85.

Høeg, P. (1996) *Borderliners*. London: Harvill.

Hoggett, P. (1996) 'Emotion and politics', in I. Parker and R. Spears (eds) *Psychology and Society: Radical Theory and Practice*. London: Pluto.

Holloway, J. (2002) *Change the World without Taking Power: The Meaning of Revolution Today*. London: Pluto.

Hollway, W. (1989) *Subjectivity and Method in Psychology: Gender, Meaning and Science*. London and Thousand Oaks, CA: Sage.

Hollway, W. (1991) *Work Psychology and Organizational Behaviour: Managing the Individual at Work*. London and Thousand Oaks, CA: Sage.

Hollway, W. and Jefferson, T. (2000) *Doing Qualitative Research Differently: Free Association, Narrative and the Interview Method*. London and Thousand Oaks, CA: Sage.

Hollway, W. and Jefferson, T. (2001) 'Free Association, narrative analysis and the defended subject: The case of Ivy', *Narrative Inquiry*, 11 (1), pp. 103–22.

Holzkamp, K. (1992) 'On doing psychology critically', *Theory & Psychology*, 2 (2), pp. 193–204.

Holzman, L. (1995) ' "Wrong", said Fred: A Response to Parker', *Changes: An International Journal of Psychology and Psychotherapy*, 13 (1), pp. 23–6.

Holzman, L. (1996) 'Newman's practice of method completes Vygotsky', in I. Parker and R. Spears (eds) *Psychology and Marxism: Coexistence and Contradiction*. London: Pluto.

Holzman, L. (ed.) (1999) *Performing Psychology: A Postmodern Culture of the Mind*. London and New York: Routledge.

Holzman, L. (ed.) (2006) 'What kind of theory is activity theory? Special Issue', *Theory & Psychology*, 16 (1).

Holzman, L. and Mendez, R. (2003) *Psychological Investigations: A Clinician's Guide to Social Therapy*. New York and Hove: Brunner-Routledge.

Holzman, L. and Morss, J. (eds) (2000) *Postmodern Psychologies, Societal Practice and Political Life*. London and New York: Routledge.

Hood, L. and Newman, F. (1983) 'Tools and results: Understanding, explaining and meaning (three sides of one dialectical coin)', *Practice*, 1 (2/3), pp. 154–88.

Hook, D. (2001) 'Discourse, knowledge and materiality: Foucault and discourse analysis', *Theory & Psychology*, 11 (4), pp. 521–47.

Hook, D. (ed.) (2004) *Critical Psychology*. Cape Town: University of Cape Town Press.

Hook, D. and Eagle, G. (eds) (2002) *Psychopathology and Social Prejudice*. Cape Town: University of Cape Town Press.

House, R. and Totton, N. (eds) (1997) *Implausible Professions: Arguments for Pluralism and Autonomy in Psychotherapy and Counselling*. Ross-on-Wye: PCCS.

Howitt, D. and Owusu-Bempah, J. (1994) *The Racism of Psychology: Time for Change*. New York: Harvester Wheatsheaf.

Huntington, S. (2002) *The Clash of Civilizations, and the Remaking of World Order*. New York: Free Press.

Immelman, A. (1999) 'Inside the mind of Milošević', Unit for the Study of Personality in Politics, available at www.csbju.edu/uspp/Milosevic/Milosevic.html (accessed 16 June 2006).

Immelman, A. (2003) 'Psychological profile of Saddam Hussein', Unit for the Study of Personality in Politics, available at www.csbju.edu/uspp/Research/Saddam%20profile.html (accessed 16 June 2006).

Ingleby, D. (1972) 'Ideology and the human sciences: Some comments on the role of reification in psychology and psychiatry', in T. Pateman (ed.) *Counter Course: A Handbook for Course Criticism*. Harmondsworth: Penguin.

Irvine, J., Miles, I. and Evans, J. (eds) (1979) *Demystifying Social Statistics*. London: Pluto.

Israel, J. and Tajfel, H. (eds) (1972) *The Context of Social Psychology, A Critical Assessment*. London: Academic Press.

Jackins, H. (1978) *The Upward Trend*. Seattle, WA: Rational Island.

Jacoby, R. (1975) *Social Amnesia: A Critique of Conformist Psychology from Adler to Laing*. New York: Beacon.

Jacoby, R. (1983) *The Repression of Psychoanalysis*. New York: Basic Books.

James T., Webb, P., Amend, E. and Webb, N. (2005) *Misdiagnosis and Dual Diagnoses of Gifted Children and Adults: ADHD, Bipolar, OCD, Asperger's, Depression, and Other Disorders*. Scottsdale, AZ: Great Potential Press.

James, A. (2001) *Raising Our Voices: An Account of the Hearing Voices Movement*. Gloucester: Handsell.

James, O. (2003) *They F*** You Up: How to Survive Family Life*. London: Bloomsbury.

James, W. (1892) 'A plea for psychology as a "Natural Science" ', *Philosophical Review*, 1, pp. 146–53.

Jameson, F. (1984) 'Foreword', in J.-F. Lyotard (ed.) *The Postmodern Condition: A Report on Knowledge*. Manchester: Manchester University Press.

Jameson, F. (1991) *Postmodernism, or the Cultural Logic of Late Capitalism*. London: Verso.

Janis, I. (1972) *Victims of Groupthink: A Psychological Study of Foreign-Policy Decisions and Fiascos*. Boston, MA: Houghton Mifflin.

Jaques, E. (1951) *The Changing Culture of a Factory*. London: Routledge & Kegan Paul.

Jiménez-Domínguez, B. (1996) 'Participant Action Research: Myths and fallacies', in I. Parker and R. Spears (eds) *Psychology and Society: Radical Theory and Practice*. London: Pluto.

Jiménez-Domínguez, B. (2005) 'The critical and liberationist social psychology of Ignacio Martín-Baró: An objection to objectivism', *Journal of Critical Psychology, Counselling and Psychotherapy*, 5 (2), pp. 63–9.

Johnson, R. D. and Downing, L. L. (1979) 'Deindividuation and valence of cues: Effects on prosocial and antisocial behaviour', *Journal of Personality and Social Psychology*, 37, pp. 1532–8.

Johnstone, L. (2000) *Users and Abusers of Psychiatry: A Critical Look at Psychiatric Practice*, Second Edition. London: Brunner-Routledge.

Jonckheere, L. (2005) 'Evaluation today: From the frying pan of control into the fire of growth', available at www.janvaneyck.nl/~clic/documents/LievenJonckheereevaluatieideologie.Engels.doc (accessed 15 August 2005).

Jones, R. A. (2003) 'The construction of emotional and behavioural difficulties', *Educational Psychology in Practice*, 19 (2), pp. 147–57.

Joseph, J. (2003) *The Gene Illusion: Genetic Research in Psychiatry and Psychology Under the Microscope*. Ross-on-Wye: PCCS.

Jost, J. T. (1995) 'Negative illusions: Conceptual clarification and psychological evidence concerning false consciousness', *Political Psychology*, 16 (2), pp. 397–424.

Joyce, P. (2003) *The Rule of Freedom: Liberalism and the Modern City*. London: Verso.

Kagan, C. and Burton, M. (1996) 'Rethinking empowerment', in I. Parker and R. Spears (eds) *Psychology and Marxism: Coexistence and Contradiction*. London: Pluto.

Kakar, S. (1974) *Frederick Taylor: A Study in Personality and Innovation*. Boston, MA: MIT Press.

Kamin, L. (1974) *The Science and Politics of IQ*. Harmondsworth: Penguin.

Kamin, L. (1993) 'On the length of black penises and the depth of white racism', in L. J. Nicholas (ed.) *Psychology and Oppression: Critiques and Proposals*. Johannesburg: Skotaville.

Kamin, L. J. (1995) 'Review of Herrnstein and Murray's *The Bell Curve*', *Scientific American*, 272 (2), pp. 99–103, available at www.du.edu/~psherry/bellcrv.html (accessed 10 March 2006).

Kant, I. (1784) 'An Answer to the Question: What is Enlightenment?', available at www.english.upenn.edu/~mgamer/Etexts/kant.html (accessed 24 February 2003).

Kawai, H. (1995) *The Japanese Psyche: Major Motifs in the Fairy Tales of Japan*. Putnam, CT: Spring Publications.

Kessel, F. S. and Siegel, A. W. (eds) (1981) *The Child and Other Cultural Inventions (Houston Symposium 4)*. New York: Praeger.

Kessen, W. (1979) 'The American child and other cultural inventions', *American Psychologist*, 34 (10), pp. 815–20.

Kincheloe, J. L. and Steinberg, S. R. (eds) (1997) *Changing Multiculturalism*. Buckingham: Open University Press.

Kirk, S. A. and Kutchins, H. (1992) *The Selling of DSM: The Rhetoric of Science in Psychiatry*. New York: Aldine de Gruyter.

Kitzinger, C. (1987) *The Social Construction of Lesbianism*. London and Thousand Oaks, CA: Sage.

Kitzinger, C. (1990) 'The rhetoric of pseudoscience', in I. Parker and J. Shotter (eds) *Deconstructing Social Psychology*. London and New York: Routledge.

Kitzinger, C. (1999) 'Lesbian and gay psychology: Is it critical?', *Annual Review of Critical Psychology*, 1, pp. 50–66.

Kitzinger, C. and Perkins, R. (1993) *Changing Our Minds: Lesbian Feminism and Psychology*. New York: New York University Press, and London: Onlywomen Press.

Kitzinger, C. and Wilkinson, S. (1994) 'Virgins and queers: Rehabilitating heterosexuality?', *Gender & Society*, 8 (3), pp. 444–63.

Klein, M. (1986) *The Selected Works of Melanie Klein*. Harmondsworth: Pelican.

Kline, P. (1972) *Fact and Fantasy in Freudian Theory*. London: Methuen.

Knight, C. (1976) *Sex and the Class Struggle: Selected Works of Wilhelm Reich*, Second Edition. London: Chartist.

Knight, C. (1980) *Revolutionary Consciousness: What It Is; Where It Comes From*. London: Chartist Tendency and Women and Labour Collective.

Kogan, N. and Wallach, M. A. (1967) 'Risk taking as a function of the situation, the person and the group', in G. Mandler (ed.) *New Directions in Psychology, Volume 2*. New York: Holt, Rinehart & Winston.

Kovel, J. (1981) *The Age of Desire: Case Histories of a Radical Psychoanalyst*. New York: Pantheon.

Kovel, J. (2004) 'The American mental health industry', in D. Ingleby (ed.) *Critical Psychiatry: The Politics of Mental Health*. London: Free Association Books.

Kozulin, A. (1989) *Vygotsky's Psychology: A Biography of Ideas*. Hemel Hempstead: Harvester Wheatsheaf.

Kozulin, A. (1994) *Psychology in Utopia: Toward a Social History of Soviet Psychology*. Cambridge, MA: MIT Press.

Kramnick, I. (ed.) (1995) *The Portable Enlightenment Reader*. Harmondsworth: Penguin.

Krige, J. (1979) 'What's so great about facts?', in J. Irvine, I. Miles and J. Evans (eds) (1979) *Demystifying Social Statistics*. London: Pluto.

Kuhn, T. (1962) *The Structure of Scientific Revolutions*. Chicago: University of Chicago Press.

Kumar, M. (2006) 'Rethinking psychology in India: Debating pasts and futures', *Annual Review of Critical Psychology*, 5, available at www.discourse-unit.com/arcp/5.htm (accessed 13 September 2006).

Kvale, S. (1975) 'Memory and dialectics: Some reflections on Ebbinghaus and Mao Tse-tung', *Human Development*, 18, pp. 205–22.

Kvale, S. (ed.) (1992) *Psychology and Postmodernism*. London and Thousand Oaks, CA: Sage.

Laclau, E. (2001) 'Can immanence explain social struggles?', *Diacritics*, 31 (4), pp. 3–10.

Laclau, E. and Mouffe, C. (2001) *Hegemony and Socialist Strategy: Towards a Radical Democratic Politics*, Second Edition. London: Verso.

Lambley, P. (1973) 'Psychology and socio-political reality: Apartheid psychology and its link with trends in humanistic psychology and behaviour theory', *International Journal of Psychology*, 18 (1), pp. 73–9.

LaPiere, R. T. (1934) 'Attitudes vs. actions', *Social Forces*, 13, pp. 230–7.

Laplanche, J. (1989) *New Foundations for Psychoanalysis*. Oxford: Blackwell.
Laqueur, T. (1990) *Making Sex: Body and Gender from the Greeks to Freud*. Cambridge, MA: Harvard University Press.
Latané, B. and Darley, J. M. (1970) *The Unresponsive Bystander: Why Doesn't He Help?* New York: Meredith.
Lather, P. (1994) *Getting Smart: Feminist Research and Pedagogy Within/in the Postmodern*. London and New York: Routledge.
Lather, P. (1995) 'The validity of angels: Interpretive and textual strategies in researching the lives of women with HIV/AIDS', *Qualitative Inquiry*, 1 (1), pp. 41–68.
Laurie, N. and Bondi, L. (eds) (2005) *Working the Spaces of Neoliberalism: Activism, Professionalisation and Incorporation*. Oxford: Blackwell.
Lave, J. (1988) *Cognition in Practice*. Cambridge: Cambridge University Press.
Law, I. (1998) 'Attention Deficit Disorders: Therapy with a shoddily built construct', in S. Madigan and I. Law (eds) *Praxis: Situating Discourse, Feminism and Discourse in Narrative Therapies*. Vancouver: Yaletown Family Therapy.
Law, I. (1999) 'A discursive approach to therapy with men', in I. Parker (ed.) *Deconstructing Psychotherapy*. London and Thousand Oaks, CA: Sage.
Lawlor, J. M. (1978) *IQ, Heritability and Racism*. London: Lawrence & Wishart.
Lawry, J. D. (1981) *Guide to the History of Psychology*. Totowa, NJ: Littlefield, Adams.
Layard, R. (2006) *The Depression Report: A New Deal for Depression and Anxiety Disorders*. London: LSE Centre for Economic Performance, available at http://cep.lse.ac.uk/research/mentalhealth/default.asp (accessed 23 March 2006).
Le Bon, G. (1896) *The Crowd: A Study of the Popular Mind*. London: Ernest Benn.
Leonard, P. (1984) *Personality and Ideology: Towards a Materialist Understanding of the Individual*. London: Macmillan.
Levett, A. (1994) 'Problems of cultural imperialism in the study of childhood sexual abuse', in A. Dawes and D. Donald (eds) *Childhood and Adversity: Psychological Perspectives from South African Research*. Cape Town: David Philip.
Levett, A. (1995) 'Stigmatic factors in sexual abuse and the violence of representation', *Psychology in Society*, 20, pp. 4–12.
Levett, A., Kottler, A., Burman, E. and Parker, I. (eds) (1997) *Culture, Power and Difference: Discourse Analysis in South Africa*. London: Zed.
Levine, A. (2007) 'Collective unconscionable: How psychologists, the most liberal of professionals, abetted Bush's torture policy', *Washington Monthly*, January, available at www.washingtonmonthly.com/features/2007/0701. levine.html (accessed 9 January 2007).
Lewis, R. (1996) *Gendering Orientalism: Race, Femininity and Representation*. London and New York: Routledge.
Lewis, S. and Cooper, C. (2005) *Work-Life Integration – Case Studies of Organizational Change*. Chichester: Wiley.
Lewontin, R. (2001) *It Ain't Necessarily So: The Dream of the Human Genome and Other Illusions*. London: Granta.

Lifton, R. J. (1989) *Thought, Reform and the Psychology of Totalism: A Study of 'Brainwashing' in China*. Chapel Hill, NC: University of North Carolina Press.

Lincoln, Y. S. and Cannella, G. S. (2004) 'Dangerous discourses: Methodological conservatism and governmental regimes of truth', *Qualitative Inquiry*, 10 (1), pp. 5–14.

Lipietz, A. (1987) *Mirages and Miracles: The Crises of Global Fordism*. London: Verso.

Littlewood, R. (1992) 'How universal is something we can call "therapy"?', in J. Kareem and R. Littlewood (eds) *Intercultural Therapy: Themes, Interpretations and Practice*. Oxford: Blackwell.

Littlewood, R. and Lipsedge, M. (1993) *Aliens and Alienists: Ethnic Minorities and Psychiatry*, Third Revised Edition. London and New York: Routledge.

Löwy, M. (1988) *Marxism and Liberation Theology*. Amsterdam: IIRE.

Lubek, I. (1976) 'Some tentative suggestions for analysing and neutralizing the power structure in social psychology', in L. Strickland, F. Aboud and K. J. Gergen (eds) *Social Psychology in Transition*. New York: Plenum.

Lubek, I. (1980) 'The psychological establishment: Pressures to preserve paradigms, publish rather than perish, win funds and influence students', in K. Larsen (ed.) *Social Psychology: Crisis or Failure?* Monmouth, OR: Institute for Theoretical History.

Lubek, I. (1993) 'Social psychology textbooks: An historical and social psychological analysis of conceptual filtering, consensus formation, career gatekeeping and conservatism in science', in H. J. Stam, L. P. Mos, W. Thorngate and B. Kaplan (eds) *Recent Trends in Theoretical Psychology*. New York: Springer-Verlag.

Lucey, H. and Reay, D. (2000) 'Social class and the psyche', *Soundings*, 15, pp. 139–54.

Luepnitz, D. A. (1992) 'Nothing in common but their first names: The case of Foucault and White', *Journal of Family Therapy*, 14, pp. 281–4.

Lynch, T. (2004) *Beyond Prozac: Healing Mental Suffering*. Ross-on-Wye: PCCS.

Lynn, R. (1982) 'IQ in Japan and the United States shows a growing disparity', *Nature*, 297, pp. 222–3.

Lynn, R. and Irwing, P. (2004) 'Sex differences on the Progressive Matrices: a meta-analysis', *Intelligence*, 32, pp. 481–98.

Lyotard, J.-F. (1984) *The Postmodern Condition: A Report on Knowledge*. Manchester: Manchester University Press.

Macey, D. (1994) *The Lives of Michel Foucault*. London: Vintage.

Macpherson, C. B. (1964) *The Political Theory of Possessive Individualism*. Oxford: Clarendon.

Madigan, S. (1999) 'Inscription, description, and deciphering chronic identities', in I. Parker (ed.) *Deconstructing Psychotherapy*. London and Thousand Oaks, CA: Sage.

Madigan, S. and Epston, D. (1995) 'From "psychiatric gaze" to communities of concern: From professional monologue to dialogue', in S. Friedman (ed.) *The Reflecting Team in Action: Collaborative Practice in Family Therapy*. New York: Guilford.

Madigan, S. and Law, I. (eds) (1998) *Praxis: Situating Discourse, Feminism and Discourse in Narrative Therapies*. Vancouver: Yaletown Family Therapy.

Maiers, W. and Tolman, C. (1996) 'Critical psychology as subject-science', in I. Parker and R. Spears (eds) *Psychology and Marxism: Coexistence and Contradiction*. London: Pluto.

Malson, H. (1997) *The Thin Woman: Feminism, Post-structuralism and the Social Psychology of Anorexia Nervosa*. London and New York: Routledge.

Malson, L. and Itard, J. (1972) *Wolf Children* and *The Wild Boy of Aveyron*. London: New Left Books.

Mama, A. (1995) *Beyond the Masks: Race, Gender and the Subject*. London and New York: Routledge.

Mamdani, M. (2004) 'Race and ethnicity as political identities in the African context', in N. Tazi (ed.) *Keywords, Identity: For a Different Kind of Globalization*. New Delhi: Vistaar.

Mamdani, M. (2005) *Good Muslim, Bad Muslim: America, the Cold War, and the Roots of Terror*. Houston, TX: Three Leaves.

Mandel, E. (1974) *Late Capitalism*. London: New Left Books.

Mandel, E. (1977) 'The Leninist theory of organisation', in R. Blackburn (ed.) *Revolution and Class Struggle: A Reader in Marxist Politics*. London: Fontana.

Mandel, E. (1978) *From Stalinism to Eurocommunism: The Bitter Fruits of 'Socialism in One Country'*. London: New Left Books.

Mandel, E. (1979) *Revolutionary Marxism Today*. London: New Left Books.

Mandel, E. (1992) *Power and Money: A Marxist Theory of Bureaucracy*. London: Verso.

Mandel, E. and Novack, G. (1970) *The Marxist Theory of Alienation*. New York: Pathfinder.

Marcus, S. (1974) *Engels, Manchester, and the Working Class*. New York: W. W. Norton.

Marks, D. (1999) *Disability: Controversial Debates and Psychosocial Perspectives*. London and New York: Routledge.

Marsden, J. (1999) 'Cyberpsychosis: The feminization of the post-biological body', in Á. J. Gordo López and I. Parker (eds) *Cyberpsychology*. London: Palgrave.

Martín-Baró, I. (1994) *Writings for a Liberation Psychology*. Cambridge, MA: Harvard University Press.

Marx, K. (1844) 'Introduction to A Contribution to the Critique of Hegel's Philosophy of Right', available at www.marxists.org/archive/marx/works/1843/critique-hpr/intro.htm (accessed 10 August 2006).

Marx, K. (1845) 'Theses on Feuerbach', available at www.marxists.org/archive/marx/works/1845/theses/theses.htm (accessed 24 March 2006).

Marx, K. and Engels, F. (1965) *Manifesto of the Communist Party* (originally published 1848). Beijing: Foreign Languages Press.

Masling, J. (ed.) (1983) *Empirical Studies of Psychoanalytical Theories*. Hillsdale, NJ: The Analytic Press.

Masson, J. (1990) *Against Therapy*. London: Fontana.

Matthews, G., Davies, D. R., Westerman, S. J. and Stammers, R. B. (2000) *Human Performance: Cognition, Stress and Individual Differences*. Hove: Psychology Press.

Maturana, H. R. and Varela, F. J. (1980) *Autopoiesis and Cognition: The Realisation of the Living*. Dordrecht: D. Reidel.

May, R. (2000) 'Taking the Plunge', *Asylum*, 12 (3), pp. 4–5.

McClintock, A. (1995) *Imperial Leather: Race, Gender and Sexuality in the Colonial Contest*. London and New York: Routledge.

McDougall, W. (1927) *The Group Mind* (originally published 1920). New York: G. P. Putnam.

McLaughlin, K. (2003a) 'Agency, resilience and empowerment: The dangers posed by a therapeutic culture', *Practice*, 15 (2), pp. 45–58.

McLaughlin, K. (2003b) 'Identities: Should we survive or surpass them?', *Journal of Critical Psychology, Counselling and Psychotherapy*, 3 (1), pp. 48–58.

McLaughlin, K. (2004) 'Stressing vulnerability: Stress discourse in the public sector', *Journal of Critical Psychology, Counselling and Psychotherapy*, 4 (4), pp. 223– 32.

McLaughlin, T. (1996) 'Hearing voices: An emancipatory discourse analytic approach', *Changes: An International Journal of Psychology and Psychotherapy*, 14 (3), pp. 238–43.

McLaughlin, T. (2003) 'From the inside out: The view from democratic psychiatry', *European Journal of Counselling, Psychotherapy and Health*, 6 (1), pp. 63–6.

Mercer, K. (1986) 'Racism and transcultural psychiatry', in P. Miller and N. Rose (eds) *The Power of Psychiatry*. Cambridge: Polity.

Michie, S. (1979) 'The psychiatric hospital in Havana', *Bulletin of the British Psychological Society*, 32, pp. 143–4.

Middlemist, R. D., Knowles, E. S. and Matter, C. F. (1976) 'Personal space invasions in the lavatory: suggestive evidence for arousal', *Journal of Personality and Social Psychology*, 33 (5), pp. 541–6.

Milgram, S. (1963) 'Behavioral study of obedience', *Journal of Abnormal and Social Psychology*, 69, pp. 371–8.

Miller, A. (1998) *Thou Shalt Not Be Aware: Society's Betrayal of the Child*, Second Edition. London: Pluto.

Miller, G. A. (1966) *Psychology: The Science of Mental Life* (originally published 1962). Harmondsworth: Penguin.

Miller, G. A. (1969) 'Psychology as a means of promoting human welfare', *American Psychologist*, 24, pp. 1063–75.

Miller, J.-A. (originally published 1989) 'Michel Foucault and psychoanalysis', in T. J. Armstrong (ed.) (1992) *Michel Foucault: Philosopher*. New York: Harvester Wheatsheaf.

Miller, J.-A. (2001) *The Tenderness of Terrorists*. New York: Wooster.

Miller, L., Rustin, M., Rustin, M. and Shuttleworth, J. (eds) (1989) *Closely Observed Infants*. London: Duckworth.

Miller, M. (1998) *Freud and the Bolsheviks: Psychoanalysis in Imperial Russia and the Soviet Union*. New Haven, CT: Yale University Press.

Miller, P. (1986) 'Psychotherapy of work and unemployment', in N. Rose and P. Miller (eds) *The Power of Psychiatry*. Cambridge: Polity.

Millett, K. (1977) *Sexual Politics*. London: Virago.

Millett, K. (2000) *The Loony-Bin Trip*. Urbana, IL: University of Illinois Press.

Milligan, D. (1979) *The Politics of Homosexuality* (originally published 1973). Edinburgh: Gay Information Centre.

Mills, J. A. (1998) *Control: A History of Behavioral Psychology*. New York: New York University Press.

Minuchin, S. (1974) *Families and Family Therapy*. London: Tavistock.

Mitchell, R. (2003) 'Ideological reflections on the DSM-IV-R (or Pay no attention to that man behind the curtain Dorothy!)', *Child & Youth Care Forum*, 32 (5), pp. 281–98.

Mixon, D. (1974) 'If you won't deceive, what can you do?', in N. Armistead (ed.) *Reconstructing Social Psychology*. Harmondsworth: Penguin.

Moerman, D. E. (2002) *Meaning, Medicine and the 'Placebo Effect'*. Cambridge: Cambridge University Press.

Moncrieff, J. (2006) 'An unholy alliance: Psychiatry and the influence of the pharmaceutical industry', *Asylum*, 15 (2), pp. 14–16.

Moncrieff, J. (in press) 'Neoliberalism and biopsychiatry: A marriage of convenience', in C. Cohen and S. Timimi (eds) *Liberatory Psychiatry*. Cambridge: Cambridge University Press.

Monk, G., Winslade, J., Crocket, K. and Epston, D. (eds) (1997) *Narrative Therapy in Practice: The Archaeology of Hope*. San Francisco, CA: Jossey-Bass.

Montero, M. (2004) *Leadership and Organization for Community Prevention and Intervention in Venezuela*. New York: Haworth.

Montero, M. and Montenegro, M. (2006) 'Critical psychology in Venezuela', *Annual Review of Critical Psychology*, 5, available at www.discourseunit.com/arcp/5.htm (accessed 13 September 2006).

Morawski, J. G. (1982) 'Assessing psychology's moral heritage through our neglected utopias', *American Psychologist*, 37, pp. 1082–95.

Morawski, J. G. (1997) 'The science behind feminist research methods', *Journal of Social Issues*, 53 (4), pp. 667–81.

Morgan, R. (2006) *Fighting Words: A Toolkit for Combating the Religious Right*. New York: Nation Books.

Morris, C. (1972) *Discovery of the Individual, 1050–1200*. London: SPCK.

Morris, J. (ed.) (1996) *Encounters with Strangers: Feminism and Disability*. London: The Women's Press.

Morss, J. (1990) *The Biologising of Childhood*. Hillsdale, NJ: Lawrence Erlbaum.

Morss, J. (1996) *Growing Critical: Alternatives to Developmental Psychology*. London and New York: Routledge.

Moscovici, S. (1986) *The Age of the Crowd*. Cambridge: Cambridge University Press.

Mowbray, R. (1995) *The Case Against Psychotherapy Registration: A Conservation Issue for the Human Potential Movement*. London: Transmarginal Press.

Moynihan, R. and Henry, D. (eds) (2006) *Public Library of Science Medicine*, 3 (4), available at http://medicine.plosjournals.org/perlserv?request=get-toc&issn=1549-1676&volume=3&issue=4 (accessed 14 September 2006).

Murray, B. (2002) 'Wanted: politics-free, science-based education', *APA Monitor on Psychology*, 33 (8), available at www.apa.org/monitor/sep02/wanted.html (accessed 10 August 2006).

Nadar, L. (1997) 'The phantom factor: Impact of the Cold War on anthropology', in N. Chomsky (ed.) *The Cold War and the University*. New York: The New Press.

Neel, A. (1977) *Theories of Psychology: A Handbook*, Revised and Enlarged Edition. Cambridge, MA: Schenkman.

Neisser, U. (1967) *Cognitive Psychology*. Englewood Cliffs, NJ: Prentice-Hall.

New, C. (1996) *Agency, Health and Social Survival: The Ecopolitics of Rival Psychologies*. London: Taylor & Francis.

Newman, F. (1999) 'One dogma of dialectical materialism', *Annual Review of Critical Psychology*, 1, pp. 83–99.

Newman, F. and Holzman, L. (1993) *Lev Vygotsky: Revolutionary Scientist*. London and New York: Routledge.

Newman, F. and Holzman, L. (1996) *Unscientific Psychology: A Cultural-Performatory Approach to Understanding Human Life*. Westport, CT: Praeger.

Newman, F. and Holzman, L. (1997) *The End of Knowing (And a New Developmental Way of Learning)*. London and New York: Routledge.

Newman, F. and Holzman, L. (2003) 'All power to the developing!', *Annual Review of Critical Psychology*, 3, pp. 8–23.

Newnes, C. and Radcliffe, N. (eds) (2005) *Making and Breaking Children's Lives*. Ross-on-Wye: PCCS.

Newnes, C., Holmes, G. and Dunn, C. (eds) (1999) *This Is Madness: A Critical Look at Psychiatry and the Future of Mental Health Services*. Ross-on-Wye: PCCS.

Newnes, C., Holmes, G. and Dunn, C. (eds) (2001) *This is Madness Too: Critical Perspectives on Mental Health Services*. Ross-on-Wye: PCCS.

Newton, T. (1999) 'Stress discourse and individualization', in C. Feltham (ed.) *Controversies in Psychotherapy and Counselling*. London and Thousand Oaks, CA: Sage.

Nightingale, D. J. and Cromby, J. (eds) (1999) *Social Constructionist Psychology: A Critical Analysis of Theory and Practice*. Buckingham: Open University Press.

Nissen, M., Axel, E. and Bechmann Jensen, T. (1999) 'The abstract zone of proximal conditions', *Theory and Psychology*, 9 (3), pp. 417–26.

Norton, D. F. (1981) 'The myth of "British empiricism" ', *History of European Ideas*, 1 (4), pp. 331–44.

Novack, G. (1975) *Pragmatism versus Marxism: An Appraisal of John Dewey's Philosophy*. New York: Pathfinder.

Novatore, R. (n.d.) *Toward the Creative Nothing*. San Francisco, CA: Venomous Butterfly Publications, Elephant Editions.

O'Donnell, J. M. (1979) 'The crisis of experimentalism in the 1920s: E. G. Boring and his uses of history', *American Psychologist*, 34, pp. 289–95.

O'Donnell, P. (1982) 'Lucien Sève, Althusser and the Contradictions of the PCF', *Critique*, 15, pp. 7–29.

O'Reilly Byrne, N. and Colgan McCarthy, I. (1999) 'Feminism, politics and power in therapeutic discourse: Fragments from the Fifth Province', in I. Parker (ed.) *Deconstructing Psychotherapy*. London and Thousand Oaks, CA: Sage.

Oe, K. (1996) *Nip the Buds, Shoot the Kids*. New York: Grove.

Oliver, M. (1990) *The Politics of Disablement*. Basingstoke: Macmillan.

Oliver, M. (1996) *Understanding Disability: From Theory to Practice*. London: Macmillan.

Orbach, S. (2001) *Towards Emotional Literacy*. London: Virago.

Orne, M. T. (1962) 'On the social psychology of the psychology experiment: With particular reference to demand characteristics and their implications', *American Psychologist*, 17, pp. 776–83.

Osborne, P. (2006) 'The dreambird of experience: Utopia, possibility, boredom', *Radical Philosophy*, 137, pp. 36–44.

Papadopoulos, D. (2002) 'Dialectics of subjectivity: North-Atlantic certainties, neo-liberal rationality and liberation promises', *International Journal of Critical Psychology*, 6, pp. 99–122.

Papadopoulos, D. (2003) 'The ordinary superstition of subjectivity: Liberalism and technostructural violence', *Theory & Psychology*, 13 (1), pp. 73–93.

Papadopoulos, D. and Schraube, E. (2004, September) ' "This world demands our attention": Ian Parker in conversation with Dimitris Papadopoulos and Ernst Schraube' [33 paragraphs], *Forum Qualitative Sozialforschung / Forum: Qualitative Social Research* [online journal], 5 (3), Art. 14, available at www.qualitative-research.net/fqs-texte/3–04/04–3–14–e.htm (accessed 12 November 2005).

Paré, D. and Larner, G. (eds) (2004) *Collaborative Practice in Psychology and Therapy*. New York: Haworth.

Parker, I. (1989) *The Crisis in Modern Social Psychology, and How to End it*. London and New York: Routledge.

Parker, I. (1995a) 'Everyday behaviour(ism) and therapeutic discourse: Deconstructing the ego as verbal nucleus in Skinner and Lacan', in J. Siegfried (ed.) *Therapeutic and Everyday Discourse as Behavior Change: Towards a Micro-analysis in Psychotherapy Process Research*. New York: Ablex.

Parker, I. (1995b) 'Michel Foucault, psychologist', *The Psychologist*, 8 (11), pp. 214–16.

Parker, I. (1995c) ' "Right", said Fred, "I'm too sexy for bourgeois group therapy": The case of the Institute for Social Therapy', *Changes: An International Journal of Psychology and Psychotherapy*, 13 (1), pp. 1–22.

Parker, I. (1996) 'The revolutionary psychology of Lev Davidovich Bronstein', in I. Parker and R. Spears (eds) *Psychology and Society: Radical Theory and Practice*. London: Pluto.

Parker, I. (1997) *Psychoanalytic Culture: Psychoanalytic Discourse in Western Society*. London and Thousand Oaks, CA: Sage.

Parker, I. (1998a) 'Against postmodernism: Psychology in cultural context', *Theory & Psychology*, 8 (5), pp. 621–47.

Parker, I. (1998b) 'Constructing and deconstructing psychotherapeutic discourse', *European Journal of Psychotherapy, Counselling and Health*, 1 (1), pp. 77–90.

Parker, I. (1999a) 'Critical reflexive humanism and critical constructionist psychology', in D. J. Nightingale and J. Cromby (eds) *Social Constructionist Psychology: A Critical Analysis of Theory and Practice*. Buckingham: Open University Press.

Parker, I. (ed.) (1999b) *Deconstructing Psychotherapy*. London and Thousand Oaks, CA: Sage.

Parker, I. (1999c) 'Deconstructing diagnosis: Psychopathological practice', in C. Feltham (ed.) *Controversies in Psychotherapy and Counselling*. London and Thousand Oaks, CA: Sage.

Parker, I. (1999d) 'Qualitative data and the subjectivity of "objective" facts', in D. Dorling and L. Simpson (eds) *Statistics in Society: The Arithmetic of Politics*. London: Edward Arnold.

Parker, I. (1999e) 'Against relativism in psychology, on balance', *History of the Human Sciences*, 12 (4), pp. 61–78.

Parker, I. (2000) 'Four story-theories about and against postmodernism in psychology', in L. Holzman and J. Morss (eds) *Postmodern Psychologies: Societal Practice and Political Life*. New York: Routledge.

Parker, I. (2002) *Critical Discursive Psychology*. London: Palgrave.

Parker, I. (2003) 'Foreword', in R. House, *Therapy Beyond Modernity: A New Paradigm Insight for a Post-Professional Era*. London: Karnac.

Parker, I. (2004) 'Discursive practice: Analysis, context and action in critical research', *International Journal of Critical Psychology*, 10, pp. 150–73.

Parker, I. (2005a) *Qualitative Psychology: Introducing Radical Research*. Maidenhead and New York: Open University Press.

Parker, I. (2005b) 'Lacanian ethics in psychology: Seven paradigms', in A. Gülerce, A., Hofmeister, J. Kaye, G. Saunders and I. Steauble (eds) *Theoretical Psychology*. Toronto: Captus.

Parker, I. and the Bolton Discourse Network (1999) *Critical Textwork: An Introduction to Varieties of Discourse and Analysis*. Buckingham: Open University Press.

Parker, I., Georgaca, E., Harper, D., McLaughlin, T. and Stowell Smith, M. (1995) *Deconstructing Psychopathology*. London and Thousand Oaks, CA: Sage.

Peters, D. P. and Ceci, S. J. (1982) 'Peer-review practices of psychological journals: The fate of published articles, submitted again', *The Behavioural and Brain Sciences*, 5, pp. 187–255.

Piercy, M. (2000) *Woman on the Edge of Time*. London: The Women's Press.

Pilgrim, D. (1997) *Psychotherapy and Society*. London and Thousand Oaks, CA: Sage.

Pilgrim, D. and Rogers, A. (1993) *A Sociology of Mental Health and Illness*. Buckingham: Open University Press.

Pilgrim, D. and Treacher, A. (1992) *Clinical Psychology Observed*. London and New York: Routledge.

Pinkard, T. (2000) *Hegel: A Biography*. Cambridge: Cambridge University Press.

Plant, S. (1993) *The Most Radical Gesture: The Situationist International in a Postmodern Age*. London: Routledge.

Plekhanov, G. V. (1946) *The Role of the Individual in History* (originally published 1898). Moscow: Foreign Languages Publishing House.

Poster, M. (1978) *Critical Theory of the Family*. London: Pluto.

Potter, J. (1996) *Representing Reality: Discourse, Rhetoric and Social Construction*. London and Thousand Oaks, CA: Sage.

Potter, J. (1998) 'Fragments in the realization of relativism', in I. Parker (ed.) *Social Constructionism, Discourse and Realism*. London and Thousand Oaks, CA: Sage.

Potter, J. and Wetherell, M. (1987) *Discourse and Social Psychology: Beyond Attitudes and Behaviour*. London and Thousand Oaks, CA: Sage.

Precarias a la Deriva (2005) 'Housewives, maids, cleaning ladies and caregivers in general: Care in the communication continuum', *Annual Review of Critical Psychology*, 4, pp. 188–98.

Prilleltensky, I. (1990) 'On the social and political implications of cognitive psychology', *Journal of Mind and Behavior*, 11 (2), pp. 127–36.

Pringle, R. (1989) 'Bureaucracy, rationality and sexuality: The case of secretaries', in J. Hearn, D. L. Sheppard, P. Tancral-Sheriff and G. Burrell (eds) *The Sexuality of Organization*. London and Thousand Oaks, CA: Sage.

Pringle, R. (1991) *Secretaries' Talk*. London: Verso.

Proctor, G., Cooper, M., Sanders, P. and Malcolm, B. (eds) (2006) *Politicizing the Person-Centred Approach: An Agenda for Social Change*. Ross-on-Wye: PCCS.

Pyszczynski, T., Solomon, S. and Greenberg, J. (2002) *In the Wake of 9/11: The Psychology of Terror*. Washington, DC: American Psychological Association.

Rack, P. (1982) *Race, Culture and Mental Disorder*. London: Tavistock.

Ramon, S. and Giannichedda, M. (eds) (1989) *Psychiatry in Transition: The British and Italian Experiences*. London: Pluto.

Ratner, C. (1971) 'Totalitarianism and individualism in psychology', *Telos*, 7, pp. 50–72.

Raymond, J. (1980) *The Transsexual Empire*. London: The Women's Press.

Read, J. (2005) 'The bio-bio-bio model of madness', *The Psychologist*, 18 (10), pp. 596–7.

Reason, P. and Rowan, J. (eds) (1981) *Human Inquiry: A Sourcebook of New Paradigm Research*. Chichester: Wiley.

Redding, R. E. (2001) 'Sociopolitical diversity in psychology', *American Psychologist*, 56, pp. 205–15.

Reed, E. (1971) *An Answer to 'The Naked Ape' and Other Books on Aggression*. New York: Pathfinder.

Reed, E. (1996) 'The challenge of historical materialist epistemology', in I. Parker and R. Spears (eds) *Psychology and Society: Radical Theory and Practice*. London: Pluto.

Reich, W. (1972) *Sex-Pol: Essays, 1929–1934*. New York: Random House.

Reich, W. (1975) *The Mass Psychology of Fascism* (originally published 1946). Harmondsworth: Pelican.

Reicher, S. (1982) 'The determination of collective behaviour', in H. Tajfel (ed.) *Social Identity and Intergroup Relations*. Cambridge: Cambridge University Press.

Reicher, S. (1984) 'The St Paul's riot: An explanation of the limits of crowd action in terms of a social identity model', *European Journal of Social Psychology*, 14, pp. 1–21.

Reicher, S. (1988) 'Essay review of *Arguing and Thinking*', *British Journal of Social Psychology*, 27, pp. 283–8.

Reicher, S. (1991) 'Politics of crowd psychology', *The Psychologist*, 4 (11), pp. 487–91.

Reicher, S. (1997) 'Laying the ground for a common critical social psychology', in T. Ibáñez and L. Íñiguez (eds) *Critical Social Psychology*. London and Thousand Oaks, CA: Sage.

Rice, C. E. (1997) 'The scientist–practitioner split and the future of psychology', *American Psychologist*, 52 (11), pp. 1173–81.

Rich, A. (1976) *Of Woman Born: Motherhood as Experience and Institution*. New York: W. W. Norton.

Richards, B. (1995) 'Psychotherapy and the injuries of class', *BPS Psychotherapy Section Newsletter*, 17, pp. 21–35.

Richards, G. (1996) *Putting Psychology in its Place: An Introduction from a Critical Historical Perspective*. London and New York: Routledge.

Richards, G. (1997) *'Race', Racism and Psychology: Towards a Reflexive History*. London and New York: Routledge.

Richardson, K. and Spears, D. (eds) (1972) *Race, Culture and Intelligence.* Harmondsworth: Penguin.

Riger, S. (1993) 'What's wrong with empowerment?', *American Journal of Community Psychology*, 21 (3), pp. 279–92.

Riley, D. (1983) *War in the Nursery: Theories of the Child and Mother.* London: Virago.

Ritzer, G. (2004) *The McDonaldization of Society.* London and Thousand Oaks, CA: Sage.

Roberts, R. and Groome, D. (eds) (2001) *Parapsychology: The Science of Unusual Experiences.* London: Edward Arnold.

Rodney, W. (1973) *How Europe Underdeveloped Africa.* London: Bogle-L'Ouverture, London and Dar es Salaam: Tanzanian Publishing House, available at www.marxists.org/subject/africa/rodney-walter/how-europe (accessed 10 August 2006).

Rodríguez Mora, I. (2005) 'Contesting femininity: Women in the political transition in Venezuela', *Annual Review of Critical Psychology*, 4, pp. 39–53.

Roemer, J. (ed.) (1986) *Analytical Marxism.* Cambridge: Cambridge University Press.

Roiser, M. (1974) 'Asking silly questions', in N. Armistead (ed.) *Reconstructing Social Psychology.* Harmondsworth: Penguin.

Roiser, M. and Willig, C. (2006) 'Marxism, the Frankfurt School, and working-class psychology', in I. Parker and R. Spears (eds) *Psychology and Marxism: Coexistence and Contradiction.* London: Pluto.

Romme, M. and Escher, A. (1989) 'Hearing voices', *Schizophrenia Bulletin*, 15 (2), pp. 209–16.

Romme, M. and Escher, A. (1993) *Accepting Voices.* London: MIND.

Romme, M., Honig, A., Noorthoorn, E. and Escher, A. (1992) 'Coping with hearing voices: An emancipatory approach', *British Journal of Psychiatry*, 161, pp. 99–103.

Rose, H. and Rose, S. (2001) *Alas Poor Darwin: Arguments Against Evolutionary Psychology.* London: Vintage.

Rose, N. (1985) *The Psychological Complex: Psychology, Politics and Society in England 1869–1939.* London: Routledge & Kegan Paul.

Rose, N. (1999) *Powers of Freedom: Reframing Political Thought.* Cambridge: Cambridge University Press.

Rose, S. (2006) *The 21st Century Brain: Explaining, Mending and Manipulating the Mind.* London: Vintage.

Rose, S., Lewontin, R. and Kamin, L. J. (1990) *Not in Our Genes: Biology, Ideology and Human Nature.* Harmondsworth: Penguin.

Rosenhan, D. L. (1973) 'On being sane in insane places', *Science*, 179, pp. 250–8.

Rosenhan, D. L. (1975) 'The contextual nature of psychiatric diagnosis', *Journal of Abnormal Psychology*, 84, pp. 462–74.

Rosenthal, R. (1965) 'The volunteer subject', *Human Relations*, 18, pp. 389–406.

Rosenthal, R. (1966) *Experimenter Effects in Behavioral Research.* New York: Appleton-Century-Crofts.

Rosenthal, R. and Rosnow, R. (1975) *The Volunteer Subject.* New York: Wiley.

Rousset, P. (1987a) *The Chinese Revolution – Part I: The Second Chinese Revolution and the Shaping of the Maoist Outlook.* Amsterdam: IIRE.

Rousset, P. (1987b) *The Chinese Revolution – Part II: The Maoist Project Tested in the Struggle for Power*. Amsterdam: IIRE.

Rowan, J. (2005) *The Transpersonal: Spirituality in Psychotherapy and Counselling*. London and New York: Routledge.

Rowbotham, S. (1973) *Hidden from History: 300 Years of Women's Oppression and the Fight Against It*. London: Pluto.

Rustin, M. (1982) 'A socialist consideration of Kleinian psychoanalysis', *New Left Review*, 131, pp. 71–96.

Rustin, M. (2000) 'States of Mind Special Issue', *Soundings*, 15.

Ryle, G. (1949) *The Concept of Mind*. London: Hutchinson.

Saarni, S. I. and Gylling, H. A. (2004) 'Evidence based medicine guidelines: A solution to rationing or politics disguised as science?', *Journal of Medical Ethics*, 30, pp. 171–5.

Sacks, O. (1973) *Awakenings*. London: Duckworth.

Sacks, O. (1991) *Seeing Voices: A Journey into the World of the Deaf*, Revised Edition. London: Picador.

Said, E. (1978) *Orientalism*. London: Routledge & Kegan Paul.

Sale, A. E. (2006) 'They were victims too', *Community Care*, 26 January, pp. 30–1.

Salecl, R. (1994) *The Spoils of Freedom: Psychoanalysis and Feminism After the Fall of Socialism*. London: Routledge.

Samelson, F. (1974) 'History, origin myth and ideology: Comte's "discovery" of social psychology', *Journal for the Theory of Social Behaviour*, 4, pp. 217–31.

Samelson, F. (1992) 'Rescuing the reputation of Sir Cyril Burt', *Journal for the History of the Behavioral Sciences*, 28, pp. 221–33.

Sampson, E. E. (1981) 'Cognitive psychology as ideology', *American Psychologist*, 36 (7), pp. 730–43.

Sampson, E. E. (1985) 'The decentralization of identity: Towards a revised concept of personal and social order', *American Psychologist*, 40, pp. 1203–11.

Sampson, E. E. (1988) 'The debate on individualism: Indigenous psychologies of the individual and their role in personal and societal functioning', *American Psychologist*, 43, pp. 15–22.

Sampson, E. E. (1989) 'The deconstruction of the self', in J. Shotter and K. Gergen (eds) *Texts of Identity*. London and Thousand Oaks, CA: Sage.

Sampson, E. E. (1990) 'Social psychology and social control', in I. Parker and J. Shotter (eds) *Deconstructing Social Psychology*. London and New York: Routledge.

Sampson, E. E. (1993) *Celebrating the Other: A Dialogical Account of Human Nature*. New York: Harvester Wheatsheaf.

Samuels, A. (1992) 'National psychology, National Socialism, and analytical psychology: Reflections on C. G. Jung and anti-Semitism', *Journal of Analytical Psychology*, 37, pp. 23–64.

Samuels, A. (1993) *The Political Psyche*. London: Routledge.

Sanin, D. (2006) 'Critical psychology in Austria', *Annual Review of Critical Psychology*, 5, available at www.discourseunit.com/arcp/5.htm (accessed 13 September 2006).

Sarbin, T. R. (1986) 'The narrative as a root metaphor for psychology', in T. R. Sarbin (ed.) (1986) *Narrative Psychology: the Storied Nature of Human Conduct*. New York: Praeger.

Sargant, W. (1959) *Battle for the Mind: A Physiology of Conversion and Brain-Washing*, Revised Edition. London: Pan.

Sawacki, J. (1991) *Disciplining Foucault: Feminism, Power and the Body*. London: Routledge.

Sawer, M. (1990) *Sisters in Suits*. Sydney: Allen & Unwin.

Sayers, J. (1986) *Sexual Contradictions: Psychology, Psychoanalysis and Feminism*. London: Tavistock.

Schacht, T. E. (1985) 'DSM-III and the politics of truth', *American Psychologist*, 40, pp. 513–21.

Scheff, T. J. (1995) 'Academic gangs', *Crime, Law, and Social Change*, 23, pp. 157–62.

Schlemmer, B. (2000) *The Exploited Child*. London and New York: Zed.

Scruggs, D. and Breggin, P. (2001) *Talking Back to Ritalin: What Doctors Aren't Telling You about Stimulants and ADHD*. Cambridge, MA: De Capo.

Sears, D. O. (1986) 'College sophomores in the laboratory: Influences of a narrow data base on social psychology's view of human nature', *Journal of Personality and Social Psychology*, 15 (3), pp. 515–30.

Sedgwick, P. (1974) 'Ideology in modern psychology', in N. Armistead (ed.) *Reconstructing Social Psychology*. Harmondsworth: Pelican.

Sedgwick, P. (1982) *Psycho Politics*. London: Pluto.

Seligman, M. E. P. (1998) 'Message from the President of the APA', in *APA Annual Convention Program*. Washington, DC: American Psychological Association.

Selvini, M., Boscolo, L., Cecchin, G. and Prata, G. (1978) *Paradox and Counterparadox*. New York: Aronson.

Selvini-Palazzoli, M., Boscolo, L. Cecchin, G. and Prata, G. (1980) 'Hypothesizing-circularity-neutrality: Three guidelines for the conductor of the session', *Family Process*, 19, pp. 3–12.

Sennett, R. and Cobb, J. (1972) *The Hidden Injuries of Class*. London: Faber & Faber.

Sève, L. (1978) *Man in Marxist Theory, and the Psychology of Personality*. Hassocks: Harvester Press.

Sey, J. (1999) 'The labouring body and the posthuman', in Á. J. Gordo López and I. Parker (eds) *Cyberpsychology*. London: Palgrave.

Shakespeare, T. (ed.) (1998) *The Disability Reader: Social Science Perspectives*. London: Cassell.

Shallice, T. (1984) 'Psychology and social control', *Cognition*, 17, pp. 29–48.

Shames, C. (1981) 'The Scientific Humanism of Lucien Sève', *Science and Society*, 45 (1), pp. 1–23.

Sharp, P. (2001) *Nurturing Emotional Literacy: A Practical Guide for Teachers, Parents and Those in the Caring Professions*. London: David Fulton.

Shaw, W. (1995) *Spying in Guru Land: Inside Britain's Cults*. London: Fourth Estate.

Shephard, B. (2001) *A War of Nerves: Soldiers and Psychiatrists in the Twentieth Century*. Cambridge, MA: Harvard University Press.

Shore, C. and Wright, S. (1999) 'Audit culture and anthropology: Neo-liberalism in British Higher Education', *The Journal of the Royal Anthropological Institute*, 5 (4), pp. 557–75.

Shotter, J. (1987) 'Cognitive psychology, "Taylorism", and the manufacture of unemployment', in A. Costall and Still (eds) *Cognitive Psychology in Question*. Brighton: Harvester.

Simblett, G. J. (1997) 'Narrative approaches to psychiatry', in G. Monk, J. Winslade, K. Crocket and D. Epston (eds) *Narrative Therapy in Practice: The Archaeology of Hope*. San Francisco, CA: Jossey-Bass.

Sivanandan, A. (1985) 'RAT and the degradation of black struggle', *Race & Class*, 25 (4), pp. 1–33.

Skeggs, B. (2003) *Valuing Class*. London and New York: Routledge.

Skinner, B. F. (1957) *Verbal Behavior*. New York: Appleton-Century-Crofts.

Skinner, B. F. (1962) *Walden Two* (originally published 1948).Toronto: Macmillan.

Skinner, B. F. (1969) *Contingencies of Reinforcement*. New York: Appleton-Century-Crofts.

Skinner, B. F. (1973) *Beyond Freedom and Dignity* (originally published 1971). Harmondsworth: Penguin.

Slater, H. (2003) 'Evacuate the leftist bunker', *Annual Review of Critical Psychology*, 3, pp. 116–36.

Slater, L. (2005) *Opening Skinner's Box: Great Psychological Experiments of the Twentieth Century*. London: Bloomsbury.

Sloan, T. S. (1990) 'Psychology for the Third World?', *Journal of Social Issues*, 46 (3), pp. 1–20.

Sloan, T. S. (1996) *Damaged Life: The Crisis of the Modern Psyche*. London and New York: Routledge.

Sloan, T. S. (ed.) (2000) *Critical Psychology: Voices for Change*. London: Palgrave.

Smith, D. (1988) *The Everyday World as Problematic: A Feminist Sociology*. Milton Keynes: Open University Press.

Smith, D. (1990) *Texts, Facts, and Femininity: Exploring the Relations of Ruling*. London: Routledge.

Smith, J. (2004) 'Reflecting on the development of interpretative phenomeno-logical analysis and its contribution to qualitative research in psychology', *Qualitative Research in Psychology*, 1, pp. 39–54.

Smith, R. (1988) 'Does the history of psychology have a subject?', *History of the Human Sciences*, 1, pp. 147–77.

Smith, S. (1983) 'Taylorism rules OK? Bolshevism, Taylorism and the techni-cal intelligentsia in the Soviet Union, 1917–41', *Radical Science Journal*, 13, pp. 3–27.

Sohn-Rethel, A. (1978) *Intellectual and Manual Labour: A Critique of Epistemology*. London: Macmillan.

Soldevilla, C. (1999) 'Vertiginous technology: towards a psychoanalytic genealogy of technique', in Á. J. Gordo López and I. Parker (eds) *Cyberpsychology*. London: Palgrave.

Southgate, J. and Randall, R. (1989) *The Barefoot Psychoanalyst: An Illustrated Manual of Self Help Therapy*. London: Gale Centre.

Soyland, A. J. (1994) *Psychology as Metaphor*. London and Thousand Oaks, CA: Sage.

Spandler, H. (1996) *Who's Hurting Who? Young People, Self-Harm and Suicide*. Manchester: 42nd Street.

Spandler, H. (2006) *Asylum to Action: Paddington Day Hospital, Therapeutic Communities and Beyond*. London and Philadelphia, PA: Jessica Kingsley.

Spiegel, A. (2005) 'The dictionary of disorder: How one man revolutionized psychiatry', *New Yorker*, 3 January, available at www.newyorker.com/fact/content/?050103fa_fact (accessed 23 August 2006).

Squire, C. (1989) *Significant Differences: Feminism in Psychology*. London and New York: Routledge.

Stam, H. J., Lubek, I. and Radtke, L. (1998) 'Repopulating social psychology texts: Disembodied "subjects" and embodied subjectivity', in B. Bayer and J. Shotter (eds) *Reconstructing the Psychological Subject: Bodies, Practices and Technologies*. London and Thousand Oaks, CA: Sage.

Stephenson, N. (2003) 'Rethinking collectivity: Practising memory-work', *International Journal of Critical Psychology*, 8, pp. 160–76.

Stephenson, N. and Papadopoulos, D. (2006) *Analysing Everyday Experience: Social Research and Political Change*. London: Palgrave Macmillan.

Stern, D. N. (1985) *The Interpersonal World of the Infant: A View from Psychoanalysis and Developmental Psychology*. New York: Basic Books.

Stirling, J. (1999) *Cortical Functions*. London and New York: Routledge.

Stirner, M. (1995) *The Ego and Its Own* (originally published 1844). Cambridge: Cambridge University Press.

Strathern, M. (2000) 'The tyranny of transparency', *British Educational Research Journal*, 26 (3), pp. 309–21.

Sutton, C., Utting, D. and Farrington, D. (eds) (2006) 'Nipping Criminality in the Bud, Special Issue', *The Psychologist*, 19 (8).

Swan, V. (1999) 'Narrative, Foucault and feminism: Implications for therapeutic practice', in I. Parker (ed.) *Deconstructing Psychotherapy*. London and Thousand Oaks, CA: Sage.

Swartz, L. (1986) 'Carl Rogers in South Africa: The issue of silence', *Psychology in Society*, 5, pp. 139–43.

Symington, N. (1990) 'Religion and psychoanalysis', *Free Associations*, 19, pp. 105–16.

Tajfel, H. (1970) 'Experiments in intergroup discrimination', *Scientific American*, 223, pp. 96–102.

Tatchell, P. (1997) 'Hans Eysenck: Obituary', available at www.petertatchell.net/psychiatry/aversion.htm (accessed 10 August 2006).

Taylor, F. W. (1911) *Scientific Management*. New York: Harper & Row.

Tazi, N. (ed.) (2004) *Keywords, Identity: For a Different Kind of Globalization*. New Delhi: Vistaar.

Teo, T. (1999) 'Methodologies of critical psychology: Illustrations from the field of racism', *Annual Review of Critical Psychology*, 1, pp. 119–34.

Terre Blanche, M. and Durrheim, K. (eds) (1999) *Research in Practice: Applied Methods for the Social Sciences*. Cape Town: University of Cape Town Press.

Therborn, G. (1976) *Science, Class, Society: On the Formation of Sociology and Historical Materialism*. London: Verso.

Thomas, E. (1967) *The Women Incendiaries*. London: Secker & Warburg.

Timimi, S. (2002) *Psychological Child Psychiatry and the Medicalization of Childhood*. Hove and New York: Brunner-Routledge.

Timimi, S. (2005) *Naughty Boys: Anti-Social Behaviour, ADHD and the Role of Culture*. London: Palgrave Macmillan.

Timms, E. and Segal, N. (eds) (1988) *Freud in Exile: Psychoanalysis and its Vicissitudes*. New Haven, CT and London: Yale University Press.

Timpanaro, S. (1976) *The Freudian Slip: Psychoanalysis and Textual Criticism*. London: New Left Books.

Tolkien, J. R. R. (1969) *The Lord of the Rings*. London: George Allen & Unwin.

Tolman, C. (1994) *Psychology, Society and Subjectivity: An Introduction to German Critical Psychology*. London and New York: Routledge.

Tolman, C. and Maiers, W. (eds) (1991) *Critical Psychology: Contributions to an Historical Science of the Subject*. Cambridge: Cambridge University Press.

Totton, N. (2000) *Psychotherapy and Politics*. London and Thousand Oaks, CA: Sage.

Totton, N. (ed.) (2006) *The Politics of Psychotherapy: New Perspectives*. Maidenhead and New York: Open University Press.

Tourish, D. and Wohlforth, T. (2000a) *On the Edge: Political Cults Right and Left*. Armonk, NY: M. E. Sharpe.

Tourish, D. and Wohlforth, T. (2000b) 'Fred Newman: Lenin as therapist', available at www.timwohlforth.com/edge.html (accessed 12 March 2005).

Townshend, J. (1998) *Possessive Individualism and Democracy: C. B. Macpherson and His Critics*. Edinburgh: Edinburgh University Press.

Triplett, N. (1898) 'The dynamogenic factors in pacemaking and competition', *American Journal of Psychology*, 9, pp. 507–33.

Trotsky, L. (originally published 1938) 'The Death Agony of Capitalism and the Tasks of the Fourth International (The Transitional Programme)', in W. Reisner (ed.) (1973) *Documents of the Fourth International: The Formative Years (1933–1940)*. New York: Pathfinder.

Trotsky, L. (1973) *The Revolution Betrayed: What Is the Soviet Union and Where Is It Going?* (originally published 1936). London: New Park.

Trotsky, L. (1975) *The Struggle Against Fascism in Germany*. Harmondsworth: Pelican.

Trotsky, L. (1977) *The History of the Russian Revolution* (originally published 1934). London: Pluto.

Trotter, W. (1919) *Instincts of the Herd in Peace and War*, Second Edition. London: Ernest Benn.

Trower, P., Bryant, P. and Argyle, M. (1978) *Social Skills and Mental Health*. London: Methuen.

Tuffin, K. (2004) *Understanding Critical Social Psychology*. London and Thousand Oaks, CA: Sage.

Turner, B. S. (1987) *Medical Power and Social Knowledge*. London and Thousand Oaks, CA: Sage.

Turner, J. C., Hogg, M. A., Oakes, P. J., Reicher, S. D. and Wetherell, M. (1987) *Rediscovering the Social Group: A Self-Categorisation Theory*. Oxford: Blackwell.

Ulman, J. D. (1991) 'Toward a synthesis of Marx and Skinner', *Behavior and Social Issues*, 1 (1), pp. 57–70.

Ulman, J. D. (1996) 'Radical behaviourism, selectionism, and social action', in I. Parker and R. Spears (eds) *Psychology and Society: Radical Theory and Practice*. London: Pluto.

Urwin, C. (1998) 'Power relations and the emergence of language', in J. Henriques, W. Hollway, C. Urwin, C. Venn and V. Walkerdine (1998)

Changing the Subject: Psychology, Social Regulation and Subjectivity, Second Edition. London and New York: Routledge.

Ussher, J. (1989) *The Psychology of the Female Body*. London and New York: Routledge.

Ussher, J. (1991) *Women's Madness: Misogyny or Mental Illness?* Hemel Hempstead: Harvester Wheatsheaf.

Ussher, J. (2005) *Managing the Monstrous Feminine*. London and New York: Routledge.

Vandenburg, B. (1993) 'Developmental psychology, god and the good', *Theory & Psychology*, 3 (2), pp. 191–205.

Vanheule, S. and Verhaeghe, P. (2004) 'Powerlessness and Impossibility in Special Education: A qualitative study on professional burnout from a Lacanian perspective', *Human Relations*, 57, pp. 497–519.

Virden, P. (2006) 'The sexual abuse of psychiatric patients: The cover-up and the government whitewash', *Asylum*, 15 (1), pp 9–33.

Vološinov, V. N. (1973) *Marxism and the Philosophy of Language*. New York: Seminar Press.

Vygotsky, L. S. (1962) *Thought and Language*. Cambridge, MA.: MIT Press.

Vygotsky, L. S. (1966) 'Development of the higher mental functions', in A. N. Leont'ev, A. R. Luria and A. Smirnov (eds) *Psychological Research in the USSR*. Moscow: Progress Publishers.

Walkerdine, V. (1982) 'From context to text: A psychosemiotic approach to abstract thought', in M. Beveridge (ed.) *Children Thinking Through Language*. London: Edward Arnold.

Walkerdine, V. (1986) 'Video replay: families, films and fantasy', in V. Burgin, J. Donald and C. Kaplan (eds) *Formations of Fantasy*. London: Methuen.

Walkerdine, V. (1987) 'No laughing matter: Girls' comics and the preparation for adolescent sexuality', in J. M. Broughton (ed.) *Critical Theories of Psychological Development*. New York: Plenum.

Walkerdine, V. (1988) *The Mastery of Reason*. London and New York: Routledge.

Walkerdine, V. (1990) *Schoolgirl Fictions*. London: Verso.

Walkerdine, V. (ed.) (1996) *Feminism and Psychology Reader: Class*. London and Thousand Oaks, CA: Sage.

Walkerdine, V. (ed.) (2002) *Challenging Subjects: Critical Psychology for a New Millennium*. London: Palgrave.

Wann, T. W. (ed.) (1964) *Behaviorism and Phenomenology: Contrasting Bases for Modern Psychology*. Chicago: Chicago University Press.

Warner, R. (1994) *Recovery from Schizophrenia: Psychiatry and Political Economy*, Second Edition. London and New York: Routledge.

Waterhouse, R. (1993) ' "Wild women don't have the blues": A feminist critique of "person-centred" counselling and therapy', *Feminism & Psychology*, 3 (1), pp. 55–71.

Weizman, E. (2006a) 'The art of war: Deleuze, Guattari, Debord and the Israeli Defence Force', *Mute Magazine*, available at www.metamute.org/?qen/node/8192 (accessed 22 August 2006).

Weizman, E. (2006b) 'Walking through walls: Soldiers as architects in the Israeli–Palestinian conflict', *Radical Philosophy*, 136, pp. 8–22.

Went, R. (2000) *Globalization: Neoliberal Challenge, Radical Responses*. London: Pluto.

Westen, D., Novotny, C. and Thompson-Brenner, H. (2004) 'The empirical status of empirically supported psychotherapies: Assumptions, findings, and reporting in controlled clinical trials', *Psychological Bulletin*, 130 (4), pp. 631–63.

Wetherell, M. and Potter, J. (1992) *Mapping the Language of Racism: Discourse and the Legitimation of Exploitation*. Hemel Hempstead: Harvester Wheatsheaf.

Wexler, P. (1983) *Critical Social Psychology*. Boston, MA: Routledge & Kegan Paul.

Whitaker, B., Campbell, D. and Cowan, R. (2005) 'A chilling message to Britons', *Guardian*, 5 August.

White, M. (1986) 'Anorexia nervosa: A cybernetic perspective', in J. Elka-Harkaway (ed.) *Eating Disorders*. Rockville, MD: Aspen.

White, M. and Epston, D. (1989) *Literate Means to Therapeutic Ends*. Adelaide: Dulwich Centre.

White, M. and Epston, D. (1990) *Narrative Means to Therapeutic Ends*. Adelaide: Dulwich Centre.

Widdicombe, S. (1995) 'Identity, politics and talk: A case for the mundane and the everyday', in S. Wilkinson and C. Kitzinger (eds) *Feminism and Discourse: Psychological Perspectives*. London and Thousand Oaks, CA: Sage.

Wilkinson, S. (1997) 'Prioritizing the political: Feminist psychology', in T. Ibáñez and L. Íñiguez (eds) *Critical Social Psychology*. London and Thousand Oaks, CA: Sage.

Wilkinson, S. and Kitzinger, C. (eds) (1993) *Heterosexuality: A Feminism and Psychology Reader*. London and Thousand Oaks, CA: Sage.

Wilkinson, S. and Kitzinger, C. (eds) (1995) *Feminism and Discourse*. London and Thousand Oaks, CA: Sage.

Williams, R. (1976) *Keywords: A Vocabulary of Culture and Society*. London: Fontana.

Willis, P. (1980) *Learning to Labour: How Working Class Kids Get Working Class Jobs* (originally published 1977). Aldershot: Gower.

Wilson. E. (1999) 'Critical/cognition', *Annual Review of Critical Psychology*, 1, pp. 136–49.

Woolfe, R., Dryden, W. and Strawbridge, S. (eds) (2003) *Handbook of Counselling Psychology*, Second Edition. London and Thousand Oaks, CA: Sage.

Worchel, S. and Austin, W. G. (eds) (1986) *The Social Psychology of Intergroup Relations*. Chicago: Nelson-Hall.

World Health Organization (2006) *International Statistical Classification of Diseases and Related Health Problems, Tenth Revision, Version for 2006*. Geneva: WHO, available at www3.who.int/icd/currentversion/fr-icd.htm (accessed 23 August 2006).

Yardley, K. M. (1979) 'Social skills training – A critique', *British Journal of Medical Psychology*, 52, pp. 55–62.

Young, R. M. (1992) 'Science, ideology and Donna Haraway', *Science as Culture*, 15 (3), pp. 165–207.

Young, R. M. (1996) 'Evolution, biology, and psychology from a Marxist point of view', in I. Parker and R. Spears (eds) *Psychology and Society: Radical Theory and Practice*. London: Pluto.

Zajonc, R. (1965) 'Social facilitation', *Science*, 149, pp. 269–74.

Zaretsky, E. (1976) *Capitalism, the Family, and Personal Life*. London: Pluto.

Zavos, A., Biglia, B., Clark, J. and Motzkau, J. (eds) (2005) 'Feminisms and Activisms, Special Issue', *Annual Review of Critical Psychology*, 5.

Zhang, S. X. (1995) 'Measuring shaming in an ethnic context', *British Journal of Criminology*, 35 (2), pp. 248–62.

Zimbardo, P. G. (1969) 'The human choice: Individuation, reason, and order vs. deindividuation, impulse and chaos', in W. J. Arnold and D. Levine (eds) *Nebraska Symposium on Motivation, Volume 17*. Lincoln, NE: University of Nebraska Press.

Zimbardo, P. G. (1973) 'On the ethics of intervention in human psychological research: With special reference to the Stanford prison experiment', *Cognition*, 2, pp. 243–56.

Zimbardo, P. G. (2002) 'Mind control: psychological reality or mindless rhetoric?', *APA Monitor on Psychology*, 33 (10), available at www.apa.org/monitor/nov02/pc.html (accessed 23 August 2006).

Index

psychologist(s) – *continued*
  and change   205–7
  and collusion   206–7
  and error   91–3
  networking   185
  perception of own role   30–2
  safe-guarding expertise   207
  study of   208–9
  and subjects   17–18, 27–8, 31,
    41–2, 116, 127, 155
  and terminology   204–5
  and 'tried and tested' knowledge
    207
psychology
  and abnormal distribution of
    power   52–4
  at work   55–73
  and capitalism   22, 30, 31, 53,
    55, 112, 173–4, 202
  and class   64, 114–16, 186, 188–9
  competing areas of study   10–11
  and competing methodologies
    28
  conditions for existence of
    11–16
  development of discipline   16–22
  differentiating from rival
    approaches   22–6
  disagreement over definition of
    9–10
  identifying abnormalities   74–5
  as ideology   33–54
  male dominance   38, 66, 139
  need for resistance   163–5
    see also psychological struggles
  new approaches   130–47
    see also alternative psychology
    (alt-psy)
  political analysis of   202–3
  and politics   209–11
    see also political psychology;
    psychological culture, on
    the left
  reinforcing Western images of
    human being   45–8
  and revolution   147–65
  and state definition   211
  training   27
  using and abusing   203–5

and 'white' values   39, 51, 139
psychopharmacology   96
psychosis   98, 118, 160
psychotherapy *see* counselling and
  psychotherapy

queer politics   160, 211

racism   15, 21, 35, 52–3, 63, 89,
  123–4, 128, 129
  anti-racist movement   143, 153,
    156, 159, 166, 171, 182, 199
  and capitalism   60
  and education   187
  institutionalised   191–2
  racial unconscious   125
rationality   92, 112, 117, 121–2,
  177
  and emotion   63, 66
  see also madness
reductionism   77, 79, 87, 92, 118,
  163, 181
  challenges to   185–8
reflecting teams   197
reflexivity   34, 137–8, 155, 161,
  171, 204
Reich, W.   176–7
reification   18, 45, 47, 116, 150,
  154
reintegrative shaming   109, 110n
repression   117, 153, 169, 176,
  177
research
  assumptions   29–30
  based on undergraduate students
    39–40
  effect of methodological
    procedures   41–4
  and participation   113–14
  perception research   45–6
  qualitative   114, 132, 139, 162
  tension between US and
    European modes   36–8, 39
  and transparency   205
revolution, challenge to dominant
  ideologies   147–8
'risky shift'   89
Rogers, K.   126–7
Romme, M.   192